45

A BOOK OF SCOTLAND

THE ISLAND OF RUM, FROM ARISAIG

A BOOK
OF SCOTLAND

by

GEORGE ROWNTREE HARVEY

WITH THIRTY-ONE PLATES IN COLOUR
AND THIRTY-TWO PHOTOGRAPHS

LONDON
ADAM AND CHARLES BLACK

FIRST PUBLISHED 1949
BY A. AND C. BLACK LTD.
4, 5 AND 6 SOHO SQUARE LONDON W.I
REPRINTED 1950 AND 1953

To
my inn-mates at Broadstraik
WILLIE, MALLY *and* ANNIE BAIRD
LIZA PROFEIT
but for whose care this book
could never have been finished
and to
NORMAN CATTANACH
in exile
for whom this book was written.

MADE IN GREAT BRITAIN
PRINTED BY R. & R. CLARK, LTD., EDINBURGH

CONTENTS

v

ILLUSTRATIONS

Plates in Colour

Photographs

PROLOGUE

THIS book I have called "A Book of Scotland". That, for me, means more than highways and byways, towns and villages, mountains and hills, glens and carses, rivers and lochs and the sea. It means also, people—those who exist today, those who existed in old time, and especially those who, for good or bad, made Scotland more Scottish, added to its loveliness and liveliness.

I have not attempted to write an all-covering guide-book in the ordinary sense of the words, just as the illustrations are not all the time illustrative of what I have written, but complementary. Such a guide-book is a job for people with more of a certain kind of sense than I possess, and more extensive and intensive knowledge. Even so, the all-covering guide-book does not exist. It couldn't. It is possible only by a synthesis of all the books, good and bad, that have been written on Scotland and parts of Scotland—and now they are very, very many.

Yet, in another sense, I hope this is a guide-book, not only to parts of the surface of Scotland, but to something more than the surface.

You can look with enjoyment of a kind upon the mountains of Scotland, from a distance, from the outside, as it were. But you will never know those mountains, love them in reality, until you have penetrated to their fastnesses, lain for summer days or nights in their bosoms. Then and thus only you get to know their inner secrets. And they have them.

I leave that implication as it is, and what I have tried to do is to implement it, to readers and critics, but more especially to men and women like myself. One thing, I think—however badly or inadequately it may be expressed—is clear. I love all that is Scotland to me, with all my heart and soul, yet not beyond idolatry, and not to the exclusion of not being able to love other places. For instance, in England, I love Shropshire, Worcestershire, Gloucestershire, the Wye, the Severn, Devonshire, Kent and the Lake District. But I cannot love them as the men of those places love their own districts. So is it between their love of Scotland—if it is there—and mine.

As a Scotsman I can, of course, completely understand the Scot's, perhaps rather intense, love of Scotland—firstly, because there is so much that is worth loving to love: there is the particular and peculiar beauty of so much of our country. Secondly, Scotland is a very individual nation. Its ways, its mode of living, its thought, its character belong to the centuries, have been shapen by natural as well as historical circumstances and events.

Scotland was never more alive, generally, politically and culturally, than she is today. Whether they be or be not financial propositions, art, literature, the theatre, music are all being pursued by both makers and appreciators. The cinema, even, has discovered Scotland, and will find more and more that is of interest and use. We have already produced artists, in many branches, of quality and, here and there, of international reputation, and we shall produce more and better as time goes on. A great feature, too, is that many of these artists are founding their work on a genuine Scottish basis, more or less intense, but, in the best of them, not too narrowly. In any case, if art, however national, is of true value, it will find its international standing. It is basic quality that we need most of all; the rest is there. Another good aspect of this revival, or renaissance as it is more generally called, is that, though it is all intensely national, it is not separating us from other countries and other peoples, but rather is bringing them to us in a fraternisation that has not been so strong for a century or more.

It must not be overlooked that a considerable factor in this Scottish renaissance has been the cultural use of wireless. It reaches so far, so easily. But there are still possibilities for the propagation of the best in Scottish life and art, and for a better understanding of what is going on in Scotland now, on the part of those far furth of her lands and coasts.

Scotland, being what she is and what she has been, is still in some ways a distressed country. But then there are so many other countries in the world today that are even more distressed, and likely to be so for generations. Scotland has, at least, nominal peace and the chance to build and reconstruct in all aspects of national life and living. Whatever may or may not be in matters material, Scotland has rediscovered her soul. She may never be rich or luxurious—perhaps better not; it would not be in the nature of things, anyway—perhaps there will always be more than a tang of austerity. But there is, it seems to me, a new vision, and with that on our side we shall not perish.

CARTER BAR

TEVIOTDALE

I

PLACES AND HISTORY

MELROSE ABBEY

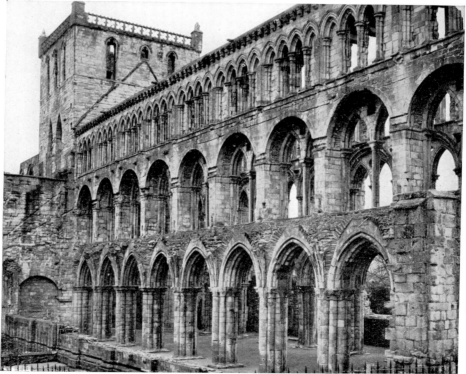

JEDBURGH ABBEY

OVER THE BORDER

THERE are several gateways into Scotland from the south, from England, but if I had to choose or suggest one—it would be Carter Bar. One reason is because, I think, such gates as Berwick-on-Tweed and Gretna are too flat. Berwick has its history, its river, its bridges and the sea, Gretna its aura or former romance—runaway marriages and the famous smithy, where, on the anvil, links were forged that lasted short or long, just like those of any other marriages in any other conditions—but Carter Bar lands you at once in characteristic Scotland.

I will not say that everyone would find the way by Carter Bar, especially on a bad day, superficially glamorous. My own first journey over the long stretches was made on a summer day that was cold as early spring, and I was seated in the open side-car attached to an old-fashioned motor bicycle. Even then, however, with all discomfort included, as soon as we had reached the Bar, I should have allowed of no other choice—for entry into Scotland.

It is true, as has been written, that here on this height one has the feeling of being on top of the world and, as you look upon Scotland below, this first landscape seems, to a Scotsman, to be something of what might be called a little epitome of the country we are entering. The greatest grandeur is still far away, but here is prologue and introduction. So, too, those lands beneath us have that other tang of Scotland besides scenery—history, over the centuries, and they have been the inspiration of much song and story. We are going to the Scots Borderlands, and few parts of Scotland for so long and so often were cockpits of strife and international rivalry.

Of course, all borderlands, everywhere almost in the world, are places of strife and bloodshed and cruelty. We have known that only too well in the last twenty-five years and more, and, alas, may not have seen the end of such strife by any means. The difference between the Scots Borderlands and other borderlands such as I have just mentioned is that our strife and bloodshed belong now to the realm of "old, unhappy far-off things and battles long ago". As I shall point out later, what happened has, for some of us, left its aftermath. But that is for romantic minds; is, it may be, only their creation.

For an Englishman coming to Scotland or a Scotsman going south, there is another reason for the choice of Carter Bar as the way in or out—it was the scene of the last Border battle, in 1575. It seems only right to say here that the Scots were the victors. The affray was no more than a skirmish and ended amicably. A portent?

This skirmish of the Redeswire, as it was called, and as you read it in Sir Walter Scott's *Minstrelsy of the Scottish Border*, has in it some things that rather remind you of a football international today.

It came out of a meeting held to redress wrongs. "In the course of the day . . . a bill, or indictment, at the instance of a Scottish complainer, was fouled (*i.e.* found a true bill) against one Farnstein, a notorious English freebooter." It was stated by the English representative at the meeting that Farnstein had fled from justice. The Scots representative took this as an attempt to evade compensation. There was a call to "play fair". The English representative said rude things about the family of his opponent. And then the battle began, with a flight of arrows sent among the Scots by the English. The Scots representative was made prisoner and the battle seemed to pass into the English hands. But they were too intent on their plunder. Up came the men of Jedburgh to the aid of the Scots, and the Scots won the day. A few days after the actual skirmish there was mutual readjustment, anything like war was avoided, and so it has been in Border matters general ever since.

It would not have been a Border fray, however, and no song about it. Here in one verse the Provost of Jedburgh, who led the reinforcements, is succintly set out for all time:

> Bauld, he was fou stout,
> Wi' a' his nine sons him about;
> He led the toun o' Jedburgh out,
> All bravely fought that day.

Not far away, below where meet Jed Water and Carter Burn, is all that is left of the old church of Southdean. Here again lingers history. In the church, in 1588, Douglas and his counsellors met before the Battle of Otterburn. Douglas died in that battle and was buried in Melrose Abbey.

Thinking over the Border history and Redeswire, we cannot repress a smile when we remember that in Southdean manse was reared James Thomson, author of not only *The Seasons*—who reads it now besides students?—but also of "Rule Britannia".

Well, we are now in the Scottish Borders, and my own choice leads me to Melrose first of all. This was the first town of the Borders I ever entered, and it has held me ever since. I have visited almost every other, but Melrose has my heart just as its ruined Abbey has the heart of that great Scottish King, Robert the Bruce.

Melrose Abbey must have been one of the glories of Scottish architecture, perhaps the greatest in some ways. But, like so many others in the Borders—they almost seem like a line of ruined fanes—we can but guess at its full beauty. Sir Walter Scott,

So let us slip across to Galashiels, during the annual Gala Week. This is one of the least historical-looking towns of the Borders, but that the spirit is there you will find out if you happen to be in the town in June when the Braw Lads' Gathering takes place. I never saw a town so communally decorated. In that week every house seems to produce its own flags and bunting.

There are all sorts of ceremonies in connection with the Week—and Galashiels is not the only Border town that has such gatherings or events—but the climax comes on the Saturday.

Then chimes and trumpets usher in the day's doings. The Burgh Standard is given to the Braw Lad, who, along with the Braw Lass, is elected by popular vote. The procession then formed goes here and there, including Abbotsford, and returns to the Mercat Cross. Here an ancient rite is enacted. The Braw Lass receives bouquets of red and white roses, the roses of the Houses of Lancaster and York. She mingles them and then places them among thistles on the Mercat Cross. This goes back in commemoration to the time when Margaret Tudor became possessed of the lands of Ettrick Forest as dowry on her marriage to James IV of Scotland. So, you see, even in busy Galashiels you cannot always get away from Border history.

For myself, I found the last ceremony of the day the most impressive. The centre of the town's war memorial is a bronze figure of the Border Horseman. Up to this rides the Braw Lad and dips his standard in homage to the men who gave their lives in war. From overhead drop the chimes, playing the melody of that famous song which all Scotland as well as the Borders knows and sings:

> Braw, braw lads on Yarrow braes,
> They rove among the blooming heather,
> But Yarrow braes nor Ettrick shaws
> Can match the lads o' Gala Water.

Selkirk vies with Galashiels in gaiety and ceremony in its Common Riding and here again is a Standard Bearer, and so with Hawick, where the Cornet is the man of the day, Lauder and Jedburgh, in fact every Border town. In all these galas the heart of the matter is communal feeling allied with history.

Forgetting history and remembering the lives of the people of the towns and the present day—Galashiels, Hawick, Selkirk, and also Peebles—where the Feast of Beltane, largely a matter of the youngsters, is the summer gala—Innerleithen and Jedburgh are the centres of the tweed woollen trade. This, in its way, is historic, too, but modern days have seen modern ways, and, though there may be troubles in the industry in these hard economic times, no one can believe but that the trade will pull through again to more flourishing days.

I have said before that in the Borders there is almost a line of ruined fanes, and though we cannot here visit them all, we must go for a moment to Jedburgh and

Dryburgh Abbeys. Jedburgh is the best-preserved of the Border abbeys. It was another of Hertford's sackings. The building was not so ornate as Melrose, but perhaps it is slightly more impressive in its own way. Dryburgh, which stands on the Tweed some five miles from Melrose, is today as much a shrine as a ruin. Like Melrose and Jedburgh, this abbey was another of the foundations of David I, "the sair saint to the Crown". But this, again, must have been architectural loveliness in its day. Here, however, are buried Sir Walter Scott and Earl Haig of Bemersyde. They sleep here because it is their native and natural resting-place.

This has covered but a small part of the varied attractions of the Borders. Little has been said, except almost incidentally, of the loveliness of the country. That in a way centres round rivers—the Tweed, dominating, perhaps; the Yarrow, the Teviot, Ettrick, Gala Water and a myriad burns. Here should be, and is, the fisherman's paradise.

And Yarrow reminds us—if we step out of history in the Borders we almost immediately step into literature. If we think of Ettrick and Yarrow, we think of James Hogg, of Wordsworth, of Scott.

You may not care too much for literature, but if you care for exploring the quiet lands, you can combine that with a touch of literary history. James Hogg, the Ettrick Shepherd, pursued the double calling of poet and peasant. A literary descendant of Thomas the Rhymer, Hogg's most famous poem, "Bonnie Kilmeny", was a tale of faery. And Hogg had another connection with faery; his mother's father, "Will o' Phaup", was the last man who saw and spoke to the fairies!

Ettrick and Yarrow today still keep their ancient peace, still bring refreshment to the traveller weary of towns, dirt and din. Here you are out of the world and, with special beauty and fascination, as near to another century as you can be anywhere today. But I agree with a writer on the Borders that you must get out and walk if you are to get the best out of such a place as Yarrow. St. Mary's Loch, Loch Skene, Megget Water, Dryhope—they wait for the lonely lover of the solitary places.

Yes, the happiest Border holiday I ever spent was when I shouldered a knapsack and by bus and on foot wandered out from Peebles. I had that secret excitement that some of you also may know, now and again, when you are about to see a place whose name has rung in your ears for many a day like a silver chime. I was going to Traquair.

> Will ye gang wi' me and fare
>   To the bush aboon Traquair?
> Owre the high Minchmuir we'll up and awa',
>   This bonnie summer noon,
>   While the sun shines fair aboon,
> And the licht sklents saftly doun on holm and ha'.

The name of Traquair and a certain legend had, by means of that poem by John
Campbell Shairp, haunted me from childhood days. I had often meant to go there,
but I was, in a way, frightened. Would I be disappointed by the actuality, and
Traquair lose its glamour in my imagination? Now I was resolved to risk it—the
day was right, just as in the poem.

> And what saw ye there,
>   At the bush aboon Traquair?
> Or what did ye hear that was worth your heed?
>   I heard the cushies croon
>   Thro' the gowden afternoon,
> And the Quair burn singing doun to the vale o' Tweed.
>
> And birks saw I three or four,
>   Wi' grey moss bearded owre,
> The last that are left o' the birken shaw;
>   Whar mony a simmer e'en
>   Fond lovers did convene,
> Thae bonnie, bonnie gloamin's that are lang awa'.
>
> Frae mony a butt and ben,
>   By muirland, holm, and glen,
> They cam' ane hour to spen' on the green-wood sward;
>   But lang hae lad and lass
>   Been lying neath the grass,
> The green, green grass o' Traquair kirkyard. . . .
>
> Now the birks to dust may rot,
>   Names o' luvers be forgot,
> Nae lads and lasses there ony mair convene;
>   But the blythe lilt o' yon air
>   Keeps the bush aboon Traquair
> And the luve that ance was there aye fresh and green.

That was the mood in which I went to Traquair. That poem, like many others,
holds in it some part of the spirit of the Borders and of place. Was I disappointed?
I was not. I lingered a whole morning and part of an afternoon, wandering here
and there. It is not in scenery what you would call tremendous, but it is particularly
Scottish, and there is *stimmung*—created in part, I admit, by Shairp's poem.

The last touch, of course, is supplied by the closed gates of the House of Traquair
and the house itself. Those gates, according to legend, were closed in the eighteenth
century and will not be opened again until a Stuart king returns to the throne of
Scotland. A King and Queen have been at Traquair within comparatively recent
times—King George V and Queen Mary in 1923. But the gates are still closed.

That is the Borders in the aspect in which the Scot of a certain kind of Scottish temperament sees them—are we sentimental? then we are sentimental. But there must be a foundation for all this, and I have tried, in some part, to convey it.

Before we go west from what might be called the central Borders to other parts of southern Scotland let us take leave of them in two of the verses of one of the many poets of the Borders, Andrew Lang. You can see that this part of Scotland, in poetry and prose, has created a great body of literature, and in return some of that literature has, undoubtedly, helped to create the Borders you cannot help but love.

> Three crests against the saffron sky,
>   Beyond the purple plain,
> The kind remembered melody
>   Of Tweed once more again. . . .
>
> A mist of memory broods and floats,
>   The Border waters flow,
> The air is full of ballad notes,
>   Borne out of long ago.

Ballads, scenery, history—there you have the Borders.

But as soon as you have left the central Borders, and, for my convenience, stepped across Dumfriesshire, you come again into a region that, in town and country, is almost as full of history and is an inspirer of local patriotism and literature. The name of Galloway—Grey Galloway, they sometimes call it—just as much as the Borders call up special pictures, and special aspects.

It is a country of moors and sheep and cattle, of fine quiet little towns, some of them full of history, but not living only on that, of lochs and hills. It is not a district of superficial attraction, but once let it get hold of you and you will not easily be let go.

With the entrance of Galloway comes also the entrance of another aspect of Scotland—the religious aspect. The south-west, from earliest days, has been a cockpit of religious movements.

The first famous Christian figure in Scotland—St. Ninian—is associated with Whithorn, which lies on the little peninsula between Wigtown Bay and Luce Bay, inlets of the Solway Firth. He was ordained Bishop of the Southern Picts by Pope Siricius in 394 and died somewhere about 432. His church, built of stone, was known as Candida Casa, "White House". Nothing remains of it now, but on its site stands a roofless ruin, all that remains of a chapel built about the thirteenth century and attached to the Priory of Whithorn. Little remains of the Priory itself, but there is a fine Norman doorway in the south wall. Dundrennan Abbey is the oldest house of religion in the area, and enough remains of its ruins to give some idea of this twelfth-century edifice. One other of the area's ruined churches may be

DRYBURGH ABBEY

THOMAS CARLYLE'S BIRTHPLACE, ECCLEFECHAN

mentioned now, for convenience—Lincluden Abbey. Here you will find some lovely late Gothic, and, finest of all, there is a magnificent tomb in which was buried Margaret, wife of the fourth Earl of Douglas who became Duke of Touraine.

This south-west corner of Scotland has been important more than once in the religious life of Scotland. St. Ninian, it is claimed, took the torch of Christianity as far as the Grampians. Even today scholars carry on heated arguments as to which meant more to the Christianising of Scotland—St. Ninian or St. Columba.

After, the Reformation came to Scotland, and in the fight for the Covenant the moors and hills of Galloway became the hiding-places of hunted men and women. The Pentland Rising of 1666 was planned in Dalry, in the north of the Stewartry. In those days when religious controversy divided, not only the country but even households, cruel things were done, on both sides, though the name of martyr is associated more usually with the Covenanters, and you will find martyrs' graves in many places. In Wigtown is one which tells a story that still can pain the heart. An old woman, Margaret McLauchlan, who was 63, and Margaret Wilson, only 18, were tied to a stake in the Solway and left to drown as the tide came up.

Just as in the Borders, literature has come out of the history of Galloway, though, perhaps, not so extensively. There was a time when the books of S. R. Crockett were everyone's reading, though their vogue has somewhat passed. But they do give the spirit of Galloway, in people and place. It was, too, to S. R. Crockett that Robert Louis Stevenson—a devotee of the Covenanters from his early days—sent, from Samoa in the South Seas, the lines in which he bade farewell to his native country, knowing instinctively that he would never see it again.

> Blows the wind to-day, and the sun and the rain are flying,
>   Blows the wind on the moors today and now,
> Where about the graves of the martyrs the whaups are crying,
>   My heart remembers how!
>
> Grey recumbent tombs of the dead in desert places,
>   Standing stones on the vacant wine-red moor,
> Hills of sheep, and the howes of the silent vanished races,
>   And winds austere and pure:
>
> Be it granted to me to behold you again in dying,
>   Hills of home! and to hear again the call;
> Hear about the graves of the martyrs the peewees crying,
>   And hear no more at all.

That, I think, is a tense, wonderful calling-up of the Galloway landscape; the lines can set me at once among those wide moors. They can be beautiful, even in their desolation, but they can also in certain weather conditions almost make you run for the nearest town or village.

But there are bits of Galloway that, once visited, call you back again and remain in your memory until you revisit them. You have the hills, the lochs—Trool is the best known—the rivers, the little glens, the little towns and the sea coast. So you see, there is no lack of variety in this corner of Scotland. I have seen it both in summer and in winter, and I have seldom found that I could not find beauty somewhere at any season of the year, though that beauty is often stern and wild.

Most of the towns have something, in themselves and their setting, to attract. Not without reason Kirkcudbright has become a haunt of artists, and so might other places, and, not least, the Isle of Whithorn. I love the Galloway bays, especially Luce Bay, with its lovely sands leading to water that seems to have a sheen of its own.

As you go west in Wigtownshire—at least, I found it so—you begin to realise what is that county's across-the-water neighbour, Ireland. The speech takes on something of a brogue. I have listened to amateur drama teams from Wigtownshire and been delighted by the soft lovely accent. And in the town of Stranraer—the port for Ireland—look at the names above the shop doors, the most wonderful collection of curious "Macs". Then from Stranraer go down to little Portpatrick, and from its headlands you can see Ireland.

Galloway is largely an agricultural region, and among its noted products are belted cattle—known as "Galloway Belties" and sheep. It is also a region of cream and cheese.

Some of the modern literature that has come out of Galloway, and particularly Wigtownshire, is rather grimly realistic and paints its people as of the earth, earthy. That may be as you seek for and find.

Let me mention two personalities before we leave this peculiarly attractive area—one old and one of this day. The latter is the Galloway-born composer, J. B. McEwen. In his music you will find the counterpart of R. L. Stevenson's lines. The older personality is Paul Jones, born John Paul who, in 1778, at the time when America rebelled against Britain, became head of America's first naval force and made a raid on his own native coast. He was an adventurer of a most picturesque kind and has been much written-up in recent years.

Now let us take our way to Dumfriesshire, and the reason for this late visit will become clearer in time.

Dumfriesshire means for me the way from Carlisle, by Gretna, to the north. I like this start of Scotland. I like to look at that plain house at Ecclefechan where came into this world, in 1795, a writer whose name, not so much lauded now, was to ring through the historical and philosophical world—Thomas Carlyle. There's nothing very pretty about Ecclefechan, there was nothing very pretty about Thomas

THE BACHELORS' CLUB, TARBOLTON
BEFORE RESTORATION

BARRIE'S BIRTHPLACE, KIRRIEMUIR

Carlyle. His birthplace seems to me wrong. He should have been born amid more rugged landscape—we have plenty of that in Scotland and to spare. But we should give passing tribute to this humble dwelling, the kind of house in which so many Scots who have become famous first saw the light. The wind of genius bloweth where it listeth. They have not forgotten Carlyle in Ecclefechan and preserve the house and relics. But he was not the kind of personality to attract thousands on thousands of pilgrims.

Dumfriesshire also means to me the county town—Dumfries. Ecclefechan saw the birth of one of Scotland's geniuses; Dumfries saw the death of another, Robert Burns. How different the two were in their work. Burns, the democrat, has today a reputation almost greater than at any time since his death. He is in accord with the times; he was before his time.

Englishmen look with wonder and, not unseldom, with scorn at what has been called "Bardolatry" or "Burnsolatry". That outburst of celebration that occurs round about the time of Burns's birth anniversary—January 25—is something they just cannot understand.

But do not let it be forgotten that Burns died in 1796, and the first of those Burns celebrations began only five years after that and have been going on ever since. More of these in time, when we reach Ayr!

There are anti-Burnsians who will try to tell you that Scotsmen have made for Burns a fake immortality. What rubbish! It is just the other way round. Burns was born an immortal. It was Scotland's luck and fortune that he was born a Scot. He, if any, has helped to make Scotsmen and Scotland immortal. While he lasts we last, while we last he lasts, and it could be that he will outlast both Scotland and the Scots. He may have began as a parochial poet, but today he is universal.

Burns came into this world in a humble home, and he died in almost as humble circumstances, at the age of 37. His last days were, I think, miserable. Illness and next-door-to-poverty were the last lot of the man who became Scotland's idol. It has not been unusual among men of genius. Think of that other great singer, Franz Schubert, or of Mozart. Burns had failed in almost everything except poetry. He had many good friends and one great enemy, himself.

Dumfries contains Burns's mausoleum and the house where he died, but it is any-thing but a mournful town. It is, indeed, a brisk and mentally alert place. And it should be remembered that in Dumfries Burns spent happy enough days and, perhaps, too happy nights.

The house in the Meal Vennel—now Burns Street—where he died, can be visited and, of course, no visitor passes through without paying tribute at the mausoleum. If they have any artistic flair they will not think too much of what they see there. While you look, for looking's sake, remember, instead, the work of the man commemorated. Think of the simple perfection of, for instance, the second verse of his song, "Mary Morison".

> Yestreen, when to the trembling string,
>   The dance gaed thro' the lighted ha',
> To thee my fancy took its wing,
>   I sat but neither heard nor saw;
> Though this was fair and that was braw,
>   And yon the toast o' a' the town,
> I sat and sighed among them a',
>   "Ye are na Mary Morison."

What a perfect little cameo of place and feeling, said without ever an unnecessary word, taut as the very fiddle-string to which we are listening.

While you are in Dumfries, and if the day is good, make your way to Sweetheart Abbey, some seven miles out of the town, at the village of New Abbey. I like the approach to this ruin. You go through a green cathedral of trees to come to the red ruin. Its name is romantic, so was its foundation. Devorgilla, widow of John Balliol, who himself founded Balliol College, Oxford, was Sweetheart Abbey's founder. When her husband died she had his heart embalmed and carried it with her wherever she went. When Devorgilla died she was buried near the high altar of the abbey and the embalmed heart was laid upon her breast.

Part of Dumfries is Maxwelltown, and, if you remember "Annie Laurie", a Scots song that has become the possession of the world, you will recall that the song begins—"Maxwellton braes are bonnie". This is that Maxwelltown, but in name only nowadays. The years have changed it, as they have changed so much else that belongs to the literary and romantic past of all countries.

One more of Scotland's littérateurs has a Dumfries connection. J. M. Barrie spent school-days there.

Our journey from the town in which Burns died to the place in which he was born—Alloway, on the outskirts of the town of Ayr, is for some time along the banks of one of the loveliest rivers in southern Scotland, the Nith.

Not far from Dumfries you will pass the farm of Ellisland. Here came Burns to try his last experiment in farming. Like his father and his brother, Burns was a failure as a farmer. But what did come out of Ellisland were some of the finest poems Burns ever wrote, including one that has linked the whole English-speaking world hand to hand, "Auld Lang Syne". That comic and satiric masterpiece that rushes along like a burn in spate, "Tam o' Shanter", was also written at Ellisland. "Willie Brewed a Peck o' Maut", "John Anderson, my Jo", "Ae Fond Kiss", the moving "Lament for James Earl of Glencairn"—all, in their diversity, were written here, and Ellisland and the land about it are undoubtedly one of the real Burns

ON THE RIVER AYR

EDINBURGH FROM "REST AND BE THANKFUL"

shrines, and, for me, even as the place is now, so different from the poet's day, a place where I would rather bide a wee than in others that are crowded and somewhat manufactured.

But, let's on through the Cumnocks, and so west to Ayr.

Had we gone north from Stranraer, by Girvan and the coast, there would have been less literary history and different scenery. Then we should have passed through country best seen in good weather, by Ballantrae, and so to the first of the golfing centres, Turnberry—and do not forget that, in Scotland, golf is regarded with a seriousness second only to Association football. They have taken the place in the national consciousness and argument of religion and politics. In fact, they are almost a religion or allied. As you can judge—the famous Celtic team has an Irish background, and Roman Catholicism beyond that. The equally famous team, Rangers, may or may not be mainly supported by Orangemen and Protestants generally. Legend has it, however, that at a match between the two teams one man said to another, his neighbour in the crowd—"What are ye, a Rangers supporter?" The man replied, "No." The questioner persisted, "A Celtic supporter?" Again the man said, "No." "What are ye then, an atheist?" It could be true today.

Past Maybole and so we come, at last, to Ayr.

2

BURNS LAND

THE town of Ayr and many adjacent places land us again in literature and history, but also in a new type of country.

Ayrshire is, like Galloway, very much an agricultural county, but its appearance as a whole is very different. I should say that only in spots, not in stretches, is Ayrshire particularly impressive or beautiful. Some of it, indeed, is very, very plain.

But how dear a countryside of this kind can be to the native is best shown in the work of Robert Burns, and, given his great gift, he can make ugly names as well as plain places famous throughout the world, and that for a century and much more.

Another remark that might be passed in this connection, and it has its particular as well as its general connection, is that, if you fly through a countryside by train, bus or car, you will never know anything of it. The particular application of this remark is that if you want to link Ayr, and, even more, Mauchline, with Burns's work you must explore them at some little leisure.

But to Ayr first.

Ayr is not all "Burnsolatry". It is a pleasant little seaside resort, maybe getting a little spoiled, like so many places of the kind in these days, by its double popularity. It doesn't need to go out of its way to cater for the visitor—it can still live on the reputation Burns gave it—but it does.

And, without doubt, for the passing visitor it is the Burns atmosphere that matters. We cannot get away from that.

The people of Ayr have to live up to Burns, as people and descendants of those of whom he wrote—

> Auld Ayr, wham ne'er a town surpasses,
> For honest men and bonnie lasses.

It is not so difficult for the women nowadays when there are so many aids to bonniness. As for the men, I have never had any business dealings in Ayr.

That quotation is, as you know, from "Tam o' Shanter", which begins in an inn in Ayr—"Souter Johnny's". Today you will find that Ayr Town Council have taken over the hostelry, and tried to restore it to what it looked like in Burns's day. Perhaps it looks, like the Burns birthplace, just too good to be true, but there is a resemblance.

There are still, as in another Burns poem, twa Brigs o' Ayr, but not both of them are the twa brigs of which Burns wrote.

To reach the centre of Burns tourism in Ayr—the suburb of Alloway—you make your way along the pleasant seafront, and turn inland a very little, to where stands the present version of the auld clay biggin' in which on January 25, 1759—I give the famous date for a purpose—Robert Burns was born.

Not only Scotsmen but Britons all who were born near the sea know how much the sea fills their ears, especially in winter. Few poets have written so much and so well about winter as Burns, but how little there is of the sea in Burns's poems. There are, however, two lines in one of his songs which another great poet, the late W. B. Yeats, declared to be of the most memorable in linking the sea and emotion. The song is "O open the door" and the lines:

> The wan moon is setting behind the white wave,
> And time is setting with me, O.

Like so much in Burns, that came out of well-remembered observation.

And so we come to Burns's birthplace, not a cot in a lonely little village, but, in summer-time at any rate, a crowded spot in a modern suburb. It cannot be helped, and it is no reflection on Ayr or Robert Burns. As to the latter, the very opposite.

How many hundreds of thousands of pilgrims have passed through the portals of that now very trim little house? They have come from almost every land in the world and have been of every degree. There is not the slightest doubt that in years to come they will increase, because with every year Burns's reputation seems to increase. He was not only a poet of his time, he is a poet of our time and, it would almost seem, of all time.

The house, you can see, must have been in Burns's day of the humblest, people and kine living in closest proximity. Today it is a shrine and so, though it has its relics in comparative plenty, it is neat and burnished. It has, I think, less atmosphere now of what was than the house in which Burns died at Dumfries, and in comparison it is, in every way, rather pretty-pretty. I have always wondered, as I visited and looked, if the spirit of Burns was ever anywhere near—and I could imagine the expression on his face. After all, he was a pretty strong satirist, and life as a whole was not particularly good to him.

I have already mentioned that outburst of Burns worship that breaks out every third week in January. Well, this auld clay biggin' saw the beginnings of those annual outbursts. Only, they did not then take place in January but in July. I have been asked by people to whom I have told this fact—why July? So many people, even Scots, know that Burns was born in January; they do not know that he died in the month of July.

That is one aspect of these annual outbursts that the true Burns enthusiast has to encounter and acknowledge. There are Scots, and others, in plenty, who know every page of his poems and all else that can be read and studied about him. But for every one of those at a Burns gathering there are scores who know only a few songs, and never read him except round about the 25th of January, and then only enough not to be shown up in ignorance.

But, of course, these gatherings are not assemblies of Burns experts, but of people to whom Burns means, very largely, Scotland, in a certain aspect. In England, for instance, there is no poet whose work runs in the blood of the people as Burns does in the veins of the Scot. There are few Scots who could not recite to you certain songs of Robert Burns—"Ye banks and braes", for instance, or "Of a' the airts", or "Afton Water", and so on. But how many, I often wonder, know anything but the first verse of "Scots! wha ha'e"?

Burns is a national heritage, and if Scots are different, and better in being so, Burns takes much of the credit.

It was only five years after his death in 1796 that the first Burns memorial gathering took place, here in Alloway. That was a little gathering of admirers and friends, among them John Ballantine, Provost of Ayr, and Robert Aiken ("Orator Bob" of "The Kirk's Alarm"). The first full-fledged gathering, in the same month of the same year, 1801, is claimed by Greenock. Since then, think of the spread of Burns celebrations, in what far corners of the world, in peace and war, under what curious conditions!

Many a 25th of January I have sat and thought of what was going on all over the world on that date. The thought was impressive—to think that one man, a ploughman from the fields of Ayrshire, could create a comradeship, a banding of brothers that would circle thousands of miles of this terrestrial globe.

And I remember, particularly, one 25th of January. I was going north by the east coast route through Kincardineshire—the Mearns, as it is known locally. It was just sunset and a lovely evening, clear, cold, yet beautifully coloured. The train was passing through the lands from which the poet's father, William Burness, came to Ayrshire. All of a sudden I saw, on a ridge, silhouetted against the sunset sky, a ploughman and his team. What better could I have asked for on that particular afternoon? The perfect reminder, if reminder I had needed.

Burns for me is one of the eternal wonders of literature, not of Scotland only, but of the world, one of the greatest powers the Giftie has given us. For, as time passes, and the mortal that was Robert Burns moves into his proper perspective, the immortal that was also Robert Burns shines clearer, with ever-extending radiance. Today, as I have indicated, like the genius he was, the poet—writing not for a day but for the centuries and all lands—is greater in stature, means more to the world than ever he did. Every year Robert Burns and the ideas that were the very core of some of the best of his works take on what we can call a new topicality, a universal topicality, that attaches to few poets. That is one part of the wonder of Burns, and only one part.

Mention of Burns's topicality reminds me of another aspect of his work with a similar name—his topography. And that begins in Alloway, not far from his birthplace.

There you will find the River Doon, the Brig o' Doon and the Auld Kirk of Alloway. These are tourist places, and you must be prepared to find, at certain seasons of the year, many visitors. But they are still places with a small loveliness. He loved them, and out of that love he wrote songs that are on hundreds of thousands of lips.

At Alloway and near the Doon is one of Ayr's monuments to Robert Burns. I have found it chiefly interesting as a viewpoint.

But some of my best Burns-country wanderings have been spent in and around Mauchline, the little township eleven miles west of Ayr. Here was the centre of Burns's early days as singer and lover, the scene of that stormy courtship of the heroine, Jean Armour, the place of many of his troubles, of his friendships, of his first failures as a farmer.

Mauchline is not strikingly pretty, but it has a certain atmosphere. There are bits which, even today, must be rather like the Mauchline that Burns knew, and you can still imagine what village life was like when Burns was the ploughman poet, drinking, dancing, flirting and making love, making his cronies roar with his skits on those they did not like or respect.

"Poosie Nancy's Inn" still has its sign above the door; and if you take your way a bit you will see the lands of Mossgiel farm, out of which Burns made some of his most famous poems.

And go away a little from Mauchline, to the woods by the River Ayr, the woods of Ballochmyle, especially on a golden summer evening. Wander in these woods, sit by the river on such a night, and you cannot help feeling that the spirit of the poet haunts them still. So when you stand on any little height from which you can see the lands around the scenes which Burns himself haunted, you will understand part of his life and how he made these lands into something richer than they are or were because of his gift of song.

I have mentioned also Burns's gift of topography. How many places we know today because he sang of them—I have mentioned Ayr, Alloway, the Doon, Ballochmyle, Mauchline. But there is Tarbolton, doon the brae, as might be said, scene of his freemasonry—and there the lodge has been kept in fine preservation.

Have you noticed how Burns loved rivers, but he also had a sense of the fitness of names? In one of his songs the first line originally ran—"Behind yon hills where Stinchar flows". He changed the name of the water to Lugar. He was right, whether the Lugar as a water is or is not better than the Stinchar.

But it was not only of his native haunts that Burns was topographist in his works. He has done the same for almost every airt of Scotland.

I have written much here on Burns. I have the one excuse. This is a book on Scotland. I have already said how much of Scotland Robert Burns was, is, and is likely to be for long.

He was a great poet. He was not a good farmer. Today his native county is rich in good farmers, and as you go about you will see many fine farms, and on them many fine herds of the famous Ayrshire cattle.

I have always thought it rather a curious coincidence that Burns's father, leaving the Mearns, chose Ayrshire. Both had red loam. That loam had no richness for Burns the farmer, but for Burns the poet?

And so we take a road to Glasgow. We have a choice. We can go by the coast road—by Prestwick, Troon, Ardrossan, Largs, Wemyss Bay, Gourock and Greenock; by Dalry and Paisley; by Kilmarnock and Langside; or by Strathaven.

To Glaswegians especially, but also, in some instances, to Scotsmen generally, all these names mean something, little or much, of the past, the present and of the future.

Largs and Kilmarnock are, in this way, chiefly of the past. At Largs in 1263 was fought a battle that ended the Norse attempt to dominate Scotland in the west, and all the world knows that the first, and most valuable, edition of Burns's poems was printed at Kilmarnock and is known by that name.

Prestwick, once known only as a name in the world of golf, is now Scotland's greatest air hope, the link with all the world. In matters of aviation it has become what the Clyde was, and is, in shipping. This is not the place to speak of controversy; and time, experience and political changes may alter the civil aviation position of Prestwick. There has been bitterness in Scotland over this matter, and what has happened has driven many, who otherwise might not have been easily moved, into the growing movement for Scottish nationalism. It is only one of many foolish mistakes made by Whitehall bureaucrats and their dependants—Ministers of Government—that are keeping the Fiery Cross alight.

Scotland has never been so awake nationally as she is today, and that is being fed and nurtured by the literary and artistic renaissance. That renaissance is almost as practical as it is artistic. It may be the matter of an intense minority, and they are aware of the apathy of the majority. But remember and think of other movements of the same kind in other lands, and Scotland, as I have pointed out, has and is aware of differences, of national individualities that go deep into the roots and lives of the people. You may try, but I do not think you will ever be able to standardise Scotsmen. I can safely and gladly say that I shall be lying in—I hope—Scottish soil before that day comes—if ever it does.

Troon, Ardrossan, Wemyss Bay are lungs of Glasgow, all lying along that Firth of Clyde, which all Glaswegians, to say nothing of others, unconsciously and instinctively consider as belonging to Glasgow.

When you come to Gourock you look upon something new and very lovely. To stand on the pier there on a fine summer day—which does happen now and again!—is to have a first sight, as you come from the south, of all that lies beyond of Scotland's own peculiar beauty of water and mountain. You will also begin to realise what you are coming to in Glasgow and its environs—the commercial heart of Scotland.

3

GLASGOW

WHEN you get to know Glasgow and Glasgow people you will, at first, be inclined to say—"I like the people better than the place". Second thoughts, however, will tell you that you cannot separate the two. Glasgow is art and part of every true Glaswegian. In this he is like the Scot and Scotland, and though there are other Scottish cities which have something of the same effect—Edinburgh, Aberdeen and Inverness, particularly, it does not seem so all-possessing an effect as in Glasgow.

You may not take the trouble to know Glasgow thoroughly, but you cannot escape, even in a short visit, getting to know the Glasgow people. They must surely be among the kindliest, couthiest, most friendly people, not only in Britain, but in the world. They are so with one another, they are so with the stranger. The secret, I think, is because Glasgow, for all its size, for all its differences in worldly affairs, its rich and its terribly poor, is not a city, but a community. Strange that it should be, but true. I have mentioned its rich and its terribly poor—and, God knows, the latter fact is true and patent—but there is some curious gradation from the one to the other, as you go from low to high, from high to low. There is no sharp division in this matter.

You will find linking characteristics, particularly in speech. As you go up the social scale there is, of course, a certain refinement, but there remains in the case of a majority even on the top storey, a tang, however faint it may be. Much humour has been expended upon the speech of "refaned" Glaswegians, known as "Kelvin-sade", and there is a foundation for this humour. Your sensible Glaswegian is proud of his speech, and he is quite right. It is one of the things about him that makes him loved wherever he goes, in Scotland, England or abroad. It is distinctive. Few things are more deeply embedded than the Glasgow accent. A famous teacher of speech in Glasgow, the late Mr. A. Parry Gunn, who had worked, in stage productions, on Scots from all quarters of the country told me that he could iron out most accents, but seldom the Glasgow accent. It takes a specialist—such as an actor or an actress—and one in great earnest, to eradicate the accent. I hope there will be few of these specialists, and I think that is quite likely—few people anywhere are more delight-fully unaware of their accent than ordinary Glaswegians—it would take away half the pleasure of Glasgow to a visitor. After all, Glasgow and Glaswegians are, as I have said, so indivisible. Speech, very turns of phrase are all part of the make-up of a Glaswegian, part of his couthy friendliness. Let Glasgow flourish in everything except speech snobbery!

All through Scotland these days, among a certain set of Scotsmen and Scotswomen, speech is something of a bother, though, it seems to me, there is less speech snobbery now than there was. Perhaps a scaling down of money-making, plus the rise of nationalist feeling, have something to do with the improvement. Sense and right proportion will be there when we get back to the eighteenth-century's respect for Scots, true Scots.

In speech, Scotland goes one better than Caesar's Gaul—it is divided into four parts. Glasgow and the south-west generally, with the Wigtownshire admixture I have already mentioned, is one part. Then there is Edinburgh and the south-east, to which may be linked Fifeshire and the southern fringe of Angus—the lands of the ascending scale. Aberdeen and Aberdeenshire, especially the coast lands of Buchan, and the north-east, speak what is known as the pure Doric, though there is a difference to the practised ear between the speech of Aberdeen and Aberdeenshire. The speech begins to change about Nairn, where the Highland *burr* comes in. Inverness, north of Inverness and the west coast, although with differences, really comprise one speech sect, English or Scots tinged with the tang that comes from Gaelic. And Gaelic is a language by itself.

Glasgow, in people and speech, is a clearing-house for Scotland, to say nothing of Ireland. Though the true and typical Glaswegian remains the basis of Glasgow's population, you will for ever be coming across Highlanders, Irishmen—from north and south, the north Irishman not so far from certain Scots in speech. Glasgow has for long been a kind of El Dorado of the West Highlander—a mixture of the fearful, but attractive, idea of a sink of iniquity and that other idea of streets paved with gold. That, of course, is fading, but you will still find youngsters in the north-west who have that outlook on Glasgow—until they go there. And the true Glaswegians have a very soft spot for the West Highlanders, a colony in their midst. The Highland societies and clubs in Glasgow must be legion, and it is these that keep through the generations the Highland spirit and, to some extent, the tongue of the Highlander in many who are, in every other respect, true Glaswegians.

For all this mixture, Glasgow, I assert, is a community. Not all the religious differences of Catholics and Orangemen, the presence and occasional activities of the gangs—a small minority—can take away from the friendliness of this great city. Compared with Edinburgh, Glasgow lives very much in the present and—I hope—the future. Glasgow has a history, but it is almost forgotten in the roar and pressure of life of the moment.

During the Empire Exhibition held in Glasgow in 1938 one of my greatest enjoyments was to ascend Tait's Tower in a swift lift, to step on to that balcony 300 feet above Bellahouston Park, in which the exhibition was held. The sensation of shooting up in the lift was one thing, and another was, on a windy day or night, to feel the slim tower swaying in the wind. A third was to look over Glasgow, from four sides of the balcony. By day, houses, houses, houses as far as the eye could see, by night, lights, lights, lights, miles and miles of them in the patterns of how many hundreds of streets.

I have mentioned Tait's Tower and the vista from it to give contrast. We forget in how comparatively short a space of time Glasgow has grown to what it is today. For long Glasgow was a small, quiet cathedral and university town. Today both university and cathedral are rather swallowed up in the welter of buildings, commercial and domestic, though both buildings stand out in their areas, and both are distinctive in their fashions. The cathedral was founded in 1136 and the University in 1451. Up to the middle of the seventeenth century life in the little town of Glasgow centred round these two edifices, and life was lit mainly by the torches of religion and learning.

Trade at one time in Scotland was largely with the European continent, and thus the East coast was more important than the West. Then the Atlantic and the far lands of the West became targets for trade, but not immediately for Glasgow. Scotland was united so far as Crowns were concerned, but, politically, England was England and Scotland was Scotland, until 1707. Although not in favour at first, that second Union was the beginning of Glasgow's rise to prosperity. Sugar and tobacco were the foundation commodities, but more was to come. There were textiles, there were dyeing, there were chemicals. Soon the Clyde became more than a pleasant waterway, dammed here and there by sand banks. Another important event that helped to shape Glasgow's future was the invention of the steam engine by James Watt, a Greenock youth. But Glasgow was the mother of many inventors, whose number increased as the industrial age rushed on its revolutionary way— shipping, coal, iron and steel, to name but the principals—made the Clyde one of the great waterways of the world, Glasgow and Clydeside names that, not only the Empire, but the whole world knew and still knows, changed the little cathedral and university town to the Scottish commercial metropolis I saw from Tait's Tower.

And yet, as I say, Glasgow remains a community, and, on the whole, a happy one. Another gift of the Glaswegian is that he takes his community feeling and happiness when he goes away on holiday. Some of the happiest moments I have spent in other parts of Scotland have been in the company of holidaymaking Glaswegians.

What has the Glaswegian to amuse him when he is at home and comes out of his high tenements and flatted houses, his bungalow or council house? There is, of course, football, to which all other sports in Glasgow are also-rans. That is outdoor.

For indoors, there are plenty of theatres, legitimate and variety. And that reminds me that Glasgow in more than one way has become a very important drama centre for Scotland. Here London managers try out many new plays—what Glasgow thinks today London can confirm in a week or two. In the matter of national drama Glasgow has always given a greater lead than Edinburgh. Here before the war of 1914–18 was the first Scottish repertory theatre. War circumstances closed it. After 1918 and between the two wars the Scottish National Players kept Scottish drama going, not only in Glasgow but throughout the country by means of tours. Many of those enthusiastic amateurs are now names that you know on the professional stage and the films. The Scottish theatre is, in the phrase of the day, on the up-and-up, and Glasgow is the chief centre of the movement. But, as you will find, Scotland is drama-keen from the heart of Glasgow to the most remote villages in the far north, to the islands and to the Borders.

Glasgow is also the musical centre of Scotland. Here is the home of the Scottish Orchestra, a historic body which has been in the hands of some of the world's most famous conductors, and has, indeed, helped to make some of them famous. For too long this orchestra has done only a winter season, but now there is every hope that there will be what is practically an all-round-the-year season. That is very important. It means that no longer will the players have to disband in April and be re-engaged in October, with probable loss of players and the effect of the conductor's work in one season wasted when the next season starts, all to be done over again.

There is a tendency in Scotland generally, and especially in another city some forty-five miles to the east, to consider Glasgow sheerly in terms of commerce. But, if you consider the matter, that is anything but true, and much of the money which Glasgow merchants have made has been used to foster and perpetuate the arts.

At Kelvingrove, Glasgow has one of the finest art galleries in the kingdom, and in recent years, under an expert and enthusiastic director and by means of munificent gifts, it has become greater and more valuable, not only in the monetary but in the artistic sense. At Kelvingrove you will find the classics and you will find the moderns. Among the exhibits are some of the most famous of both. The university looks benignantly on Kelvingrove from its fine situation on Gilmorehill. In a city so large as Glasgow the university is—as I have indicated—almost apt to be overlooked—unlike Aberdeen and, even more, St. Andrews. But it is there, and in culture and learning plays a great part and has produced many great men from all its faculties, not forgetting science and philosophy.

There was a time when the art of the painter that emanated from Glasgow was known throughout the artistic world, and that means not only what we call the artistic world of Britain but wherever art was practised and appreciated. Indeed, Glasgow gave its name to this famous School, which flourished towards the end of last century and existed into this one. Perhaps the most famous name of those who composed this so-called Glasgow School was that of Sir John Lavery, but the work of James Guthrie will also live; he was in the great tradition of British and Scottish portrait painters. For too long art in Glasgow was inclined to bask in the reputation of this "School", and by degrees art in Glasgow suffered a decline and an orientation. Since 1918, if not before, the centre of art progress in Scotland has shifted to Edinburgh, and seems likely to remain there for some time. There has, however, at the same time been a devolution in artistic production in Scotland, and you will find artists at work producing interesting work in every city and town of any size in Scotland today.

But the graphic arts are the only way in which Glasgow has lost precedence. In music, in drama Glasgow still leads in Scotland, and looks like doing so for some time to come. Glasgow has again, at least, one repertory theatre.

This, to a great extent, is the creation of the best, because the most Scottish and the most intelligent of Scottish dramatists, who calls himself James Bridie. So much is he identified with his pen-name and his drama that we are apt to forget that he is Dr. Osborne Mavor. What James Bridie—who is, besides a Scotsman, a grand specimen of the literary Glaswegian—has meant to Scottish literature, particularly drama, will be known better in time to come. He is as fine a personality as he is a writer: full of ideas, ready any moment for controversy, but though hard-hitting never embittered and as ready to smile as to smack. He looks like Puck come to middle-age, and anyone who knows him will tell you that there is plenty of Puck in his make-up. He fights for Scotland, not the Scotland that such as Barrie miscreated, but a Scotland that takes itself intelligently, yet with humour and with truth, never caricature. He does not write Scots plays for the English and the Americans. It is to be hoped that he has killed that for ever. His example has led to the growth of a new school of Scottish playwrights and most of them, as yet, belong to Glasgow. The longer Bridie lives, the greater the hope for a Scottish theatre—I use the word in the literary, the French sense. The Barrie and worse tradition is hard to kill. But the new spirit in Scotland is slowly putting it to death. James Bridie is one of the biggest men in Scottish culture and life, generally, in Scotland today. His name, I believe, will live, and, as I say, he is essentially of Glasgow, the best of Glasgow.

Bridie would look down his nose, and he is rather given to that in certain moods and circumstances, at the comedian who carries on the wrong tradition. But Glasgow has and sends forth throughout Scotland and even into England, though not often as far as London, a band of music-hall comedians who carry with them the tang of Glasgow. Like Lancashire, Glasgow seems to breed comedians. Like Lancashire, they come inevitably out of the folk from which they spring, from the lives which that folk lead. They are so representative of Glasgow and Glaswegians that it is understandable if, as you travel in a Glasgow tram, sit in a Glasgow café or elsewhere of the kind, you have the impression that Glasgow consists of brothers and sisters of the comedians, not so well organised in "gag" and situation, but just as grandly humorous in their speech and comment on life. The Glasgow comedians are the joy of other parts of Scotland. They even "go down" in Edinburgh.

Like Manchester, Glasgow weather is one of the jokes of the country. But the legend of perpetual rain is just one more joke. I have seen some of the loveliest sunsets I have ever seen above Glasgow's high rooftops, from one or the other of those heights that lie just beyond Sauchiehall Street.

The "Rue de Sauchie", as it is so often called, is not exactly what Princes Street is to Edinburgh, in one way, but it is in another. There are no gardens here, but shops, shops, shops all the way along its straightish length. The other street in Glasgow, of importance and dearness to the Glaswegian, is Argyle Street, and I am not sure that Argyle Street is not dearer to me than Sauchiehall Street. Here, it always seems, is the crowded, loud-beating heart of Glasgow. On a Saturday afternoon or evening it is, in some ways, like no other street in any other city in the British Isles. Here is the fascination of humanity. Step off Sauchiehall Street and you step into streets of comparative quiet, still essential Glasgow, but from Argyle Street, with few exceptions, wherever you turn you encounter only more humanity, and it is a long, long thoroughfare, and as noisy as any lover of noise could wish. And its companion is the River Clyde, the Glasgow Clyde, and all that that means and, either way, leads to.

Glasgow is the kind of city that compels you to wander in parts of it that are not superficially attractive in any way—it is life that lures you, and the life of the Glaswegians.

But Glasgow is also a city from which it is sometimes good and easy to escape. It has grand outlets, and not so far away. On one side, however, to leave Glasgow is like going through an artist's idea of Dante's Inferno. That is the foundry side. On a soft night the whole atmosphere is lit up, red, and never still.

But there is the estuary of the Clyde and there is Loch Lomond and there is the Clyde as a nice beginning of a river. If you go up the Clyde in spring-time, you will suddenly come out of a drab, industrial area into a land of blossom that can be almost breath-taking in its delicate loveliness.

Down the Clyde, however, has always been the Glaswegian's idea of pleasure in holidaying. "Doon the watter" is how it is spelt, with two *t*'s, comically, I think, because your true Glaswegian has not got a *t* in his vocabulary. The "watter" does not, perhaps, attract so much as once upon a day, but it is still a legend.

Rothesay was the centre of attraction at one time; why, I have never quite fathomed. I cannot see that Rothesay is very attractive, though the way thither is. It seems to me that it was almost a matter of habit. Sailing down the Clyde on a fine day, or, even better, at sunset, is something to remember, perhaps because of the contrast between the firth and the city left behind.

All about the Firth of Clyde and just beyond are places dear not only to the Glaswegian but to Scotsmen generally—Dunoon, the island of Arran, haunt of artists, Machrihanish, and beyond Kintyre the islands of Islay, Jura, Colonsay, Ardrishaig, Tarbert, Loch Fyne.

Easier of access, perhaps, a great playground for Glasgow young and old are the shores of Loch Lomond, beginning at Balloch, going on by Luss, Arrochar, Tarbert, and so to Ardlui and into the heart of the hills. That is one side of Loch Lomond. On the other shore there is no great highway, and in the shadow of Ben Lomond are lovely little places, culminating in Inversnaid which Wordsworth the poet made famous by his poems:

> Sweet Highland girl, a very shower
> Of beauty is thy earthly dower!
> Twice seven consenting years have shed
> Their utmost bounty on thy head;
> And these grey rocks; that household lawn;
> Those trees, a veil just half withdrawn;
> This fall of water that doth make
> A murmur near the silent lake;
> This little bay; a quiet road
> That holds in shelter thy Abode—
> In truth together do ye seem
> Like something fashioned in a dream. . . .

And still today, when more than a century has passed, Inversnaid has the atmosphere that fascinated Wordsworth. I love its quiet, the great stretch of the loch that mirrors blue sky, green banks and trees and the great mountain. After even a week-end at Inversnaid you can say with Wordsworth:

> Now thanks to Heaven! that of its grace
> Hath led me to this lonely place.
> Joy have I had; and going hence
> I bear away my recompence. . . .

And that is only the beginning of many spots near and far in Scotland that leave their deep impression upon the lover of natural beauty and solitude.

Let us return to Glasgow, only to say goodbye to it and cross the waist of Scotland to "Auld Reekie", the capital and history.

The country between Glasgow and Edinburgh is among the least interesting in the whole country. It has its commercial riches and they leave their mark everywhere, but not in beauty.

4

EDINBURGH

EVERY Scottish youth of any sensibility comes to Edinburgh on, at least, his first visit with his head in the clouds of history. But this is not, I have found, confined to youth, nor to Scots. It is so with many people from over the Border, and, during the war of 1939–45, when Edinburgh was the most polyglot city in Britain, serving men from the Empire, Americans, Czechs, Poles, Frenchmen and many others who assisted the Allied cause came to Edinburgh, ready to admire, and left even more full of admiration.

Edinburgh is, indeed, a romantic and a haunted city, a city of the centuries, but not a sad city. For anyone with any sense of the past, however, the atmosphere is coloured and thronged with ghosts in what is to us the motley of their periods, from good Queen Margaret, by several Jameses to that most memorable, world-shaking female ghost, Mary of Scots, and her grey antagonist, John Knox, and then by a long procession of artists, in literature and other mediums—Raeburn, Sir Walter Scott, to one who loved and made Edinburgh in writing one of the darling cities of the world, Robert Louis Stevenson.

When I first came to Edinburgh—oh, how many years ago!—I remember being glad that I was approaching the city in the same way that Mary of Scots had done —by the Forth and Leith. The day I came, however, was not as the day she came, grim and foggy, but a day of brilliant sunshine, the Forth looked its violet best and the city, though still with its halo of reek, was lit and clear. There was a thrill as my feet touched the quay. I was about to put my years of reading to the test. I could not believe that I should be disappointed. In all the years between and hundreds of visits I never have. Edinburgh, in sun and cloud, in summer and winter, daylight or moonlight, never lets you down, but is for ever adding to your memories of her. She never withers, and certainly custom cannot stale her infinite variety. There are cities, I have found, that cloy the appetites they feed, but Edinburgh makes hungry where most she satisfies.

It was between twelve and one when I set up the streets of Leith, the famous Leith Walk, and when I arrived at the east end of Princes Street, and stood there entranced by my first sight of the castle on its rock, the apex, the apotheosis of

Edinburgh's appearance, I nearly leapt into the air. The one o'clock gun sounded from the castle!

But it is exactly that skyline of the castle on the rock—even before you know all that the castle contains—that begins the magic of Edinburgh for the visitor. It is for the castle that every person, newly under the enchantment of Edinburgh, makes. But I did have one companion on one visit to Edinburgh, who, when I asked, "Well, where shall we go first?" replied at once—"The Zoo." He was only six years of age, and has since changed his attitude.

Whichever way you take to the castle, you are passing through scenes of history of one century or another. But the castle is your aim. You pace across the broad esplanade that brings you to the portal, and, for once, that seems the right word. This esplanade has been for years a drilling ground for the castle garrison, but in its day it saw many executions. Now, with its ring of statues, its surface is worn by the feet of myriads of visitors.

Atmosphere begins at once within the portal and never ceases until you leave again by the same way. Inevitably, as your steps have led you first to the castle, once inside you are led to the ramparts, and you are again rewarded. The view from the highest platform on a fine day is something you are not likely to forget. Immediately below is the city, thronged, busy, colourful, the old and the new, and when you look beyond you see the Forth—that ancient royal waterway, across which, between the south and north ferries, so many kings and queens of Scotland passed and repassed on journeys, public and pageantried, or secret and so often sorrowful. Centuries later, here, after the war of 1914-18, came the German Fleet, pride of the Kaiser, to surrender. Beyond the Forth are the shores and laws—or hills—of Fife; and before Edinburgh and along with it, later, Fife was the Royal county of Scotland, Dunfermline and other places their seats of court.

On one of the castle's high platforms stands an ancient cannon, called "Mons Meg", so called, some say, because it was forged at Mons in the year 1486. Others assert it was the work of a Galloway blacksmith in his shop at Mollance. Meg was not always stationary here. Not only did she take part in battles long ago, but for a time her abiding place was the Tower of London, whither she went as a punishment for the Porteous Riots of the seventeenth century. But Meg and the castle now seem one and indivisible.

From memories of wars and riots let us step into a little, a tiny haven of peace and beauty, Saint Margaret's Chapel, which stands high on this high rock. This is one of Edinburgh's most ancient antiquities, and yet it has been found that the chapel is built upon even older foundations. Queen Margaret, the wife of King Malcolm Canmore, was a saint in her life and works and is in the calendar of saints. The golden legend of her life still persists after eight-and-a-half centuries. She needed

THE PALACE OF HOLYROOD, EDINBURGH

LINLITHGOW PALACE

all her fortitude at the end of her good life. It was to this eyrie in Edinburgh that there came the news of the death of her husband and eldest son in battle at Alnwick, a battle in which the old alliance between Scotland and France, that persists to this day, was manifested.

Still hobnobbing with Royalty we go into the Regalia Room in the castle's Crown Square. Here is the old treasure of Scotland when it was a kingdom by itself: the crown that goes back to the days of Robert the Bruce, sceptre, orb, sword and many another relic of the kind. In the Banqueting Hall on the south side of the Square, those who care for the weapons and accoutrements of warriors of old can gaze their fill, and there is a lovely old fireplace worth examining. Below this banqueting hall, which has a long history, are vaults where the prisoners of the French wars were confined.

But the crown of the castle, for all Scotland, is on the north side of the Square. This is the Scottish War Memorial. Whatever noise and bustle there may be outside on a day of many visitors to the castle, when you step inside you will find as impressive a quietness as you will in any ecclesiastical building during a service. That is, it has always seemed to me, as fine a tribute as could be to the success of the artists and those who conceived this national shrine. It is no compensation for the thousands of lives lost which the shrine memorialises, but the shrine has some sort of consolation. Navy, Army, Air Force, Merchant Navy, miners—all who contributed to victory are remembered here, and the name of every Scot who gave his life between the years 1914 and 1918, and whose sacrifice was recorded, can be read in the books in this edifice.

The memorial is a combination of many arts, but, apart from the architect, Sir Robert Lorimer, I feel I must mention the stained glass work of Douglas Strachan, one of the geniuses of our day, who, not only here, but in many places throughout Scotland and in other parts of the kingdom, has brought the art of stained glass to a new standard of beauty and poetry, even mysticism, that sets him with and beyond the old masters in this medium.

At the centre of the memorial you come to the inmost shrine. Here, too, is the crowning touch of the conception of the shrine. The bare rock on which the castle is built, something that is of the very heart of Scotland, is a visible part of this *sanctus sanctorum*. Here, too, is the casket of fine and lovely workmanship in which are the names of the Scottish dead. There are other shrines in Scotland, in Edinburgh, but this one has greatest call on the heart and feelings of every man and woman, and never fails. The Scot is a fighting man when the call comes, a bonnie fechter, but that the Scot can be a man of finer feeling and great artistry is here made clear and true.

Older history will claim your attention in the castle—such as the Royal apartments, the smallest of which is the most important—the bedroom of Mary of Scots, in which, at a time of trouble and discord, was born the prince who became James VI of Scotland and First of Britain, with whom came about the Union of the Crowns.

But, inevitably, before you leave the castle you will go again to look from the castle down on the city and all that lies within sight beyond it. It is a lure and a tribute to those who conceived and set this castle upon its rock. They, too, had their genius.

As you go towards the Royal Mile, which lies between the castle and the Palace of Holyrood, as historical a mile of street as can be found in the whole country, if not the world, you will pass a quaint house on which there was—and, I hope, will continue to be—the notice "Camera Obscura". This was always one of my Edinburgh delights, something of an epitome of the city.

You climbed and climbed until you reached the real Outlook Tower and found yourself in a curious chamber, dim and small. Before you stood a circular table covered with something like oilcloth, but through it shot up some kind of pillar and above was a contraption of mirrors. The attendant adjusted certain "gadgets" and there came on to the table before your wondering eyes, in soft, beautiful colours the Edinburgh that you had been looking at from the castle ramparts, the actual life that was going on while you were standing in that little tower. All the traffic of Princes Street, all the old and the new town buildings. Then the angle was changed and you were out over the Forth and looking over the lands of Fife. Another change, and you were away across the centre of Scotland. On a fine day you could be taken as far as the hills that look down on the bonnie banks of Loch Lomond. It was with difficulty that I could drag myself away from something that seemed to hover between loveliness and magic.

And so on to that Royal Mile which has seen so much of Scottish history through the centuries, so much pageantry, which, so often, at one time, was a tragic road for so many. The Mile has left in it many examples of Edinburgh's older architecture—it all looks rather "slummy" now and many of the people you will meet in it accord with the houses—but for history's sake it is right that this Mile should be left.

On it you will come to the Tolbooth Kirk, not so old comparatively in Edinburgh —it dates only from 1637. But as you go you will, bit by bit, come deeper into the remnants of history, Royal, religious and domestic. What a wealth of names suggestive of an even greater wealth of history comes out of the houses and closes you pass! But these are too numerous to mention here—they range from the Stuart kings and more than one queen to Burns and Scott.

Not very far down the Mile you'll find another Edinburgh and Scottish shrine—the Cathedral of St. Giles. Today it belongs to the Established Church of Scotland, which seems right, because in it was laid part of the beginnings of the

Reformed Religion in Scotland. The cathedral still has beauty and atmosphere, indeed, I think that within the last score of years it has gathered more atmosphere than it had had for many a day. Not only in matters material, but otherwise, its present guardians have not only kept but added to their sacred trust.

It is a place of dim religious light, but not so dim as to prevent you from seeing what architectural beauties it has—though one of the chief of these is without and above—the crown tower. Here again, as in the War Memorial you walk in hush and quiet, but St. Giles in its day has heard tumult enough. One memorial is to Jenny Geddes, and as you look at it you hear sounding through the place the thud of the stool she flung at the representative of the Old Religion and her cry—"Daur ye say Mass at my lug!" That was a cry that rang down many years of religious controversy.

Aisles and chapels and monuments and all the names and history connected with them make St. Giles a truly national monument. The monuments range from John Knox—equally revered and hated in Scotland even now—the Marquises of Argyll and Montrose, to Robert Louis Stevenson, who is depicted sitting in bed, as his life so often compelled him to do, busy at the making of the literature which linked Edinburgh and Scotland with the world.

In St. Giles is the Chapel of the Order of the Thistle with a stall for each Knight and his coat of arms above it. The years are taking away its newness, mellowing it and bringing it more and more into keeping with other parts of the cathedral.

And still in the still atmosphere hang the flags of the Scottish regiments, not new standards, but mostly those which have seen the wearing, tattering service of war in days when war was something of a pageant as well as a time of slaughter.

Nearer than a stone's throw to the cathedral stands Parliament House, now the centre of law in Scotland. Here is the old Scottish Parliament Hall, a place to be seen for more than itself. The Scottish Parliament ceased to exist in 1707, and today you will find the Hall being paced by gowned and wigged King's Counsel and those who hope to be, in time. If you were to listen, you would find that their talk is not all of briefs and cases. The tradition of the days of Cockburn and Scott has not yet departed.

So into the Mile again. Very trim and neat is the house which is known as John Knox's House. Between the castle and Holyrood and near to St. Giles, it seems so appropriate to the stormy history of this man, who flouted the law, roused the people to religious rebellion and all but spat in the faces of Royalty. But Scotland owes a large debt to John Knox—not even his greatest antagonist would entirely deny that. Yet the artistic will tell you that not only did he encourage the destruction of much sacred art that Scotland had accumulated over the years, if not centuries, before he was a leader of religious and other rebellion—some say in the manner of the Duke of Plaza Toro—but he destroyed the impulse towards artistic effort in Scotland and retarded its development for so long time that we are only now getting into line. All the same, it may be that, without that part of the achievement of Knox for the Scottish people—education for all—Scotland today would not be where she is culturally, and the people would be unable to appreciate the upcome of the arts that is now so great and growing a feature of our national life. The whirligig of time, John. Yet it should be noted that only as Scotland gets away from almost all that Knox stood for and left as a heritage is Scotland really coming into her own as a generally artistic nation.

So, leaving Knox's house behind, we come, but not as stormily and menacingly as he so often did, to the Palace of Holyrood, and the end of the Royal Mile.

If you are blessed, or cursed, with an imagination, you may feel, on ordinary days and occasions, that about this place still hangs and broods an after-air of the unhappiness and tragedy that for too long possessed it. If you are of that mind—and I have known people who felt that the sunshine that can so beautifully flood it without and within was a lie—you will liken the atmosphere to that of a Greek tragedy in progress or a performance of Eugene O'Neill's dark, dark play, *Mourning Becomes Electra*.

For myself, I love roving the palace, trying to reconstruct this and that event and occasion, though I have also thought that I should not like to have to live here on a certain kind of night. I know those who have done so, and they have laughed the idea to scorn.

Anyway, there is plenty to see. There are the great rooms of the seventeenth-century part of the building; there is a portrait gallery with a great collection of ancient Scottish monarchs in which you will not and need not put a single moment of belief as to their authenticity. But your interest comes to a peak in the really historical apartments, which, with their furniture relics, have an atmosphere as near authenticity as the portraits mentioned have not. Here we are in no way Jacobean but Marian. Mary, Darnley, Rizzio, John Knox, Moray and a host of conspirators and counsellors, the Four Maries—they haunt these rooms. There is Queen Mary's bedroom, with the little workbox that seems, as much as the bed with its faded covering, to bring back that ghost, not little but tallish and slim, that has haunted literature for so many years and goes on haunting it. Then there is that Supper Room in which Rizzio was slain; the winding stair that leads down to Darnley's bed-chamber. This was the way the assassins came. There is the Audience Chamber whither they dragged his mutilated body that never was in life a thing of beauty. But it was never so twisted as the minds and lives of those who killed him. Yes, there is atmosphere here in plenty, and according to your mood and mind you can make it.

Holyrood nowadays comes back to life as a Royal Palace once a year, when the reigning monarchs keep their Scottish court. That is a bright if not so picturesque time of display and pageant. The precincts of the palace in Mary's time knew evenings when a howling mob shouted their threats, demands and imprecations. Now when a King and Queen are there it is filled with men, women and youngsters who fill the air with community singing and cheer after cheer when the King and Queen come out upon a balcony.

You must not go away from Holyrood without visiting that sad-looking Abbey, older than the palace, and now showing only the skeleton of what it once was. But there is enough to impress you with what must have been. There is the western doorway, the nave, the west aisle. And for a moment or two stand apart and look at the shape of what is left and imagine all that once was.

Holyrood is curiously set. At one set of gates are something very near slums, at the other you are almost in the country, and towering over it are Salisbury Crags and Arthur's Seat. Anyone who wishes to look over Edinburgh should not fail to climb the latter. There below you is the definite picture you will take away of "Auld Reekie". As you get to know the city you will go again and again, to pick out this and that aspect and peak of architectural and other interest. Arthur's Seat and its view form the complement to the table of the "Camera Obscura" and its softly coloured table of moving pictures.

So, from the old and the view, to the close-up and the new, to the modern centre of Edinburgh—Princes Street, where we began. I have looked on many urban prospects in many great cities, but I can say that there is none that can thrill me— and it is not only a matter of patriotic sentiment—as when I look along Princes Street on a fine spring, summer or autumn morning and on a certain kind of winter forenoon. As you all know, there is a wind—or is it a bunch of them?—that can blow along Princes Street in the winter. Once upon a time there were ropes at the top of Waverley Steps to which the pedestrian could cling when he felt he would be blown off his feet or away. Now they are so certain of the permanency of the coming of those winds that they have put up iron rails instead of the ropes. But such winds do not always blow, far from it. I have met people who have been in Edinburgh over and over again, and think the wind legend is something like the Aberdeen story or the Loch Ness monster, deliberately invented as an advertising trick.

But Princes Street at its best? When you try to analyse its attraction, it is somewhat difficult. Of course, undoubtedly, part of the pleasure is that, in opposition to its width and the buildings on the one side, there is the openness of the other, the gardens and, always, that marvellous skyline of the castle. On its two sides Princes Street is almost an epitome of Edinburgh itself. On one side commerce, as exemplified by the shops, entertainment and hospitality by the cinemas (I wish there had been a theatre on Princes Street; Edinburgh seems to hide her theatres and halls for music); community life in the clubs and tea shops (apart from the hotels, is there a "pub" in the street?); literature in the bookshops.

On the other side, for the main part, are beauty and art. Art is there in the Royal Scottish Academy Galleries and the Scottish National Gallery on the Mound, and in the many statues—I don't know a city of its size with as many statues as Edinburgh; they are everywhere, in every square, round every corner it seems.

Life in Edinburgh for the incomer who is there for only a short visit will seem to centre in and around Princes Street. It is only as you stay on or come again and again and get to know the general life of the citizens that you realise that Princes Street for the Edinburgh man and woman is a mere, if lovely, thoroughfare. Life for them really goes on in those other streets, crescents, circuses and squares beyond "The Street". Some of those quarters are very beautiful, the Edinburgh that arose at the end of the eighteenth century and the beginning of the nineteenth. Others are no better than any other city of the kind. But always you will be coming across corners and vistas to which you will say "Oh!" and "Ah!" That is Edinburgh.

And as you get to know something of the private life of Edinburgh you will discover that this city is not like Glasgow, not a graduated community, but a series of classes and coteries. The classes are pretty sharply divided, in speech, work and ways. The coteries consist of business-men generally, the law, the arts and what is known as "society". Into the last the "high yins" of all the coteries long to get, and there is a sort of merger in this way. Pride and poverty has always been the gibe flung at Edinburgh and its *rentiers*, and, more especially, its *rentières*. Nowadays, the *rentières* cannot but display something of their poverty to the world. Life is very hard for the indigent gentlewoman. Edinburgh, as I have said, is a city of antiquities, and many of them can be seen on Princes Street on a fine forenoon or afternoon; they may be brave, but they are pathetic. They will pass away, as a class, while the castle and Holyrood will still stand.

I have said there is no doubt that within the last quarter of a century or more there has been a reorientation of the arts of painting and sculpture in Scotland, and that Edinburgh has once again stolen what the Glasgow School gave to Glasgow. Glasgow artists know this, and some of them know the reason and are striving to achieve a new balance. Art is very much alive in Edinburgh, though you will find men there who say that the city has become utterly deculturalised. The Scottish School, for Edinburgh draws her artists from every airt of the country, was for rather too long an echo, an aftermath of the Paris and southern France cafés and studios, but today there is coming up, I think, a fairly distinctive native school.

Edinburgh's art collections are something that no visitor should miss. There is the

National Gallery of Scotland, where you will find certain pictures that, in the general history of art, cannot be matched in the world. There are also the pictures that tell the history of Scottish art, especially that glorious collection of Raeburn portraits. Then there is the Portrait Gallery, in Queen Street, where, if you are like myself, you will spend hours of fascination, conjecture and imagination. In the Mound Gallery is the collection of contemporary Scottish art, and that should certainly be visited.

Time may alter it, and it would almost seem that alteration is on the way, but there is that rather dreadful occasion—the Edinburgh Sunday. Of course, every other Scottish city and town is pretty much the same, but it seems to come to a height—or depth—of depression in Edinburgh. For myself, I have done more churchgoing in Edinburgh than anywhere else, and I advise you to do the same. Choose your church and your preacher—anyone will help you towards that; they still know their kirks in Edinburgh.

Of course, on the other hand, you can get out of Edinburgh on a Sunday, though curiously, you are not so near the better scenes of Scotland in Edinburgh as you are in Glasgow. But there are, not too far away, many pleasant haunts, especially the hilly ones, where, on a fine day, you can steep yourself in romance and history, feel something of Scotland's lesser beauties, or just bask for a day.

One of my own favourite jaunts from Edinburgh is the famous little chapel at Roslin, with its fantastically wrought Prentice Pillar and its legend. The pillar, it is alleged, was made by a prentice genius, and so jealous was the master builder that he murdered the young lad. But I would advise that you go to Roslin on a week-day. On Sunday the chapel is open only at service times.

If you are going west or north in Scotland, you will leave Edinburgh, I think, only to come back to it. The city is a love and a lure. See it at morning, see it at sunset, but, most of all, see it at night and arrange for the moon to be over or behind the castle. That is something unforgettable. Or see it on an autumn evening, early, when the lights begin to twinkle on the heights and in the hollows, when the air is crisp and has a tang of dead and dying leaves. Alas, it is no use now going round to Heriot Row and waiting for a leerie to come and light a lamp in front of the Stevenson house there. But, for all the changes, the spirit of Robert Louis Stevenson still haunts the Edinburgh that lies away beyond Princes Street and George Street. You will not find Mary Queen of Scots here, but along with R. L. S., that will-o'-the-wispy figure, you may see Walter Scott, limping slightly as he goes, or the finer figure of Raeburn, just finished with a sitter on whom he has conferred immortality and good company, going from his studio to home or a meeting of friends.

Yes, Edinburgh, we always come back!

STEPPING WESTWARD

NOW shall we strike west by Falkirk to Stirling, and so, with some steps aside here and there, to Aberfoyle and the Trossachs—some of the loveliest of Scottish scenery, but like most lovely and accessible spots, not exactly deserted.

As we go, the first place of interest soon after leaving Edinburgh is, not inappropriately, the Palace of Linlithgow. Here was born Mary Queen of Scots, and along this road between Edinburgh and Stirling she went not a few times in days of what happiness she had and also when life was clouded and dangerous.

Stirling, like Edinburgh, has a castle set on a height and it also was once the Scottish capital. The town is, as it were, the capital of the waist of Scotland, and is in itself and its surroundings a central spot of Scottish history. Apart from that, today it is a centre of areas of industry and agriculture—the Carse of Stirling has long been famous in the history of beef, mutton and cereals.

As with Edinburgh, so in Stirling, most people on a visit make for the castle. It is not only the history of the edifice, but the setting. You cannot get away from the idea that, from that wonderful situation, you are bound to look over miles and miles of country. And you do.

One has only to look at the setting of the castle and at once understand that, from earliest times and so long as trouble lasted, it was one of the great strategic points of Scotland. The rock on which it is built rises 250 feet above the level of the plain. It still carries an interesting and impressive "bourach" of buildings.

As you enter you will see a statue of King Robert the Bruce, and he looks towards the site of the Battle of Bannockburn. That famous battlefield lies in the county of Stirling, not very far from the capital town. Unless you are an expert you will find the scene of the battle rather difficult to trace, but you can, if you desire, find help in doing so. It is interesting that the finest set-out of the battle has been done by a woman, Dr. Mure MacKenzie, as part of the great work she has done in recent years for Scottish history. As with the site of the battle, so with the feeling about it. Once upon a time Bannockburn could raise almost bad blood between a Scot and an Englishman. We have, however, fought side by side in two of the greatest wars the world has ever seen and, apart from a friendly joke, the best attitude today towards Bannockburn and the feeling it used to engender is best summed up in the cinema phrase—"Forget it!"

The view gives you some idea of the diversity of Stirlingshire. The shire stretches and varies, from the flat and industrial lands which include mining and iron works, a narrowing section of the River Forth—these towards the east—until in the north Stirlingshire meets with Perthshire and the start of the characteristic beauties of that neighbouring county, and, on the western boundary, is the long line of mountains which overlook Loch Lomond and stretch back again to look on Loch Katrine. There are other hills in Stirlingshire, the Kilsyth and Campsies, which are very dear to more than the Stirlingshire folk; indeed have maybe roused more local patriotism and literature than the mountains; and so again with the Ochil Hills at the north-east edge of the county.

But we are in the castle, which, for me, has best been delineated by a great Scottish artist who, for many a year, made his home in one of the quaintest townships in the county. This was Sir D. Y. Cameron, painter and poet combined, and the place of his abode was Kippen. There is a saying which runs—"Into Kippen and out o' the world". At least, I think that is how the saying goes, and if it does not, it should, for that was, for me, the delight of Kippen, and I quite understand Sir D. Y. Cameron finding in Kippen the right place to dream and work.

But do not let us forget the castle and its history. It has both military and domestic buildings, including a palace. This palace dates from the days of James IV and James V, and its architecture is a mixture of Gothic and Renaissance detail, much of it the work of French masons. The interior, unfortunately, has lost much of its best work. The Chapel Royal was built in 1594, by James VI, for the christening of Prince Henry, the loved and lost son.

Stirling Castle was first a royal residence in the time of Alexander I, who died there in 1124. It was a favourite residence of William the Lion and he also died there in 1214. By the time the fourteenth century arrived it was the main royal residence of Scotland.

It was also one of the main targets of the invading English kings. Edward I captured it first in 1291, and after that the castle changed hands several times and was more than once dismantled and rebuilt. Two of the greatest names in the Scottish fight for independence are closely allied with Stirling and the Castle— William Wallace and Robert the Bruce. It was at the famous Stirling Bridge—in September 1297—that Wallace fought and won the fight for Stirling, a battle that Scots chiefly remember because it is enshrined in a song that you will hear declaimed by Scottish baritones even today. There is a picturesque monument to Wallace on Abbey Craig, near Stirling, 220 feet in height. It is not difficult to understand why Stirling is one of the favourite rallying places of members of the Scottish Nationalist Movement.

It is interesting for instance to recall that it was at Cambuskenneth Abbey, in Stirlingshire, that Bruce convened a parliament, the first to which representatives of burghs were summoned.

The last time on which Stirling Castle was in English hands was in 1342. The English garrison were starved out. Thereafter the castle became the scene of very varied Scottish history. James II stabbed his guest, Earl Douglas, in the castle in 1452. The Douglases then burned the town. That was the way in those days, though not unlike some modern instances, but not in Scotland. James III was born here and beneath its walls was defeated and killed. James IV and James V both lived steadily in the castle and, as has been stated, it owes much of its apparent appearance to them. You remember how James V used to wander incognito among his people under the name of the "Gudeman of Ballengeich". The name Ballengeich was taken from a hollow behind the castle. The infant Queen Mary was here crowned, and here James VI was baptised in 1566. In 1567 he was crowned in the parish church of Stirling. James VI and I spent his boyhood in Stirling Castle. His son, the already-mentioned Prince Henry, was the last Scottish prince to spend any time at Stirling Castle, though both Charles I and Charles II visited it.

Both Stirlingshire and the castle saw history at the time of the rebellions of 1715 and 1745; on neither occasion did the castle fall to the rebels. At Falkirk in 1746 was Stirlingshire's last piece of military history, when the Jacobites won the day.

So we come down again into the pleasant town of Stirling, past the lovely Church of the Holy Rude, and set out away from history towards natural beauty and, not so much history, as romance.

As we go now, whether in Stirlingshire or in Perthshire, for quite a distance and time we shall be in the land which belongs, in legend, to a Scottish figure that still today is better known by name and exploit to every Scots man, woman and child than many a far greater and more important person. He was called Rob Roy MacGregor.

Rob Roy certainly led an adventurous and, in the matter of other people's property, not too conventional life. Had he lived earlier or later—in the twentieth century, for instance—his exploits would, on the one hand, have been very much like those of men who had his daring, and, on the other, like those who had the same disregard for the decenter rules of conduct. It is not so much *autre temps, autres mœurs*, as that each age, by the behaviour of a forceful minority, implants on that age a different regard for the conventions, the decencies—call them what you will. The chief difference seems to be that as the centuries pile up, the thief, racketeer, or whatever we call him, becomes less picturesque, more despicable in his ways and manners.

But Rob Roy, even disregarding the way in which he has been romanticised, was, undoubtedly, a noted figure in many ways, physical and otherwise. Scott, in the novel which bears Rob's name, was the first to give us a full-length portrait, touched up, as was usual. Then someone turned the novel into a play, and the play reached an even larger public than the novel. It went round and round the theatres for goodness knows how many years. Even today I meet old men who sit in the sun in their declining years and argue the one with the other as to which has seen the play most often, and about all sorts of points that interest only them now. For the play has gone almost completely out of fashion. Now and again a revival has been attempted, but always with lessening success. Now and again in villages and little towns where the old ideas of drama still exist you will find amateur productions, but these have to be seen to be believed.

For all that, Rob Roy is a name that still conjures up romance to the youth of Scotland. He made raids on his southern neighbours' cattle, but he turned up at the raising of the Standard of the Old Pretender on the Braes of Mar in September 1715. His attitude towards Mar and the Pretender's protagonists had, however, undergone a change by the time Sheriffmuir—which lies not far from Dunblane—is reached. It was a silly battle, made sillier by the famous rhyme about it:

> Some say that we wan,
> Some say that they wan,
> An' some say that nane wan at a', man!
> But o' ae thing I'm sure,
> That on Sheriffmuir
> A battle there was that I saw, man,
> And we ran and they ran,
> And they ran and we ran,
> And we ran and they ran awa', man!

Anyway, Rob Roy became an occupant of a little no-man's-land along with his band of MacGregors. They lived to fight another day. But Rob Roy's name remains, as I say, even now, when others of men far greater mean far less.

As can be guessed, it was a life that had many turbulent times. Nothing, however, could be quieter than his last resting-place. Beside an ancient church, said to date back to the twelfth century, and near to long, narrow and often "sullen"—as Scott called it—Loch Voil, Rob Roy sleeps his longest and most unbroken sleep. Helen MacGregor, his wife, who was sturdy in mind and body, and several of his sons lie beside Rob Roy. Down the glen past Loch Voil and Loch Doine Rob Roy died, at Inverlochlaraig, on January 9, 1735.

A holiday happy in many ways can be spent exploring—if that is the right word now—the Rob Roy country. Perhaps it is a holiday best for younger folk. It was one of mine, spent in perfect weather, mostly under canvas. Given that kind of weather and such country as that associated with Rob Roy, then we see Scotland at its most lovely, evening and morning and noon.

Some think that the Rob Roy country has been overdone by the romancers. I doubt if it could be. In any case, it is not only the Rob Roy country; he chose well; it includes some of the loveliest of Scottish scenery of the kind that everyone likes, or should like. There are prigs who have written against its popularity; they cannot see the beauty for the people. That does not alter the beauty. It is not the fault of the scenery that it has so moved the heart of poets and writers that what they have written has brought the lovers of poetry, romance and scenery in their train. Anyway, beauty was not made for a few of these prigs. And in Scotland there is plenty to choose from. They can go and find their own little solitary heavens. What these people are going to do in the next world, if they think that the presence of folk will turn heaven into hell, is their problem.

But to end with Rob Roy and pass on to his country—and, as I say, not his alone —in it are places whose names conjure up to the Scot and those who have visited them, memories of beauties of many kinds—Inversnaid, the Trossachs, Loch Katrine, Loch Achray, Balquhidder, Loch Lubnaig and Ben Ledi, Lochs Chon and Ard, Aberfoyle—and these but a few.

HOLYROOD ABBEY

DOUNE CASTLE

6

PERTHSHIRE

PERTHSHIRE is, in some ways, one of the most remarkable counties in the length and breadth of Scotland. One would almost think it had been created to be a tourist's paradise. Its diversity of scenery is unusual, its points of interest, historic and otherwise, almost without end. There are parts of it which attract the lover of solitude, others which the tourist who is never quite happy if he is utterly alone can enjoy to the full. You think what you want, and you can choose as you desire.

Before we get into the heart of the county, let us take a passing look at Dunblane Cathedral, lying near the banks of Allan Water, and with the Ochil Hills not far away. It is a mixture of pre- and post-Reformation. Ruskin went out of his way in his enthusiasm over it: "I know nothing so perfect in its simplicity and so beautiful so far as it reaches, in all the Gothic with which I am acquainted". Of the inspiration of the architect and his west window at Dunblane, he writes: "Why beautiful? Simply because in the great contours it has the form of a forest leaf, and because in its decoration it has nothing but forest leaves. He was no common man who designed that cathedral of Dunblane."

There is not much to occupy attention in Dunblane besides the cathedral, but as we pass towards the Trossachs we should give a look at the half-village, half-town of Doune, and especially its castle. To most Scotsmen, accustomed to their country's songs and ballads, mention of Doune immediately brings to mind the refrain of the "The Bonnie Earl of Moray"—

> O lang will his ladie
> Look frae the Castle Doune
> Ere she see the Earl o' Moray
> Come soundin' through the toun.

The music fits the words so well that melody and verse are almost indissoluble. The Earl of Moray who was slain by the Earl of Huntly at Donibristle Castle, in Fifeshire, in 1592, was, according to the song, "a braw gallant"—

> And he played at the glove;
> And the bonnie Earl o' Moray
> He was the Queen's true love.

45

When you see the situation of the castle, you understand the fitness of the song's refrain. You can imagine the countess looking doun the toun, and seeing her husband riding through it. The castle is finely set, on a mound between the River Teith and the Ardoch burn. It is now only a ruin, but still a massive one, and within there is enough left to give you the feeling of what it once was. Its history extends from the early fifteenth century, through the troubled time of Queen Mary to the days of Prince Charlie and the '45, when it was used as a prison for Hanoverian captives. Perhaps the most famous of these was the Edinburgh student, John Home, who afterwards became a parson and author of that now unreadable tragedy, *Douglas*.

Doune today is quiet, something of a backwater, but, with its hospitality, I found it a haven of rest.

On the way to Aberfoyle, which is the route by which I prefer to approach the Trossachs, for perhaps sentimental reasons of my own, we can look, in passing, at the Lake of Menteith and the village that goes by the Port of the same name.

The lovely lake has its islands and the ruins of the ancient abbey of Inchmaholme, founded somewhere about 1240. Its chief connection with Scottish history is that here Mary Queen of Scots spent part of her childhood before being sent to France.

Four miles from the Port of Menteith we come to the famous clachan of Aberfoyle, one of the chief centres of the story or legend of *Rob Roy*. The name of one of the chief characters in Scott's romance, Bailie Nicol Jarvie, is still preserved in the clachan as the designation of the chief hostelry.

There is something about Aberfoyle that gets and keeps you, and if you go there once you will go again. The clachan is no longer the collection of "miserable little bourach" of houses it once was, but a very tidy little village. It is not the village that is important, but its setting and surroundings. It is ramparted by hills on one side, and on the other flows the River Forth.

My happiest memory of Aberfoyle is of my first visit. Two of us were on a tramping and camping holiday, exploring, as I have already told you, the Rob Roy country. We pitched our tent by the river a short distance up the Duchray road. It was to be for one night only. The next day we should be up and away across the Duke of Montrose's road—then a walk or horse road—to the Trossachs. The weather was ideal. It was June. Night after night we sat and watched the moon rise beyond the trees, listened to the last calls of the cuckoo and gazed at Ben Lomond which closed in the far end of our river vale. Night after night, too, we sat and gazed at the delicate lights of the glow-worms like a widespread kaleidoscope on the grass around our tent door. My young companion would insist, absent-mindedly, on calling them "ring-worms". That was youth.

Day after day we meant to set out for the Trossachs, but it was so hot and lovely that we were in and out of the river a dozen times, walked a little here and walked a little there, and always the thought of shouldering our packs and carrying the tent postponed our departure. If ever there was a *dolce far niente* existence it was that one!

Our time, however, was limited, and, finally, as the elder of the party I said we must get on if we were to report at the end of our itinerary that we "had done" the Rob Roy country. Then an idea struck me—why not cross the hill road from Aberfoyle to the Trossachs during the cool hours of the night. The decision was made.

The last note of the last cuckoo had died away along the Duchray road when we began to strike camp. By the time we had finished packing, the dusk was deeply settled, and, as we set out towards Aberfoyle, the moon was high above Ben Lomond. We stood for a moment or two before setting our knapsacks right to look down the valley we had known and loved for nearly a week. The Forth was flowing gently, almost without murmur. Once a fish leaped with "a lonely cheer". The trees were uttering sibilant nothings. Heat, mist and moonlight combined to hang veils of silver between hills and hills. It was inevitable. "Goodbye, happy valley," we said, half laughing, half serious, and resolutely set out to cross the strip of moor, by Lochan Spling, towards the road to the clachan.

We rested for a moment or two on the bridge at Aberfoyle. The village was almost in darkness and completely in silence. The scene before us was an extension of the moonlit beauty to which we had said an intimate farewell a mile or two behind. Then we looked towards the hills behind Aberfoyle, over which lay our way to the Trossachs. They seemed even higher and steeper than in daylight. Resolutely squaring our shoulders, we set out on the stiffish road upwards, the crunch and tramp of our footsteps echoing loudly in the deep stillness.

We toiled on and up the road to the heart of the hills, taking no short-cuts and following the white railing carefully. After a week without knapsack drill we found it hot work in the close June night. A mile or so up we rested—to view the landscape! Though it had become familiar to us in daylight, in the light of the moon it was vague and strange and fascinating—that wonderful, wide agricultural plain towards Stirling. Then on again, into the hills and moorland. We had plenty of time for the journey; we did not intend to pitch our tent before dawn.

Whenever the fancy took one or the other of us—and that was fairly frequent—we sat down by the roadside, listened to the silence and told the stars as far as we knew them, or looked over the vague outline of unknown moors to hills we should never climb, the loveliest hills of all. Past the first mile or so of that road there is—or was—no human habitation until the Trossachs were in sight.

If ever we sought for solitude and quiet—and these were at the heart of the holiday we had planned—we had them then, under the faint stars and the increasing mistiness of the moon. After the broiling heat of the warmest day in many Junes, the earliest morning air on that high road struck chill. There was, however, never a complete feeling of night. Always on one horizon or its opposite there was a faint tinge of colour rather than of actual light. Out of some such experience, surely, Shakespeare fashioned the battlement scenes of *Hamlet*.

Towards dawn, however, we had at last crossed the ridge of the road, and though we could not see them, beneath us, we knew, must lie the Trossachs. We sat down to wait for sunrise and our introduction to the centre point of our fortnight's tramping, camping expedition.

As the light grew we could see the valley hollows, looking very far away, filled with mist. Gleaming through the mist and pale as the gems of brooches lying on dark smoke-blue chiffon was the chain of lochs—Vennachar, Achray, Katrine and, nearest of all, one whose name has fled my mind, if ever I knew it—a lochan rather than a loch, set in the hills. Around us rose height on height, culminating in the stern summit of Ben Venue. We smoked a little, ate a little, drank a little, slumbered a little, and talked least of all. We buttoned our thin coats; the dawn was chill and dewy.

A few stars were still to be seen, faint and far from opulent. The moon had gone behind a veiling of cloud, and that was spreading. The lochs were far, but the peaks seemed near and had no friendly feeling at that hour. From them came the cold breath that too easily pierced our light clothing. Talk died down altogether. We felt two very lonely souls, small and of no account to God or man, up there, shelterless, among those mysterious and almost menacing forces of huger nature. The day before with its light and its cloudless blue, the quiet, friendly, singing river, the shady trees, the cuckoos' sonata and our camp on the lush, green sward seemed very far away and very desirable. A joke and a laugh would have broken the silly spell that was on us, but a long day, the climb with knapsack and tent, after a week's loafing, and a night without sleep and every desire for it had dulled our sense of humour. We were as silent as the scene around us.

Then we sat up suddenly out of our last slumber. During it something had happened—a metamorphosis of the valley. The far hills beyond it—they had been only vaguely decipherable in the half-dark—were now plain shapes and ever so faintly tinged with colour, a flush that gave them the artificiality of a stage setting by a master of scenic lighting. There was no visible source of this light. The sky had become a shade of equally unnatural blue; a blue with a touch of only sub-artistry in it, and this effect was completed by the gauzy wifts of fiery-coloured cloud, which drifted more than usually haphazardly across the unblending blue. The sky, especially, reminded me of one of those cheaply coloured, glass-covered photographs which sailors used to bring back from foreign ports.

STIRLING CASTLE FROM THE KING'S KNOT

LOCH ACHRAY, THE TROSSACHS, PERTHSHIRE

Beauty that thrilled with artistic authenticity was there, however, in the hollows. The mist was touched and changed with the "roseate hues of early dawn", and the valley was full of the veritable light of dreamland; a cloudy underheaven of most delicate sheen and texture.

We set off down the hill and were soon in full view of Loch Achray and the tree-crowded slopes beyond. Even in that dim and lovely hour the Trossachs had the maidenly—and, I am sorry to describe it so—that almost simpering beauty which scarcely ever leaves them, is there at the fullest blaze of noon, becomes rueful and almost irritating in rain, and is touched to the loveableness of the appropriate only by the silver of full moonlight. Now, however, the birches beyond the farther margin of the loch were flushed from top to toe like spell-bound nymphs who had been surprised by Phoebus and his crew. Again, even in the growing light, there was that air of unreality, of fine theatricality.

But now there was beauty of a richer, more robust and full artistic kind, in the sky. The blue had lightened and seemed less like an amateur's colouring, and the fiery wifts were fleeces of burning gold. At the heart of all this, reflecting all like a mirror microcosm, was Loch Achray.

Framed in dark green, all the colours of earth and sky were repeated in the water, and by the still water given a new subtle sheen, less artificial than enamel and yet akin to it in opulent surface. Loch Achray then was the very symbol and active analogy of Sidney's definition of the poet's duty and that of poetry—"to make this too-much-loved earth more lovely". Just as in poetry the poets—Wordsworth and Scott come particularly to mind here—have given to certain scenes a new aspect, a loveliness which ordinary eyes might not perceive, so for us that morning did Loch Achray become the revealing poet of the beauties of sunrise on the Trossachs. That was our first burst of love for Achray. The days that followed, of sun and rain, the nights of moonlight and mystery only added, though never quite surpassed, that first glamour of wordless poesy; that seems a more appropriate description of its spell than any borrowed from painting. "The silver depths of Achray hold heights of golden silence"—that was as far as our poem got, but its virtue for us lies in its brevity, something like a Japanese *hokku*, its completeness and power of evocation.

A Sunday spent by Loch Achray has, somehow, about it the very epitome of a certain aspect of Scotland. The scene about you is fairly essential Scotland—the hills, the mountains, the lochs. There is that quiet, that peculiar quiet, that lies about still water. The church is on the edge of the loch, reflected in it. As you sit in the sun after the church is in, there comes suddenly across the still water, as if skimming its surface, the sound of voices singing one of the Scottish psalms as only Scots can sing them. If the windows are fully open you will hear the minister's voice lifted in prayer—those Scottish prayers—and later you will hear his voice

4

rise and fall in the periods of the sermon. Then the church skails, with friendly voices raised in that *ave atque vale* that comes at the end of services. The churchgoers disperse, and you sit in the deeper silence and still seem to hear the ghost of the singing of the psalm skimming the water now, seemingly, stiller than ever.

There are—as I have said—those who are inclined to turn up their noses at such places as the Trossachs and Loch Katrine. Certainly they are popular and, nowadays, when transport is comparatively easy, sometimes rather overcrowded. But that cannot take away from their original beauty. Nor does the fact that Glasgow Corporation draws its water supply from Loch Katrine make any great difference to the beauty of that loch. There have been certain changes; there are certain structures which do not quite belong; but here, as elsewhere in Scotland, there is so much of natural beauty that surely we can spare the slight intrusions so that hundreds of thousands may have their water supply.

You can still walk the road by Loch Katrine and be utterly alone, if that is your wish. Better than that, you can climb Ben Venue and be even more alone, and from that height you can sit and look on beauties that must move even the hardest of hearts to praise of their Creator. Countries such as Scotland should, I think, leave no man or woman an unbeliever. You cannot penetrate to the heart of her hills, or even look on them from the level, and not feel that somewhere in the heart of their green and purple is the very secret of Eternity.

And so we move away from the Trossachs, by the road that leads to Callander, a neat, clean, open, tidy town.

From Callander you can move farther into Perthshire by the road that goes by the Pass of Leny and through "Bonnie Strathyre", along by Loch Lubnaig and under the shadow of Ben Ledi. These are names that ring through Scottish song and story. Every man, woman and child in Scotland will, if he or she has even half a musical ear, sing you the melody and some of the words of the song, "Bonnie Strathyre". It is one of the songs that have sung themselves into Scottish hearts, and long are likely to remain there.

I have talked of the green Braes of Balquhidder and Loch Voil. Soon we come to Lochearnhead, and within a comparatively small area are some of the most popular holiday places, both in Perthshire and Scotland. These include St. Fillans, Comrie, Crieff. Loch and glen and hill are there for you to gaze on and wander by. Ben Vorlich, Loch Earn, Glen Ogle, the Falls of Dochart, up by Killin and you come to long Loch Tay, with Ben Lawers and Glen Lyon, Kenmore, Aberfeldy. Then you can turn back to Amulree. These are other names that ring through Scottish history and Scottish song. For me, Amulree leads my thoughts to the Sma' Glen. See it in heather time when you stand in a small purple world.

And so on to the fair city of Perth, before we go west and north.

THE BRAES OF BALQUHIDDER

BIRNAM WOODS

Perth is a city of which I never tire. It's not that there's a great deal to the city itself, but Perth, with its history and its associations, has an atmosphere all its own. To many people, I know, Perth means merely a railway junction and all the annoying business of changing trains. In that way it is, night or day, like most places of its kind in this country, a cold, draughty place. I have felt lonelier and colder on Perth station than almost anywhere else I have been. Why is it that in this country our railway stations, for the most part, are the last word in discomfort? And ugly, so ugly. If it were not for the kindliness of the human beings who work there, I could imagine Perth station being quite a haunt of people with suicidal tendencies.

But get out of the station, into the town, and all changes. If you want to view Perth, have the city lying fair and sweet at your feet, climb Kinnoull Hill. There by the monastery you may still see a monk digging, just as his predecessors did centuries ago, when Perth was the centre of pageant and battle, murder and sudden death. Up there, however, it is all so quiet. That is what even the most turbulent history eventually comes to. When you look on this once-Royal city and remember all that its streets and vennels, its churches and houses, its palaces and environs have seen—from the crowning at Scone of the Kings of Scotland, seated on the black Stone of Destiny, brought from holy Iona, and now in Westminster Abbey, to the murder of king and nobles, the rioting of the Reformation mobs, the coming and going of Bonnie Prince Charlie, you can make Perth a dream city, a place of phantasmagoria. But up here in the peace of Kinnoull there comes to my mind the words of an English poet, Thomas Hardy:

> Only a man harrowing clods
> In a slow silent walk. . . .
>
> Only thin smoke without flame
>   From the heaps of couch-grass;
> Yet this will go onward the same
>   Though Dynasties pass.

From Kinnoull you can see some of the finest agricultural land in Scotland, and you can remember that, down yonder in Perth streets, in an early and usually cold month of the year, bulls that will go to the Argentine, the United States, Canada are sold at almost fabulous prices.

Yes, Perth is now a fairly quiet place, with work for most of her people, with finely set playgrounds and a repertory theatre for their leisure. It is a military town —as it has always been—and you will see soldiers in the streets, but not now dressed in the gay tunic and swinging sombre kilt that used to attract so many lads to the shilling. And Perth is also the centre and starting place for lovely lands and places.

Some fifteen miles away is Dunkeld-with-Birnam, as might be said. Birnam, of course, sets one's mind at once to Shakespeare and *Macbeth*. It could be that Shakespeare in his reputed tour with the players to Aberdeen and Inverness might have made a visit to this area, and it would not be surprising if here he got his inspiration for that last, sad, sorry scene of his Scottish tragedy.

Dunkeld is one of several places that claim to be the "Gateway to the Highlands", and Dunkeld has something that seems to entitle it to the name. Here, somehow, the Highlands do seem to begin, to come rushing upon you, heicht and howe. Again, Dunkeld has its own particular quiet, except for tourist traffic. Part of this quiet seems to come from the setting of the place—the steep, frowning glories of very near hills. The peace deepens when you visit the cathedral that stands by the River Tay. Dunkeld in high summer has its atmosphere—the wide open space of Birnam that leads to the narrow street of Dunkeld proper, a gully within a gully; but, myself, I like it best at the time when winter is turning to spring and Dunkeld has a chance to be itself.

The town has a very famous link with Scottish music. In the little outspot of Inver there was born, in March 1727, perhaps the most famous of all Scottish fiddlers, Niel Gow. Although nearly a hundred and fifty years away from us, the name of Niel Gow and the tradition of his playing are still bright in Scotland. He did a great work for Scottish national music. His collection of old tunes and tunes of his own composition ran into five volumes. The strathspey and reel are to Scotland what the waltz was to Vienna and the mazurka to Poland. For all the changes that have occurred in both music and dancing, the music which Niel Gow made, played and collected has still as strong a grip on Scotland, old and young. This is one of the matters in which Scotland is "different". No dance in Scotland is complete without an eightsome reel, and in recent years there has been a great revival of Scottish country dancing. The "Dashing White Sergeant", "Strip the Willow", "The Gay Gordons", these are only a few of those more commonly danced. This music and these dances stir the blood of every Scot, just as the striking up of the pipes could put new life into the weariest bodies and feet of men coming from battle.

Whatever has been the fate of Scottish literature, there was never diminution of the love for Scottish music and Scottish dances. Sometimes, and even yet, the dances have been somewhat debased. Instead of being danced as they should be, neat and trim and exact in every step and figure, there are those who turn them into a wild rampage, overswinging and breaking form. The old dancing masters would have said their say on this, and in no mild terms. We could do with them back again in the ballroom, though I know that part of this terpsichorean vulgarity is in part due to excess of youthful vigour.

As for the music of these dances, the spirit of Niel Gow has lived through the

DUNKELD AND BIRNAM, FROM CRAIGIEBARNS, PERTHSHIRE

LOCH KATRINE, PERTHSHIRE

century and more in the hearts and hands of many Scotsmen. There is scarcely a town in Scotland that has not its Strathspey and Reel society. Their concerts are always crowded and the audiences enthusiastic. If they care to go on tour of the country districts, the people will go miles through rain or snow, listen to three hours of a concert and then dance into the morning to the tunes that are in their blood and feet.

All this does not mean that the lads and lassies of town and country know only the native dances. In these days you will often see modern dances, the fox-trot, the modern waltz better danced in country halls than in some town palais. One of the most exciting exhibitions I ever saw of the ridiculous but amusing jitterbug was given by a sailor home on leave and a lass from a farm kitchen in a little hall away among the hills, nearly fifty miles from the nearest town. For all that, it is good to find lad after lad and lass after lass who will say right out that they prefer old-fashioned dances, and most of all their own Scottish reels and country dance. The country dance societies flourish. Like the Strathspey and Reel societies they bring their crowds.

Had there not been a Niel Gow, someone else would have taken his place, though they might have lacked his character and great gifts of the fiddle. For there is no doubt that a great part of Niel's fame in his day and after was due to native toughness and wit. The stories about him and his remarks are still known up and down the countryside, handed down by word o' mou'.

Niel liked playing, and he played in castle as well as cottage. But he also liked the trencher and the glass, and liked to sit down to them at a reasonable space. One night, having played reel after reel to please dance-daft ladies, he lost all patience and, shaking his bow, cried out to the insatiable dancers—"Awa' doun tae yer suppers, ye daft limmers, an' dinna haud me reelin' an' reelin' here. Dae ye think hunger an' drouth are unkent in the land? A body can get naething dune for ye."

I have noticed, even in my day, that there is something of this spirit about every notable Scots fiddler, and many of them have been almost as handsome figures as was Niel. What they have lacked in inches of height and breadth, they have made up in style and flourish. This brings to my mind one who was Niel Gow's successor in many ways. He was James Scott Skinner, born in Banchory in Kincardineshire. And he was as famous in his way as Niel Gow was. To speak of Niel and not of Scott Skinner seems to me to speak of Haydn and not of Mozart, just because Mozart came after Haydn. And this is the place to speak of Skinner, who is part and parcel of Scotland's particular musical history and the history of its worthies.

Skinner was born in 1843 and died in Aberdeen in 1927. In those eighty-four years he led one of the most picturesque lives and travelled much and far. He was the son of a fiddler and dancing master—a gardener by trade who was, however, better known in his spare-time job—whose nickname in his native district was "Dancie".

The young Scott Skinner followed the paternal tradition from his early years, first as fiddler and then both as fiddler and dancing teacher. From his early days there was one outstanding characteristic that he kept throughout his life—the ability to size up the mood of an audience. If he began quietly he would change to a livelier note, and then, with the touch of genius that combined the musician and showman, he would stop the tapping feet and have the people hanging upon the sad or sentimental melody in which he excelled almost as much as the stirring lilt.

He began to compose quite early in life, and his tunes are part of every musical Scot's repertory, some as well-known as any of the most famous Scottish folk-songs and as often played. One of his first was a strathspey that is a classic in its section of Scots music. It is called "The Miller o' Hirn". The mill o' Hirn stands in a quiet backland of the Aberdeenshire countryside, not far from Skinner's native Banchory. Like others of his kind, in verse and music, Skinner did good work as a collector and arranger as well as an original composer.

Scott Skinner soon became known up and down the length of Britain for his playing of Scots music. London heard him and he was associated there with some of the early ventures of another famous Scots musical artist—and it may surprise some, but not all, that I call this other man a musical artist—Harry Lauder. But that Lauder is; I knew him well and studied his technique closely for the last twenty years of his career. In 1894 and 1903 Skinner toured America, and his appeal to Scots abroad can be imagined. He also had his stage technique.

I can remember him well, though I was just a laddie at the time. A new stir went round a concert hall when it came to Scott Skinner's turn to appear. There was a pause, almost a hush. Then the fiddler came on, arrayed always in full highland costume—kilt and plaid, with jewelled sporran and dagger, the *skean dubh*. He strode on to the platform with a jaunty air, kilt a-swing, nonchalantly carrying fiddle and bow. With a flourish he played upon his fiddle and his hearers, and thunders of applause followed him off and welcomed him on, again and again.

Off the stage as well as on he was a personality. Here is a tale told of him. One day he was walking along a street in Aberdeen. He heard the feeble scraping of a gutter violinist attempting "The Bonnie Lass o' Bon-Accord", now, perhaps, the most famous of all the Scott Skinner melodies. Skinner approached the scraper— "Let's see your fiddle, laddie". He re-tuned the instrument and there and then, in the gutter, too, he played this tune as only he could play it. Handing back the fiddle to the astonished owner, Skinner said—"That's the way to play that tune. I should ken. It was me that made it."

Hero worship was Scott Skinner's to his dying day. His funeral was really a triumphal procession. Thousands lined the streets of Aberdeen as the *cortège* passed to the cemetery by the River Dee, the same river beside which he was born and which heard his first playing and melodies. On the top of the coffin was his violin in an open case. The principal wreath was in the form of a violin with a broken string. His birthplace is marked by a tablet and his grave by a tombstone erected by public subscription. It was unveiled by Sir Harry Lauder in 1931.

So passed, so is remembered, one of the greatest of Scots fiddlers, and his melodies will be unforgotten so long as there are Scotsmen to play or even whistle them.

I have never gone to Niel Gow's place but I have remembered Scott Skinner, and I am sure he too was a visitor there. What a treat it would have been could the two have met, and wouldn't every Scots fiddler have liked to have been there! And there are today, as there have been for many years, thousands of them.

Music such as Gow and Skinner made are certainly just as integral a part of Scottish life as are the songs of Burns, Lady Nairne and all those lesser lights of Scottish minstrelsy.

There are many places still in Perthshire which have their claim as much as those of which I have already written, but Perthshire really requires not one chapter, but more than one volume to itself.

From Dunkeld we could go north to Pitlochry, another favourite centre. Just beyond the town you have the Pass of Killiecrankie, beautiful in itself in a certain way and famous in history. Still further on, if you are a walker and were making for Aberdeenshire, you would come to Blair-Atholl, and from there make your way to Glentilt. This is one of the, as one might say, un-roaded glens. There is only a bridle path through the some thirty miles until you reach the road to Braemar. The mountains rise on either side of you, the Grampians, Ben-y-Gloe and Ben Dearg. It is a glorious tramp on a fine summer's day—no difficulty and yet, because there is no road, with the feeling of real mountainy country.

On the other hand, still going towards Braemar, we might have taken the road to Blairgowrie, and by Bridge of Cally, Blackwater and Bleaton Hallett to Glenshee. The Spittal of Glenshee is a place known to thousands of Scottish folk of all classes, for by this road sumptuous cars and touring charabancs "do" one of the best-known jaunts in Scotland. By this route every September come thousands of cars, buses and vehicles of all kinds from mid- and even southern Scotland, to attend the famous Royal Braemar Gathering. You have the feeling, in spite of a dip and here and there a level, that you are climbing, climbing, climbing—and you are right. Bit by bit from the meadowlands the roads winds into the hills and the sheep country. At the Spittal is the famous whitewashed hostelry, the last on the long journey over the noted Devil's Elbow, until, after the long road through house-deserted valleys deep in the heart of the towering mountains, you come to Braemar.

The Devil's Elbow, a double hairpin bend beloved of the adventurous driver and taken cannily by the wise and tender-hand, lies six miles more above the thousand feet of the Spittal. But the road has been for long kept in excellent repair, and it would be amazing to know how many cars and buses and lorries negotiate this—said to be the highest main road in the British Isles—every summer.

But it is not only the feat and unusualness of the Elbow that makes this trip attractive. There is the whole setting of the place: hills or mountains on every hand, great dips with stream or river running through them, and, because of the lack of habitations, the feeling, even when the road is thick with traffic, of elemental nature, looking with calm, eternal eyes on the passing to and fro of the very, very temporal.

We are 1,951 feet up at the Elbow and a little further on, at the Cairnwell, 2,199 feet. On the mountain called Glas Maol, near by, the three counties of Aberdeen, Angus and Perthshire meet at the end of this part of Perthshire. We shall come near to the district again when we are in Aberdeenshire.

Once again, had we gone northward from Blair-Atholl to Dalnaspidal and Dalwhinnie to the Pass of Drumochter, we should have been on one of the other famous roads of Scotland, the great road to the north. It is like the road to the Devil's Elbow, a road with long stretches of loneliness and elementary scenery that has wild beauty in it. But it is not so uninhabited, and at all seasons of the year, so far as snow will allow, it is a great traffic route. Also, here the railway marches with the road.

It is a road with history. This way to the south, in August 1745, came Prince Charlie and his men, on his way to Blair and Dunkeld. He was in great fettle then. This, again, is a road known to thousands upon thousands in Scotland and from beyond the Border, and its history today is of happy people going on or coming from holiday.

You will find that these people have the most diverse views regarding these roads, according to the number of times and the weather in which they have traversed and seen what lies on either side, before and behind them. To some they have been glorious journeys. Others think of them, in rain and mist, as the last stages to utter desolation. But, then, that is so with almost every part of the Highlands of Scotland. You must get to know them, live in them, at any rate for a while, before you can know and, more especially, pass judgment on them.

And so, on our first journey to the west. From Pitlochry we go a short distance towards Blair-Atholl and then turn off towards Loch Tummel. This is a pleasant road, and when you come to the head of Loch Tummel you will halt, as a more exalted personage did, Queen Victoria. From a high vantage point you gaze on one of the many "Queen's Views" in the Highlands. This is, however, really a glorious view. Loch Tummel lies at your feet, and as you look along its not very great length, you see the mountain with a name that rings through literature, Schiehallion. Schiehallion is one of the heights of Scotland that call forth a curious love. It does not frighten, it is there to be loved. On a fine day, at the far, far end of the view, you can catch sight of a distant mountain that is the opposite of Schiehallion, the Buchaille Etive Mhor, beyond Glencoe. And to that we shall come in time. The great Shepherd of Etive has a long history of trouble and fear.

But let's on, down the road to Kinloch Rannoch, still a pleasant easy way, with the mountains in sight but not too near. At what was once the Brig o' Tummel you will no longer see the scene that so many ladies and minor artists once upon a day loved to paint, one of the scenes that the unsophisticated loved—and why not?—but on which the Scot of a certain type frowned, just as he would frown whenever the name of Harry Lauder was mentioned. "Travesty", he would mutter. But it was not really so; merely selective though not altogether representative. But what is selection if not part of artistry? The trouble nowadays with everything from literature to life is that it is too inclusive, packed and overpacked.

Well, instead of the jolly little bridge and the little hostelry, you are faced with a power station. Here we come up against the division of Scotland, although I think it is a division that will last only until Scotland's new schemes for the commercialisation of the waters are productive. The outcry against vandalism is both true and untrue. There never were yet, in any country or any commercial scheme, men who did not commit some form or degree of vandalism. It is part of the price we have to pay for progress of the kind such schemes envisage. They are not progress for the artist as artist, or the aesthete as aesthete, but for the good of the multitude, and artists and aesthetes of a certain kind are anti-multitude. But I never yet knew an artist or an aesthete who was not readier than most to take advantage of the results of the action he and his predecessors were the first to condemn and keep on condemning.

The great outcry against the great hydro-electric schemes has come from the aesthetes and a certain type of patriot. Scotland's beauty would be ruined, they have cried. What amazes me is that these people talk as if they were over-the-Border Sassenachs who have the idea that Scotland consists of a few acres or, at most, a few square miles. When one thinks of the extent, multiplicity and variety of Scotland's natural beauty, and think how comparatively little of it is touched or changed to any great extent by the schemes, then the outcry seems just peevish and silly. Even more so when we think of what the schemes could, and, I hope and believe, will do for the material good of Scotland and the Scots who are most in need of that good. It does happen that the schemes, in part, do, of necessity, impinge upon some of the finest things in the Scottish landscape. But is there not the fact that art has come into industrialism and commercialism to a greater extent than ever before? I am one of those who would rather see a fine modern road—such as Glencoe or Loch Ness-side—than some loathsome old track, and a modernistic power house than a dirty and even more loathsome inhabited black dwelling.

But on from Tummel Brig, for all our sakes, to Kinloch Rannoch and the Loch. Kinloch Rannoch is still a haunt of ancient peace, but also of hospitality. Now, having gazed along the loch, take the road along the loch until we come to its end —at Rannoch Station, on the verge of the great Moor of Rannoch.

It has always seemed to me something of a curiosity that the railway crosses that great stretch of moorland while the road stops dead. Yet I have never heard aesthete, artist or patriot complain of the railway across Rannoch Moor. There is plenty of the moor left when the railway has been realised and forgotten.

By heavens, there is plenty of moor, enough to be as impressive and, in its way and at certain times, almost frightening. Rannoch affects one in this way as do the lonely glens and heights at their loneliest and highest. We have never, as far as I know or remember, had an author to do for Rannoch what Thomas Hardy did for Egdon Heath. Yet the same feeling, although with extensiveness added to intensiveness, is there on Rannoch. Walking it of an evening, especially towards dusk, you feel that that moor is capable of everything in nature antagonistic towards intrusive ordinary human beings. At that hour I have felt that, exactly opposite to Mary Rose's island in Barrie's play, the moor does not like to be visited. The moor seems alternately deadly quiet and full of voices. It would never surprise me, standing at the road edge of the moor, to see even strong men who had been out on it running for their lives towards the nearest human habitation. Nor would it surprise me, if you asked them why, to hear them gasp out that they didn't know. Not even at the blaze of noon can I ever imagine Rannoch Moor looking entirely friendly. There are places otherwhere that I know which have, for me at any rate, this touch of the sinister. And that, of course, is also part of their fascination.

I remember lying in a tent within a stone's-throw of the moor, in the terrific quiet of such places, and all the time, until I fell asleep from weariness after the summer day's itinerary, I was aware of the moor's proximity, its seemingly limitless extent, the spirit that I have tried to describe. I was glad of the proximity of a companion and even of the protection of the cloth wall of the tent. Curiously, I dreamt not of moorland bogles but of water kelpies.

There, but for our journey to the farther west, I must leave this great and, I think, wonderful county of Perthshire, wonderful in its variety alone. And I have given but a glimpse of it.

7

ROADS TO THE ISLES

It's by Sheil Water that the track is to the West,
By Ailort and by Morar to the sea.

SO goes Kenneth MacLeod's song, to which the lovely artist that was Margaret Kennedy-Fraser put a tune that has set Scots singing, as few other songs in the last hundred years have done. Others than Scots love it, too, but not in quite the same way. That song sums up part of our birthright and heritage, and also it leads us to another part of Scotland, different from the east and the south, different in many ways except the basic unity. Curiously enough, one of the first and noticeable differences—if you live in the west long enough to notice it—is in the folk-song, in melody, sentiment and, of course, in the language. The language is the Gaelic —a curious tongue, at once fascinating and unattractive, full of strange sounds, and yet what the Gael can do with those sounds, put into those sounds something that can alternately stir the soul, make the toes itch to dance, and—even though you may not understand a syllable—a Gael telling a tale can make you roar with laughter at the very use of sound.

The Gael in his native tongue and the Gael in Scots or English is far from being the same person. When I was a student at Aberdeen University there existed there a very strong Celtic Society. The *ceilidhs* were great affairs, but the crowning glory of the society's year was the annual dinner—for men only. Speech flowed as copiously as the *usquebaugh*—those were the days after the 1914–18 war and the United States did not drain us then of our national beverage—and that speech was both in English and Gaelic. The Celtic Society had on its books those of us who, while not speaking the tongue, loved both the tang and the tongue.

I remember one speaker, a Celt of Celts, who had first to make a speech in English. It was a good-enough speech, but just good-enough. Later, he had to propose a toast in Gaelic. What a change! Here was oratory, fire and even passion, humour, eloquence. Eric Linklater, the novelist, was one of the student band, like myself on the non-Gaelic-speaking fringe, and he rushed up after the speaker had finished and said: "By heavens, Mac, I didn't understand a word you said, but that was the finest speech I've ever heard in my life." That was true in ways deeper than the particular occasion.

I tell you these things because that is the land we are going to; still Scotland, remember, but again a different Scotland from that we have been in, and shall come back to.

We are not taking exactly the route of Kenneth MacLeod's song, but the end is the same. We shall go west by Crianlarich—lovely name in itself and introduction —Tyndrum, Dalmally, Loch Awe, Connel and so to Oban. Names, names, names —that is where, I sometimes wonder, if a Scot is the right person to write the best book on Scotland—or, shall we say, an objective book on Scotland? Name after name will come up, and set him dreaming of what is behind the name. One name will lead to another and the Scot, writing, will forget that whatever those names may mean to him, music and re-imagined beauties, he must implement the names for those who have never even heard them and do not know what lies behind them.

From Crainlarich what a great country lies before us—west, south and north— highlands and islands, surface beauty, deeper mysticism and history; history that goes back and back till history ceases.

It's a long road from Crianlarich to Oban, and when the mist or the rain is on it, it seems very long. Yet, there is, except in the very worst weather, always some compensation. On this road a great deal of the wilder landscape is always in the distance, and for superficial travelling nothing could be better. The scene is domi- nated by Ben Cruachan, and, like so many other Scots mountains, you never seem to see it twice in the same aspect. In fair weather it is something to bring a smile to the eyes. For all that, I am not sure that I do not love it best when the skies are grey, and the clouds, roaming its peaks, crown it with a ghostly crown.

There are two turn-offs from this road to Oban. One we shall take now and the other later.

The first is over the ups and downs to Inveraray, the white townlet by the water. I have never seen Inveraray except on days of utter quiet; in fact, I do not know if it is ever anything else. I have been quite content to take it as I found it. There is nothing to the domestic architecture of Inveraray, all to its setting and the woody height of Duniquaich and beyond that the heights of Dunicorbal.

Yet, in its quiet, Inveraray holds bits of Scottish history, some of it part of events that all the world knows.

It is the seat of the Duke of Argyll, and in the first part of the woods of his estate you will find a chapel and, separate from it, yet part of it, a campanile with a chime that could call over the water in a magical way.

Inveraray is a seat of justice, it is also the birthplace of one who enriched Scottish letters in an essentially Scottish way, Neil Munro. He lies now where his life began, in Inveraray. Here was a Scotsman of genius who stayed in Scotland—and he had his reward, as so many of them do.

LOCH LUBNAIG, PERTHSHIRE

MOOR OF RANNOCH, PERTHSHIRE AND ARGYLLSHIRE

If you were going on to Glasgow from Inveraray you could go by a road, one part of which is known to every Scottish motorist and hiker, at least by its name —"Rest and be thankful". That name applies to the journey from Glasgow. It is one of the most amazing dips between hills, a super-switchback, as desolate in its grandeur as the way from Braemar to the Devil's Elbow.

But now we are back on the shores of Loch Awe, on the way to Oban once more. This is a lovely loch in shore and distance. In the distance there is Kilchurn Castle, set on a greater scale—as so many Scottish castles, whole or in ruin, are—like those comic gazebos which the eighteenth-century makers of landskip were so fond of placing on their placid little sheets of water, to add, in their sweet, silly eyes, enchantment to the view. Nearer is a great turreted hotel, but not quite so enchanting as Kilchurn, though much more helpful materially to the traveller in certain circumstances.

Then we come to the Pass of Brander, where road and rail go side by side in a comparatively narrow defile. A dark bit of loch lies on your left-hand side as you go towards Taynuilt and Oban. It is seldom that I have seen that strip of water smile, it always seems slatey-grey. It's not a place where you ever want to stop, unless hunger makes you.

At Bonawe we come to Loch Etive, and there is a long, lovely stretch of riparian green and brown. But even this is not the Etive I love most. We shall reach that anon. So, by the Falls of Rora and Connel, with Dunstaffnage Castle of the Campbells and Dunolly of the MacDougalls westward as we go.

Oban is a well-set town, a centre of west-coast yachting, but, still more, a centre of west-coast tourism. There is not a great deal to the town itself, though it is pleasing and some folk on holiday never care to go far from it, except for a day here and there. It is not exactly a Genoa, and there is no Mediterranean, but there is something of the shape of Genoa in it, and the prospect from its quay walls on a summer day and, even more, on a summer evening is something you will carry in memory. Its sea seems to be full of islands, though that is not so.

The road that we have come is one of the roads to the west, but for me for many years now it has been the road to one place—to Iona, that little island lying beyond the greater Island of Mull. As Iona means so much to me—as it does and has done to Scotland—perhaps I had better get it out of my system, for it will always be haunting me, saying like a little child, "When is my turn coming?"—for one of the things that one compares Iona to is a little child, or, even better, a little lamb. When one thinks of the connotation of the Lamb in our spiritual lives, it is doubly right to make that comparison with Iona.

One of the best day excursions from Oban is by an excellent steamer to Iona. You sail one side or the other of the coast of Mull, touching at Tobermory; you call at Staffa, with Fingal's Cave; you pass the tiny island of Inchkenneth, for so long the home of Harold Boulton, who did so good work for Scottish minstrelsy in his volumes of *The Songs of the North*. You have a short while on Iona; you can see something of what lies within easy reach of the landing jetty. But—this is merely fact, not Iona snobbishness—you will never get the full feeling of Iona until you stay there. It is said that, if you visit Iona once, you will visit it three times. That is not true for all, but it is for many. Here, believe me, is a magical isle, the Tir-nan-Og of this life. Let me try to tell you what Iona has meant to me, and, in its history, suggest what makes Iona to so many of us in Scotland what it is, has been and, I think, will become more and more.

I have told you of one way to the island, direct by the daily steamer—always excepting Sunday, of course; the west knows no steamers on the Sabbath. The other is across the Island of Mull, and that is a journey that has glamour of its own. You make the comparatively short crossing from Oban across the Firth of Lorne to Craignure. There, by mail van or private vehicle, you take the road, through the Great Glen, in the shadow of Ben More to Fhionnphort and so by ferry across to Iona.

This journey is, or should be, a joy, though a great deal, of course, can depend on your driver and his vehicle. Ours was made in one of the most rickety cars I have ever driven in. Our driver was most jovial and as Highland as a peat, but the road is a single track and he seemed to think he was king of that road. The few vehicles we met gave way to him, which was good for our sakes. For all that and other circumstances of the drive, we did have a chance to appreciate the scenery through which we were passing—again long stretches of the green desolation that has its own beauty.

But our journey was broken by the physical agonies of another occupant of the car, a man to whom even the shortest sea journey was upsetting. Why he should choose Mull for a holiday in the circumstance, I cannot say, nor the journey he had performed on the last day we ever saw him. He was violently sick, over and over again, but came to when the car was stopped. Then I realised that our driver's driving was almost equal to being in a small boat in a squall. It was a relief to us as well, in many ways, when we got to Fhionnphort. The next time we saw this bad sailor was when we found him, utterly green, in the bottom of a small boat at the Iona jetty. He had been in that small boat, on a choppy sea, to visit Staffa. He smiled wanly at us and gasped: "It wis awfie like hell, but A've done it, A've seen Fingal's Cave." There was bravery in that!

From Fhionnphort, or just above it, on the Ross of Mull, you have one of the best views of Iona. There it lies, in its lovely sea, as I have said for all the world like a little lamb of an island. Wherever you are, and in sight of Iona, the outstanding

KILCHURN CASTLE

GLEN ETIVE: THE PEAKS BEHIND DALNESS

landmarks are two—the one hill of Iona, Dun-I, and the cathedral—and when you are leaving after your stay you gaze and gaze on them, and I am sure there are few who have stayed their once, twice or thrice on the island who do not gather those two landmarks into their inner being and think: "When and how soon shall I see them again?"

It is more than the idea of one of the great dreamers of Scotland, William Sharp, who called himself in his Celtic writings Fiona MacLeod, that Iona is the soul of Scotland. Its history almost proves it, Fiona MacLeod said: "A few places in the world are to be held holy, because of the love which consecrates them and the faith which enshrines them. Their names are themselves talismans of beauty. Of these is Iona."

And, again: "To tell the story of Iona is to go back to God and to end in God".

In the beginning was Iona. It is, according to the geologists, one of the oldest pieces of land in the world. Listen to Trenholme in the *Story of Iona*: "When our planet from a flaming mass of combustion like the sun, shrivelled into a globe with a solid crust, and the first oceans condensed in the hollows of its surface—then it was that the Archaean rocks of which Iona and the Outer Hebrides consist were formed on the sea bottom. They contain no fossils; for, so far as is known, no living creature as yet existed in the desolate waste of waters or on the primeval land. They were hard, rugged and twisted; and in Iona, as elsewhere, marble has been developed by the vast heat and pressure they have undergone. . . ." There you have science and poetry meeting.

From that beginning and until the present day, through all its vicissitudes, and part of the history of this little island has been ugly and bloody, Iona has kept its mystical atmosphere, the feeling that it came straight from the hand of God. Men only have despoiled it.

It is a tiny island, some three miles long and little more than a mile in breadth, and yet, however long you stay, you never get tired of it, you never feel hedged in and bound; you seem to have a variety and freedom that many places far larger never can give. Small as that island is, and apart from its famous historical and spiritual associations, it is big enough to have an eighteen-hole rough-golf course. It is a holiday as well as a holy island. There are two hotels, and the crofters accommodate as many people as they can. Some people have gone to Iona year after year for many summers; with one couple I knew the number had gone into double figures. Those who go time after time become friends, not only in the island but in their permanent home places. In winter in Glasgow there used to be meetings of "Ionians"—Iona their bond.

The people of the island are crofters, but a change is coming over the young folk. When they get to grown age they go mostly to the mainland to work. Few remain.

Labour is imported. Just before the war there were not half a dozen children at school. The future of the island in this way is very uncertain, but there could be an adaptation to changing conditions. Certainly the island will never be allowed to go back to the conditions in which Dr. Johnson found it in the eighteenth century. Then it was at its lowest ebb in every way. That is part of the material side of the island; what of its spiritual and historic side?

There we come to something almost unique in the history of Scottish places, that which has made Iona famous throughout the Christian world. Modern Scots are not the only men and women who have written of Iona and Columba. The literature of Iona goes back to the years not so very long after Columba died, which was in 597. Adamnan, the ninth Abbot of Iona, was born in 624. His *Life of St. Columba* is like other lives and history books of that and later periods, something that the modern reader takes with a very large grain of salt. It is hero-worship in the extreme, full of miracles and deeds of wonder. Read without any attitude of entire belief it is a very lovely romance of the life of a great saint of Christianity, for there is not the slightest doubt that Columba was the greatest man of his century and for many after, and today his light still shines before men with a great brightness; indeed, it is not certain that it is not shining brighter than ever before, because we realise perhaps better at this distance how great he really was in relation to his age. Iona and Columba, in some ways, have come into their own in spiritual newness and effectiveness. Another torch has been lit from that which has burned through the ages.

Among the many names which the island has had, none is more beloved than Icolumcille, or in Englished Gaelic Icolmkill, the island of Colum of the church or cell. Some of the history of the island is embodied in the various names it has borne. There are, also, many theories about the island's names. Originally the island was called Ioua, and it is said that the name Iona came from a miscopying by a monkish scribe who mistook the "u" for an "n". It is a curious coincidence that Iona in Hebrew should mean a dove, for that is what Columba means in the Latin.

It is asserted by various authorities that before the coming of Colum the island was inhabited by Druids, even that Columba and the Druids were on the island at one and the same time. The Druids would account for one of the names of the island—Innis-nam-Druidneach, though there is also Innis-nam-Druineach, the island of the cunning workmen. In the Gaelic Iona is simply "I" (pronounced "ee"). Apart from the name of the island, there are topographical matters which show the mixture of paganism and Christianity. Iona, for some people, is an island of the fairies, and there have been those who have lived there because of this association. Even in modern days there are grown folk who still believe in fairies, and, of course, it is not so long ago since many Celts believed in them.

INVERARAY CROSS AND CASTLE

OBAN BAY BY NIGHT

For myself, some twenty or more years ago I met an old man in the Highlands—he had been for two years at one of the Scottish universities—who told me, in all solemnity, that he did not believe in fairies, though he knew those who did and could prove their existence, but he asserted that there certainly were mermaids in the sea. It is a curious commentary on his statement that the old man today lies in the cemetery in Inverness, on the hill whose Gaelic name means the Hill of the Fairies. But, more of Sandy later.

However it may have been, on Whitsun Eve in the year 563, Columba and twelve disciples landed on Iona at the lovely little bay called Port a'Churaich. He was a voluntary exile from Derry in Ireland, for, though he was known as the Dove, Columba had also a fiery spirit within him which would conquer him now and again, and his exile was, perhaps, his biggest penance, for he loved his native land with a great love. He chose Iona because even from the little eminence above Port a'Churaich—called Carn-cul-ri-Erin, the hill of the back turned to Erin—he could no longer see any glimpse whatever of his beloved native land. With the coming of Columba began the long history of Iona and also a great deal of the history of what is now Scotland.

This is not the place and there is not space to tell the story of Columba on Iona, Columba on the mainland, but some of the history must be given. He was a pioneer of the Cross, and he and his followers went out, in danger and privation, converting the Pictish heathen, east and north and south. Among his converts, and this one was important in history, was Brude, King of the Picts. Here Columba by spiritual means fought the Druids and won.

In 574, on Iona, by Columba, was consecrated Aidan, King of the Dalriada Scots. This was the first coronation in Britain. For swearing and consecration was used that black Stone of Destiny which, after its wanderings, now forms part of the throne on which British kings today are still crowned. There, again, is part of the eternal importance of Iona.

The community which Columba founded and ruled was one of strictest discipline and of missionary zeal. But, for all that, his visionary and mystic qualities were what eventually have set Columba apart in the annals of Christianity. He was a great man of affairs, but greater still in his communion with God and of prophecy. Perhaps the best known concerns Iona itself:

> In Iona of my heart, Iona of my love
> Instead of monk's voice shall be lowing of kine;
> But ere the world comes to an end,
> Iona shall be as it was.

There are many signs in these days that that prophecy may come true, in our time.

5

In Iona Columba has conquered the fairies and the Druids. There are two little mounds on the island which have the fairy names of the Sithean (Sheean) Mhor and the Sithean Beg, but the most-loved name is Cnoc nan Aingeal, the hill on which Columba had his vision of angels. All little mounds in Iona—and there are many—are *cnocs* (pronounced crock). The island is haunted by association with Columba; even today they can tell you where this and that in his life occurred. There are, of course, no actual remnants of the Columban settlement, but there are ancient things which delight the heart of the antiquarian and interest even the ordinary tripper.

The man-made glory of Iona is, of course, the cathedral and its surrounding buildings. The cathedral has been restored, and has been given its right atmosphere in that restoration. The adjoining monastic buildings are in course of restoration. The cathedral, in the form of a cross and originally dedicated to the Virgin Mary, is of Continental Norman architecture, and is mainly of late fifteenth- and early sixteenth-century work.

South-west of the cathedral lies the Reilig Oran, an ancient burial ground, and within it St. Oran's Chapel, a roofless but interesting ruin. It is supposed that this was built by St. Margaret, wife of Malcolm Canmore, and it is thus linked with the little chapel in Edinburgh Castle.

The Reilig Oran is, surely, the most famous earth in all Scotland, or Britain, for that matter. Here were buried forty-eight crowned kings of Scotland, four of Ireland and seven of Norway, besides many chieftains.

One famous modern lies buried here—Margaret Kennedy-Fraser, who restored to Scotland and made famous throughout the musical world the songs of the Hebrides.

It is right that she should lie in Iona among the kings. In her way and art she was a queen. Who like her could sing the song that, tradition has it, was sung by the boatmen as they ferried the funeral barge of kings to the Reilig Oran—here is Kenneth Macleod's version:

> Iomar o, 'illean-mhara,
>   Iomair o.
> Isle of deeps, where death ne'er weepeth,
> Sails to thee a king who sleepeth,
> With thy saints the Tryst he keepeth,
> Iomair o, 'illean mhara,
>   Iomair o.

There are also traces of a nunnery in Iona, and in its garth in summer-time there is one of the brightest notes of colour in the whole island, flowers of every hue.

Celtic crosses—the finest that of St. Martin—and sculptured stones are but a few of the antiquarian delights of the island.

STAFFA

IONA CATHEDRAL

Yet, when all is said and done, it is the island itself that is the lasting delight. These things are the outward and visible signs of the uniqueness of Iona among Scottish islands. They help, but over the island hangs an atmosphere that is not uncanny but certainly pervading. I could never wander by the *machair*, penetrate the inlands, climb Dun-I, but I felt that I was surrounded by a cloud of witnesses.

One cannot leave Iona without speaking of the colours. If you were to see them only in the paintings of the many artists who, understandably, find the happiest of painting grounds here, you might think them only an artist's fancy. They are even more true than that. The rocks are coloured, the sea fringes fade from green into purple and back to green again, the sand is sheen white (actually it is not sand but the shell of a land insect). There was, too, one dreadful day when, in 806, the Danes slew sixty-eight monks at what is known as Martyr's Bay, and the red of blood was added to the sheen-white sand. I have seen dawns and sunsets on Iona that would defy the greatest of painters, and at sunset the colours of Iona are joined by the rose-red of the rocks on the Ross of Mull.

Readers of Robert Louis Stevenson's *Kidnapped* will remember the adventure of David Balfour on the half-island of Erraidh, which lies at the southern end of the Island of Mull. You remember that David Balfour thought he was on an island, and only after terrible privations did he find that at low tide the island's water boundary could be crossed and Mull reached easily. For all that, you have to be careful, and the two companions with whom I crossed to Erraidh would not take the warning and cross, as I did, far up the stream the water boundary becomes. They crossed and sank, kilts and all, up to the waist. I crossed dry-foot. Erraidh is one of the playgrounds for visitors to Iona, and a lovely playground it is. The water is of the west's translucent green, the sand again sheen-white. To lie on the cliff-top and watch the play-makers below, in all variety of coloured bathing-costumes is to see a Russell Flint water-colour brought to life in the loveliest of backgrounds.

To leave Iona after a visit is like leaving one's loveliest love. But you know that you will carry her in your heart until the day comes when you can return and be happy again in her company.

As we go towards Oban we call at Staffa. This is one of the great experiences of the west coast. You put off from the steamer in the small boat, and, as you come near, you can see something of the interior of the cave. The landing is easy, and then you begin to penetrate this—the finest of rocky sea-organs. The fluted columns are in themselves a wonder, but as you stand there and listen to the great diapason as the waves wash in and out is to experience something unforgettable. Mendelssohn has given you what might be called the lighter side of the cave in his most melodious and likeable Hebridean overture, but there is more of the quieter Hebrides than of Fingal's Cave in the music. The true Fingal's Cave overture has still to be written and, I think, some of the moderns could do it. Above the cave is a great mound of fine green turf, and many from Iona are rowed out or go by motor-boat and spend long, lovely summer days on the top of the islet.

Tobermory is what I call a paintable town. Its reflected water-front has attracted artists before now, and for the romantic there is the story of the buried treasure of the Spanish galleon which lies in the waters somewhere near.

So we come back to Oban, and say farewell to the ship with its jovial Gaelic-speaking officers and men. That is one of the differences that strike you in the west. Go on board any of the steamers and you might almost feel you were in a foreign country. A constant flow of Gaelic pleasantry goes on between crew and Gaelic-speaking passengers. But you are quite content to look and listen, it is all so gay and jolly. Who tells the tale of the drooly Celt? True, many of his songs are sad. But go to a Mod and hear a pair of men, handsome, in full Highland rig, sing, act and move through one of the Celt's more jovial songs; again, though you do not understand a word that is said, you will find yourself laughing by sheer infection.

From Oban we go north to lands as lovely as those we are leaving, yet again different. There are two ways. One is across Connel Ferry—that bone of contention. Not only the natives of the places between Connel and Ballachulish object to the railway's imposition for the crossing, but many tourists have never seen the coast road to Ballachulish because of it. If you decide against it, you will miss Benderloch, haunt of artists, Barcaldine Castle and Appin, scene of one of the most famous murders in Scottish criminology; nothing adds glamour to a murder like mystery. It is a tale that has so often been told and dramatised, it need not be told again.

We shall not pay the imposition. Our route is by Bonawe again, Taynuilt, Pass of Brander and Dalmally to the scene of—not a murder, but a massacre even better known in history than the murder in Appin—the massacre of Glencoe.

GLENCOE

GLENFINNAN AND LOCH SHIEL

8

GLENCOE

ON the way to Glencoe we pass the first of two lovely glens on the route—Glenorchy. I have never found any history attached to this glen, and, to tell the truth, I am rather glad. For me its loveliness is enough. All I know is that its name is supposed to imply "the glen of the tumbling stream", and that is true and appropriate. We made it our camping-place on a Sunday evening on our way to catch the Monday boat for Iona. I should think it is always Sabbath in Glenorchy. There is, as far as I remember, only one house in the glen proper, a keeper's house, and I have never seen more than one person in the glen. On a summer evening there, with the tumbling water the only sound—except bird song, of course—and the hills rising straight from the road and not too steep and not too frowning, you have a little paradise that might have stepped out of the hymn—"By cool Glenorchy's shady rill, how sweet the lily grows". Here beauty and meditation go hand in hand. In Glenorchy is for me the pure essence of the gentler side of Scottish natural beauty.

So on up the glen to the Bridge of Orchy, and out on to the road to Glencoe. There is now through the glen a new road. and, I think, a great piece of road-making. I had my private quarrels with one of the men who helped to create it— and I am one of many who had those fights—but that will not stop me from saying that he and his colleagues did a great job, and I hope they will have worthy successors. They made a fine way and yet they never, by road or bridge, spoiled the main features of this tremendous landscape.

For when you get into the glen proper, you have one of the most amazing pieces of mountain scenery, I am convinced, in the world. It is almost too good. It is everything that it should be of its kind. In another way, it reminds me of one of the most perfect—if that expression, which is not correct, is allowable—of Scottish ballads, "The Wife of Usher's Well". That is a ballad that has everything a ballad should have, good and bad, for part of a ballad's goodness is its badness. But, to my mind, a man, a great one, made "The Wife of Usher's Well"—Walter Scott. But no man ever made any part of Glencoe—if ever anywhere you see and feel the hand and power of the Creator it is in such a place as this. See it in sunshine, when there is great loveliness; see it in mist and shadow, when a little fear can come upon you; see it in moonlight, when it is almost incredible; see it in snow, when your heart sinks. But always, all the time, there is this feeling of greatness in natural beauty. There is only one other set of hills, if I may call them so, that has impressed me in the same way, and that is the Coolins—the Cuillin, nowadays—and they are, as Scottish scenery steadily is, different from the aspect and effect of Glencoe.

It was a chance of circumstance that added to Glencoe that Massacre of February 1692, one of the beastliest things in all British history, a deed that still fills most Scottish people, even today, after Hitler and Nazism, with rage and shame. What makes it worst of all, perhaps, is that it involved the betrayal of hospitality, the massacring of a trusting folk. The MacDonalds were not by any means themselves perfect, but compared with their slayers, who were no better than silly demons, they were angels of heaven. I think many people feel about it like that unknown reader of whom the late J. J. Bell has told. Written in pencil on the margin of J. J.'s copy of Dr. Garnett's *Tour*, published in 1811, against the name of King William, were these lines—"I trust in God he has got his reward in Hell, and that all those connected with him in this foul deed have experienced a like fate".

There is not the slightest doubt that, for almost every traveller in Glencoe, the Massacre has its effect. They cannot forget the bloodshed, but almost worse was the awful journey over the mountains of the majority who escaped—only forty out of some two hundred were done to death.

The most impressive account of that terrible trek, together with a great knowledge of the mountains on which it took place, is that given by John Buchan in his great little book on the Massacre. But then, John Buchan sojourned in Glen Etive and knew those mountains like an open book. There was always that sort of knowledge behind John Buchan's work. Look at these fearsome heights and think of men, women and children, half-clad, fleeing for their lives in the terrible snow and cold and exposure of an atmosphere that, even in high summer, has its ardours and endurances.

Yes, all that, more than 250 years after, still haunts the Glen of Weeping.

Let us turn aside from Glencoe, down a lovely sideway. Almost opposite Kingshouse Inn, which fringes on that Rannoch Moor of which I have already written, you will find a tiny signpost which says simply—"Glen Etive". It is—or was—a ridiculous signpost, giving not the slightest clue to what lay beyond. Many, perhaps, having found the glen have been secretly glad that the signpost was no more than it was. Although hundreds, if not thousands, know it, it is the kind of glen which one wants to keep to oneself.

The entrance is not very impressive, but, as you take the one-track road, the view and the area become more and more wonderful. Part of the wonders of the glen, of course, are those dominants, the great masses of the Buchaille Etive Mhor and the Buchaille Etive Beg. Even if your way lies pleasantly, as in most glens of the kind, beside a tumbling stream, you can never be unaware of what is beyond and over all.

In Glen Etive you are in the ancient Royal Forest of Dalcross, now a sanctuary in the hands of the National Trust. You are also in the land of old romance and tragedy. Up on the hill yonder, beyond Dalcross Lodge, Deirdre and Naoise, during their exile from Erin, when they were in flight from the evil desires of wicked old Conchubar, had their bower. Here they lived out the idyll of their young love, here the old wicked king's messenger found them and lured them to Erin and murder and suicide.

W. B. Yeats and J. M. Synge and others have written the dark tales of Deirdre and Naoise, but Kenneth Macleod, whom we shall recognise as the poet of the Hebrides, has in "Deirdre's Farewell to Scotland", given us the feeling of this idyll in the first stage towards the tragedy and the spirit of the place in which the idyll was at its happiness:

> Dearest Albyn, land o'er yonder,
>   Thou dear land of wood and wave,
> Sore my heart that I must leave thee
>   But 'tis Naoise I may not leave.
>
> O Glen Etive, O Glen Etive,
>   Where they builded my bridal hold,
> Beauteous glen in early morning,
>   Flocks of sunbeams crowd thy fold.
>
> Glen da Rua, Glen da Rua!
>   My love on all whose mother thou,
> From a cliff tree called a cuckoo,
>   And methinks I hear him now.
>   Glen da Rua! Glen da Rua!

That is sung to a lovely air which Mr. Macleod collected, and the second and third verse comes from the Glenmasen MS. of 1238. That gives you some idea of what Glen Etive can mean to those who know something of its history.

But the glen is lovely in itself. The road winds its way down to the head of the loch, here, I think, at its loveliest. Green herb, nowhere more lush, the still loveliness of the water, and, always, the two great Shepherds over all. A day in Glen Etive is a day well spent, and I can understand why John Buchan spent many days there. Scottish literature is the richer today for those days.

Now we are at Glencoe, at the head of the glen, a quiet easy place today, hub of many tourists, all the terrible story not forgotten, but hid in the hospitality of its present-day folk.

Then we set off up the south bank of Loch Leven, still a place of highland beauty until we come to Kinlochleven, where aluminium and commerce have their home. This is a warning to some of those who are commercialising the highlands. Do not let us have any more Kinlochlevens. I have nothing to say of the people who work and live there, but I have much to say to those who made this eyesore. Why dump a commercial suburb of Glasgow in such a place? That is what we are afraid of in Scotland, much as we want all the benefits of commercialisation for the highland places and people. The worst can be avoided. Will it be? Surely, we have men and women with more vision than existed when Kinlochleven was built—or thrown together.

With a shudder let us make our way down the north shore of the loch to Onich, and so on to Fort William.

9

NEVIS TO MORAR

FORT WILLIAM is neither village nor town. I should call it a large-sized clachan. Its long, narrow main street never gets away from what lies beyond it—Loch Linnhe and the shadow of Ben Nevis—Scotland's highest mountain. Now we are in the historic country with the lovely name—Lochaber.

We have come by road through impressive Glencoe, but, so far as Fort William itself is concerned, it is even lovelier in a way to come by steamer. I love the sail up Linnhe from Oban, past lovely green Lismore, past Morven, Sunart and beautiful Ardgour, land of tradition and song.

Fort William is a combination of the old and the new. You will find there a West Highland museum of great interest, you will meet in the hotels people from the highlands and islands of equal interest, and you will also find the cinema and the "chip shop".

Before we take the road to the west—once, as a road, one of the most fearsome journeys the motorist could embark upon—let us do the right thing as tourists and Scots; let us go up Glen Nevis and up the Ben.

You should walk Glen Nevis, I don't know why, but I just have that feeling. It is not respect for the Ben, though it is Scotland's highest peak, because, even for a rabbit in mountain climbing, Ben Nevis has been made a leisurely walk up. But there is something about the glen that is rather lovely. There are other glens as lovely, but this has a cachet that I cannot describe or explain. What makes one glen fairer than another, who can say? I have seen many glens, from Glen Affric to Glen Orchy, and I still have my admiration for Nevis. Leave it at that.

As I say, except for the mountaineer who looks for the most difficult way up a peak, Ben Nevis is dead easy. Motor bicycles and, I have heard, even a car have made the ascent. But however easy that may be, the reward is in the height and the view. You are lucky, in some ways, if you climb on a clear day, but if you climb on a day of alternate sun and mist I think you are even luckier. That is one of the peculiar joys of the Scottish mountains. You climb—if the climb is not dangerous —through the mist, and you arrive at the peak; still mist. Then, as you sit, perhaps a little dolefully because you have come 4406 feet and there is little or nothing to see, suddenly, as if a blind had been drawn up, away beyond, north, east, south or west, a sudden cameo of a view is unfolded for you—the sun shining on peaks or in a valley. If you sit long enough on a misty day on Nevis you will have one after the other of these cameos and vistas. It becomes almost a game—where will the blind be rolled up next? And you realise the height of Nevis, as you sit, on a July day, eating chocolate and picking a handful of snow to accompany the chocolate. As you descend, too, you have a certain feeling of elation: even though you have taken the easy way, you have climbed Britain's highest mountain. That's only human. Back in Fort William, you look at Ben Nevis, and it looks very different from what you found as you climbed, and you say: "I climbed there, to the very top, right to the old observatory". And, foolishly, you think more of yourself than ever.

Now we are out and away on the road to Glenfinnan, Kinlochailort, Arisaig, Morar and Mallaig. All these make this difficult road the road of romance. If only a Scottish composer could make a symphony of all that is in and behind these names, then Scotland would be set high in the realm of music. I think that will come. I think Scotland is going to produce its Dvořák and Smetana, its Tchaikovsky and Grieg. Already the promise is there, the fulfilment will follow. That is part of the Scottish renaissance.

The first part of this road is not very different from many other roads in Scotland. It is when you reach Glenfinnan station that you realise what and where you are. Glenfinnan station, I think, is one of the most extraordinary places of its kind in Scotland. It is a station that seems to be set almost among the mountain tops. I know only one other place like it, the peak of the road from Tomich to Drumnadrochit.

But now we must go down from Glenfinnan to one of the spots in Scotland that affects me, in a variety of ways, like no other except the field of Culloden. Such places as Sheriffmuir, Prestonpans mean nothing like these. Glenfinnan saw the start, Culloden saw the end of something that has united and divided Scotland as few things else have done, and all because of one man and a cause—Prince Charles Edward Stuart and the Rebellion of 1745. The division is between romance and realism. Mary Queen of Scots divides us, but in a different way. Yet, there is a curious affinity in the way in which those two royalties affect Scotland and Scotsmen. Each was born under a hapless star. Each went the way of destiny, but to how different ends. Mary died a martyr to the irresolute tantrums of an irresolute woman and queen, who had the gift of battening on the gifts of those whom she made and destroyed. Poor Charles—what a pity he did not die in battle or was not caught and executed. So lovely he was and debonair in youth; the drunken old man he became was not even pathetic.

His devotees refuse to see him except as the Prince Charming of 1745. But, it must be remembered, the seeds of the decay that came after were in him then. It is not right to ascribe to the failure of the '45 all that happened when that historical episode was over. The Hanover Georges were no angels, but I shudder to think what might have happened to this country had another of the fascinating but hapless Stuarts ascended the British Throne. Those Royal playboys were good for neither peer nor peasant. In every second Scot there is the touch of second sicht, and the hesitations, the desertions of certain Scots where Charlie's ploy was concerned were an outcome of that sicht. No Scot ever failed a fight, any more than any Irishman. But the difference between an Irishman and a Scot in such a matter is this. An Irishman enters the fight for the love of the fight, but a Scotsman likes to realise the fundamentals of the matter—is this the Shorter Catechism?—and it is not that he wishes always to be on the winning side, but he does like to be in a fight that has sense in it. Was there sense in the '45?

Well, that field at Glenfinnan with its monument and the long, narrow dark loch —even on the brightest of days—somehow depresses me. I have never yet been happy at Glenfinnan, and only when I realise that all Scotsmen look upon Charles Edward Stuart as something that belongs more to fiction and fairy tale than to history of importance shall I be happy there.

We must divorce Charles from all the fiction that has grown up around him and his exploits and get down to truth and realism. As I have said, I cannot understand that there should be Scots—they are not, I think, typical Scots—who, after two world wars such as that of 1914–18 and 1939–45 and all that those wars have entailed and brought in their train, can still worry about the little ramee of 1745. It is ridiculous and makes Scotland ridiculous. No, let us keep all the songs and the fiction, revel in them, wallow in them if you like, but do not let them affect our national lives now. That is not far short of idiocy, and we have plenty of contemporary foolishness without going to older history for more.

Let us love Glenshiel for what it is, a glen of true Scottish characteristic. I know, I know, it is like the Borders as I have described them. Something comes out of that soggy ground that is apt to make a Scotsman an intellectual weakling. I am more susceptible to it than most Scots, but I shall fight it and other Scots must do so too. Scotland will never get where she should be going until we put the past, the present and the future in proper perspective. We cannot live altogether on the past, though some do pretty well on it. But, the more the past recedes, the less we shall get out of it. That seems an obvious remark, but it is something that a certain section of the Scottish people either cannot or will not recognise. But we must recognise it, or go down the hill, because, unfortunately, the Scots whose eyes are turned backwards are among the most vocal and most persuasive. There, again, Scotland has its divisions. And yet, I cannot altogether blame them. Modern life is so damnable in most of its aspects, and the past is so like a tale of attraction. But, think, you of elder years and not so elder, who have been in the wars and seen all their horrors. Think of what Prince Charles Edward's ploy brought in its train. Think of the dead and the dying on many battlefields, think of the ruined homes, think of the block and the gallows tree. Think, and act differently.

Loch Shiel always seems to me to lead into some Never-Never Land. Of course, it is partly that '45 *stimmung*—I have never been there when a crowd of anti-Hanoverians were eloquent and enthusiastic. I have been there only when it was quiet and deserted. It is a strange contrast—the place where the standard was raised in 1715—Braemar—was alive and bracing, the place of the '45 is the very essence of what the outsider and the hopeless romantic thinks of the Celt. And both exploits were doomed, and both because of the Stuart dynasty. That ailed from the prime foundation. Why does not some dramatist give us a play that is an extension of the ghostly pageant that Clarence saw in his prison just before his death? The Kings of England, the Kings of Scotland—or of most countries, for that matter—what a historical phantasmagoria! Fiction never equalled fact in this. Think of the Stuarts, and forget not that they affected Scotland and affect it even today, profoundly. The Stuarts and the Reformation are the two king-pins of Scottish existence, plus, of course, Scotland in nature, and all three are bound up together.

That is what comes to me at lonely Glenfinnan. The winds that blow there speak of shattered hopes, only a little less poignantly than on the Moor of Culloden. It is something that we in Scotland have to fight; the Celtic in all of us, even the Low-landers, tends to get us down.

Now, we are on the road again. We are past Loch Eil and we are coming to Loch Eilt. Let me say one thing: you can do the journey by car to Mallaig, but if you dislike difficult road, you will enjoy the journey just as well by train. You will be on the opposite side of the loch, but the beauty is no less.

I went first to Morar and Arisaig when the road was, probably, the worst in Britain: and I have been down the Honister Hause in the Lake district when it was at its worst—in a motor cycle and side-car; but that was an intensive thrill. The road to Morar is, or used to be, a series of both extensive and intensive thrills. But these are made up for—if you do not like such thrills—by the beauty and the interest of the road. Still, I say, you can go by train and have your enjoyment.

The first excitement came on this road when we found that Loch Eilt and the road had joined forces. My driving partner was, fortunately, wearing a kilt. He got out, minus shoes and stockings and cranked the car, after which I gingerly steered her through the water. After that, what was most needed was careful driving, and often very careful.

JACOBITE MONUMENT, GLENFINNAN

INVERLOCHY CASTLE, NEAR FORT WILLIAM

After our splash we could take full note of the beauty of Loch Eilt, with its tree-topped islets, its great stillness: the loch was asleep in the sun and the reflections of the hills among which it lies were as lovely as any I have seen. We came down to Eilt, now we ascend again to Loch Ailort, best known to fishers, but to the passing traveller a very lonely region. I have seen it only at summer height, what it can be at winter depth I can only imagine.

We cross Ardnish and then we come upon Loch-nan-Uamh and here again is both beauty and history. The colours of all that lies about this loch are delicate and of the quality of a rare, fine water-colour, the ready-made subject of an aquarellist. This loch lies to the sea and here you will have a first glimpse of what you will see more fully when you get to Arisaig and Morar—the peculiar and essential sea vista of the west coast of Scotland. You will have seen something of it from Mull and Iona and the voyages there and back, but, somehow, this one has just that something more to it that makes it unique.

Loch-nan-Uamh is, of course, the spot to which came the *Doutelle* with Prince Charles Edward aboard on July 25, 1745. He had landed first at the little isle of Eriskay, but here he touched the mainland of Scotland. That was the beginning of Charles's "awfully big adventure". And Loch-nan-Uamh also saw its close, for here a year and a month after his landing, Charles, who had been hunted for months from peak to glen, from cave to shieling, boarded another French ship with the name *Heureux*—in English, "Happy"!—and the '45 was over, bar the fates of its many victims.

Charles came to, and went away from, one of the loveliest parts of the country he claimed and lost. There are those, indeed, who set the land and sea scene at Arisaig and Morar higher in beauty than any other in Scotland. It is not a claim I should like either to make or dispute, but I do agree that there is about this white shore with its light, green translucent water something which can hardly be put into words. In addition, there is its soft air, its lovely background, and for foreground the vista of which I have already spoken. This is often made by that west-coast haze, not offensive like our east-coast haar, but soft and with colour in it. Out of the haze loom the vague shapes of Eigg and Rum. Always when I hear the names of Arisaig and Morar mentioned, these islands swim into the ken of my memory, placid leviathans who never seek to leave their moorings, and who would blame them?

But it is at sunset that this western coast becomes even more magical. West-coast sunsets are noted, but they are never lovelier anywhere than they are here. Here is another shore of *dolce far niente*, and, lovely as it is by day, at evening dreams of an almost medieval quality in colour come true. Is that one reason why this has so long been a Catholic shore; it might have given rise to the many hymns such as the

Rhythm of Bernard of Clairvaux, full of yearning for heaven? Well, on this shore such a heaven does not seem so very far away.

In contrast, I do not care very much for Mallaig, the end of this road and rail journey, but then I am not partial to a pervasive smell of herring. But Mallaig can be the stepping-off point for many delightful visits—Skye among them.

LOCH LINNHE

RIVER AWE FLOWING INTO LOCH ETIVE, ARGYLLSHIRE

10

SKYE-ALLURE

SKYE—the Eilean-a-Cheo, the misty isle—is another of Scotland's islands that has evoked plenty of literature. That ranges from Dr. Johnson's Hebridean tour to the little guides and throw-aways of the tourist companies. As with Iona, you will never get to know anything much about Skye on a whirlwind tour. You must soak in its atmosphere, just as your garments may soak in the mist that gives the island its Gaelic name. I have approached the island by steamer from Oban, Fort William and Mallaig, and I have also come that long, lovely journey from Inverness by places with names as full of enchantment as the scenery through which you pass—Lochluichart, Achnashellach, Achnasheen, Garve, Plockton and Carron to Kyle of Lochalsh.

Do not be too much taken aback if, when you arrive, one way or the other, there is no Skye to be seen, only seemingly impenetrable grey mist, miles and miles and miles of it, up, down and across. I have a theory that the sun is always shining somewhere in Skye and, certainly, it is as much an island of rainbows as it is of mist. And when a day does come of clear sunshine in Skye, make the fullest use of it. You will never forget what you see and smell on such a day, and I have seen quite a few of them in Skye. I recommend that you should go to Skye between spring and early summer. As summer draws to its height so do the flocks, almost clouds of midges, which make life something of a misery and, at the same time, change the atmosphere to an almost unreal beauty. I remember driving towards Sligachan and the Coolins one evening. Between us and the hills hung a shimmering screen of the most ethereal kind. The scene reminded me of one of those transformation scenes that used to enchant us as children, when we were taken to the old-fashioned pantomimes—in *Robinson Crusoe*, for instance, "A Cave Beneath the Sea". And part of this shimmering screen consisted of midges. We were in an open car, and on this evening we had to hold handkerchiefs before our faces, so that we should not swallow mouthfuls of midge.

When you waken and find that it is a good day in Skye, be up and away early. Go across the moorland, but pick your steps carefully or you may find yourself up to the ankles in bog. But, as you go, your nostrils will be taking in the lovely smell of crushed bog-myrtle, and often you will be treading a golden path of marsh flowers. Then, on such a morning, you will see the Coolins, that really marvellous mountain range, outlined against the clear sky like shapes of fantasy, not reality.

On just such a day I climbed, not the Coolins but Tianavaig, the hill that over-looks the southern entrance to the harbour of Portree. It was not difficult, but when I got to the highest part of the hill there lay before me a panorama I had not expected. Skye seemed one of a group of islands, not set in the sea but in a huge inland loch. The sea looked like the most wonderfully wrought enamel, blue as blue could be, a soft, lovely blue. There were other colours, of course, especially away towards Applecross on the Ross-shire coast, but one's eyes always came back to the blue. It is something I have remembered for many a year. I have seen many lovely days in Skye since then, but never again from the top of Tianavaig. Fascinated, I lay too long looking at that view, and, when I turned to descend, I found that mist was coming at me from the other side of the hill. That was an annoying descent, because, although there are no precipices on Tianavaig, except on the sea-side, there are nasty bluffs. I have never picked my way so carefully down any height, and I eventually returned to a disturbed household, safe in limb and body. They knew the hill better than I did.

My first stay in Skye—many years ago—was at the little hamlet of Penefiler, a mile across Portree Bay but three miles round by road. Skye was not then the popular resort it has since become. There were no buses, and it needed a pretty sturdy car to negotiate some of the roads, which were of the same quality as that from Fort William to Mallaig. I rather think I liked the Skye that was more than the Skye that is. But it does not do to be selfish. In any case, you can always get away from the crowds. There is never likely to be a human traffic jam, for instance, in the Coolins. For the most part they are the expert climber's playground. Even if you are no expert, you can get your pleasure out of the Coolins, but there are many parts of them which should never be attempted by any one alone or inex-perienced. The Coolins have claimed their victims, sometimes under the most tragic circumstances. I have told you of my own little experience on Ben Tianavaig; the sudden descent of the mist. There is one story told of the Coolins. A father, who was experienced, was introducing his young daughter to one of the peaks. The mist came down suddenly and it was getting towards evening. The father thought. Then he decided. There was one way to get to a spot from which he knew he could lead his daughter safely down. He told her to keep close to the wall as he led her and to go slowly and easily. With relief he saw that they had achieved his purpose. Then the mist rose, and when the girl saw where she had crossed, she fainted. It was a narrow ledge and there were hundreds of feet of empty space and jagged mountain-side below the ledge. I dreamt of that story for nights after my

LOCH–NAN–UAMH

THE RED HILLS OF SKYE

first trip into the Coolins. All over the island of Skye you can never completely get away from the Coolins. Always those sharp, cruel-looking shapes shoot up into the heavens. And I have always felt that they are among the loneliest peaks and valleys I have ever encountered. But when you have once seen them, even if only from a distance, you will never forget them. I think if I were an artist as well as a Scot my work would be permeated with them. They haunt you, you use them as motif, as comparison, as decoration for your favourite fantasies.

There is one spot in them which seems to gather up everything about the Coolins, their fascination, their frightening beauty. That, of course, is Loch Coruisk. The best way to approach it is by motor-boat from Elgol, on the south-eastern shore of Loch Scavaig, but I hope you will not have the thrill I had on my first visit to Coruisk. The wind was fair, the day was fine and we were swiftly crossing, when the Gaelic-speaking boatman yelled something to his son, who was our steersman. The boat gave the most terrific swing, and only then did I see the sunken rock which we had just avoided.

But even that adventure did not take away from the impression that dark little loch made upon me, even on a fair summer day. I wonder if Coruisk is ever really all bright? I have seen it only when shafts lit now this part and that, and even if it were a day of blazing heat I should still think the place was sombre and cold. The colours—dark though they may be—and the lighting effects will haunt you just as the rest of the Coolins do. There are all sorts of legends about Coruisk. It is said to be haunted. Yet almost every day of my life I meet a man who spent a night alone by Loch Coruisk. He was living on the island of Raasay, and by boat had come to Sligachan and crossed the Coolins. By the time he had done that and was at Coruisk it was evening. He was alone, he could neither cross the hills nor was it possible to get a boat to Elgol. He found something like a cave and used newspapers as bed-covering. I asked whether it was not a terrifying experience. He said he didn't know; he slept. But there's one thing about this man, his hair turned grey at a very early age. I have never liked to ask whether that was before or after Coruisk. Among the hundreds of people whom I have met who have been to Skye, he is the only one I know who has slept the night at Coruisk.

But the Coolins are not the whole of Skye. The difference between the east and the west of the island is rather striking. Let us turn our eyes and steps away from the Coolins and the east for a time, forget Sgurr-nan-Gillean's fascination, in name and form. Shall we go first to the high road beneath which lies Talisker, the distillery from which comes that most famous of Scots liqueurs, Drambuie? But that is a place that, apart from its setting and fame, will not keep us long. Back we come and on to the road to Bracadale, and on past the view first of Macleod's Maidens and then of Macleod's Tables—those curious flat eminences, and so to Dunvegan.

6

I have not bothered Dunvegan much in my time in Skye, but it is an unceasing attraction to a majority of visitors.

Dunvegan Castle is the home of the Chief of Macleod, and a castle has stood on this site for, it is said, a thousand years, and has been called the oldest inhabited domicile in Britain. Admission is permitted for visitors, and here you will find a lock of Prince Charles's hair, in a glass case, and other Charlie relics, letters from Samuel Johnson and Walter Scott. But what most visitors seem to relish is the Fairy Flag, just a bit of yellow silk. But it goes back to the days of the Saracens and is said to have its special qualities. It has brought victory to the Macleods on two occasions, but—if it is unfurled a third time, away will go both standard-bearer and flag, into a Celtic Never-Never Land. This castle, like that of Macbeth's in Shake-speare's play, hath a pleasant seat, and its surroundings as well as its contents repay at least one visit. But it is apt to remind one at certain seasons of the year of places that are not Skye and of a Skye that should not resemble those places.

We can go now still northward, westwards to Vaternish. Though I have been only once to Vaternish it is one of the places in Skye I best remember, and for a sentimentally Scottish reason. With my companions we went into a little house for a cup of tea. The room we were shown into was very small, an ordinary dining-table almost completely filled it, but it was tidy and clean. What we noticed almost first of all, and certainly looked at last, was a portrait—one of those enlargements of photographs, so greatly in vogue a generation or more ago. It was of a fine-looking lad, and he was wearing the hood and gown of a Scottish university graduate. He was, of course, the son of the little house, and one of many lads from humble homes who, for many generations, have passed through the Scottish universities, sometimes to fame and fortune, more often to less distinctive posts and no worldly honour, but to jobs from which Scotland and her sons and daughters have reaped the best of benefit. This portrait reminds me of another incident during a holiday in Skye. I was walking along the road by Braes when I came upon a young fellow, in working rig, trundling a barrow. Not sure whether or not he had the English I greeted him tentatively. He had the English, in fact he was studying that subject as an Honours student at Edinburgh University and was helping on his father's croft in vacation! Yes, these things are part of Scotland that was and is.

Of the west and north of Skye, however, I love best, for more than one reason, the road by Loch Snizort, up past Kensaleyre, Castle Uisdean and so up the hill to Uig. Uig is the wick its name implies and lies in its hollow by the sea, a trim little port with modern houses.

Now we pass on to Kilmuir—one of the richest agricultural patches of Skye—and thoughts of the woman and heroine whom all the reading-world knows, Flora Macdonald. She was not exactly the Flora of foolish legend, and sometimes scandalous rubbish, but one of the finest and most faithful spirits of her own or any time. Flora was born at Milton in South Uist in 1722, and died at Kingsburgh, which we have already passed, in March 1790. It was in the middle twenties of that comparatively long life that there occurred the incidents that have made her known and dear to Scots and many others. One does not need to be either a Jacobite or anti-Jacobite to appreciate Flora Macdonald. Had she not done what she did on that late June time in 1746, what would have been the course of Stuart and even Scottish history? It is an interesting if now rather useless speculation.

Surely the world is not so preoccupied that it has either forgotten or does not know the story, how Flora, a girl of twenty-four—Prince Charles was then twenty-six—obtained passports for herself and certain others to leave the island of Uist, where she was on a visit to her brother at her birthplace, and cross to Skye. It is part of the ironic comedy of a time that otherwise knew so much tragedy, suffering and death, that the passports were given by her stepfather, who was in command of the Hanoverian troops in Benbecula. That was not looked on as treason; the whole business was as mixed as that. More, Hugh MacDonald, of Armadale, that stepfather, gave Flora a letter which was as good as the passport, if not better, telling his wife that Flora was in care of Niel MacEachainn and with them was an Irish maid, Betty Burke.

So came that twenty miles' journey in an open boat across the Minch. That Saturday night was a night of terrible thunder and lightning, and twenty miles is a long way through such a storm. But Vaternish was reached in the early morning and later Loch Snizort was crossed to the Uig shore, and the petticoated Prince was still in danger. Flora put off one military questioner, even telling him a lie—that the Prince was on his way to France. There in a cave at Dun Scudabord the Prince took refuge for a time before the party set out for Kingsburgh. It was here that the lock of hair now at Dunvegan was asked and given. And here occurred one of the acts that, in its long aftermath, reveal something of the charm that was Prince Charlie's then, even in the midst of danger and physical suffering. Remember he was an outlaw and a fugitive, with the price of £30,000 on his head—a temptation that switherers as well as enemies might yield to. Flora took away one of the sheets from the bed in which the Prince had slept at Kingsburgh, and, forty-four years later, it was her shroud. And in those long years she had been in nominal prison, to America and back, and a happy wife and a good mother.

Flora did not end her help at Kingsburgh. With Niel MacEachainn she accompanied the Prince to Portree. At what is now the Royal Hotel there the Prince said goodbye to Flora; and it was goodbye, for, though he hoped to see her when as king he enjoyed his own, they never met again and not a word of writing ever passed between the twain. Flora died two years after the Prince, and she would know his later history. Unpretty as that was, it did not take away that feeling for

Charles the young and debonair. To her he must have been the unfading Prince Charming. Of that there is no doubt; her shroud was evidence. Is there not in all this something of an epitome, a curious summing-up of the 1745—and after? It was romantic, but that romance caught even the most level-headed, and even after it was all over and done and the glory of its central figure had gone, left only the dregs of the heady cup; the memory of that headiness remained like the ghost of a mist that could still enchant those who had drunk of the original cup. And think of what happened in Scottish literature and song!

I thought of all this as I sat by Flora's grave in the lone churchyard of Kilmuir. It was a greyish day, but soft, and from that spot I could hear the sound of the little waves, the quiet brothers of those more fiercesome ones of the Minch through which the Prince and Flora came that angry night. Some would say that even the elements fought against Charles, but could not prevail. That streak of mixed luck has touched even the monuments destined for Flora's grave. The first, a marble slab, was cracked on its journey to Skye and did not long survive after it was erected. Next a large Celtic cross was erected, but was blown down and broken in two. Now there is a third cross and that has been reinforced by an iron stanchion. Again, is this synonymous? But Flora, in her own day and ever since, has been the darling of the romantics. I think she must have laughed and would still laugh at much of this, but at the heart of her own practical personality was also the Celtic glow of romance.

But as we reluctantly leave this spot we stand just for a moment and listen to "the sea's listless chime" and remember how far is this place from the Church of Frascati, in Rome, where Charles was originally buried, and how far was the life of Charles Edward Stuart from that which Flora led. Kilmuir—Rome, what worlds apart!

On, then, by the romantic ruins of Duntulm Castle, once the seat of the Lords of the Isles, by Kilmaluag to Flodigarry, where Flora spent almost half of her married life, down by the Quairaing, something of a curious relation of Macleod's Tables, past Staffin and the Old Man of Storr to Portree. It is not too desolate a road, though it has its patches that come near it, and it can be a slow pilgrimage if you meet, as I have done, a shepherd with a great flock of sheep. The shepherd never turned his head at the sound of our car, but jogged slowly on behind his flock. There was no room to pass, so we had to jog on as well. This went on for quite a distance and then, suddenly, one of the silly flock turned off the road, and the whole lot followed and were allowed to. So we passed, but still the shepherd never turned his head!

I have indicated some difference between the islands of Scotland. There is another —religion. There is not the slightest doubt that an island in which the Catholic religion is predominant is different from that in which one or several Calvinistic denominations are the vogue and tradition. I felt this latter strongly in Skye in the old days. The Sabbath was something I had not known since my boyhood—full up

GLEN SLIGACHAN, SKYE

LOCH CORUISK, SKYE

of taboos and fetishes. Agricultural work in Skye, once on a day, was done according to the dates of the two half-yearly communions. This was probably why I would see a man come out into his little hayfield, scythe a row and then either go back into his house or lie on his back where he had thrown down his scythe. Well, there was time to lie and stare, and perhaps his life in every way was better than that of those of us who are, as they say, at the ding-dong all day long.

On the only time I was ever able to make a visit to Skye coincide with the great festival of the Seceders, perhaps the most Calvinistic of Skye's Presbyterian sects, it was not weather good enough for open-air services and, thereby, I missed seeing in modern actuality a replica of something rather like that which Burns describes in "The Holy Fair". I did, however, listen from the porchway to an inside service. The singing we all now know something of, from Gaelic services on the wireless, grace notes galore that made the tunes seem allies of the melodies that Chinese coolies sing. But the sermon I heard then I have never heard equalled in a wireless service. It started quietly, but soon the preacher began to soar to his top-notes and at the climax he seemed like a man in a frenzy. All of a sudden, with an effect that did something to my spine, his voice dropped, straight as a stone into a pool of almost silence. But soon he was soaring again. And the length of the sermon! To an outsider such preaching and singing is often a strain on the risible faculties.

One other incident during my stay in those far-off days impressed me. The lady with whom I was staying set off the three miles to church one Sunday. On the way she was joined by another woman, and so they came to Portree. There my friend made for the United Free Church. The other woman said: "Do you mean to tell me you are not a Seceder?" "No, I am United Free." "Well, if I had known I wouldn't have walked the road with you." What will happen in heaven?

And there was the comment made by certain religious persons in Skye when a climber met a sad death on Sunday on the Coolins. "Well, they shouldn't have been climbing on the Sabbath. It was a judgment."

But that need not affect anyone's happiness and enjoyment to the full of the beauty, the real and eternal beauty of Skye. Skye haunts you for long after you have been there, especially if your lot is set in a city. . . .

> The road winds over the moorland to Camastianavaig,
> And now, when I'm tired of city ways, it's there I would be going
> In glint of sun or grey of rain, for there the wind that's blowing
> Has the tang of the sea, the cool of the hills and scent of bog-myrtle growing
>
> There's peace beyond understanding at Camastianavaig
> Dear name, that holds the murmur of the Hebridean breakers;
> What joy to see the rainbows span the little patchwork acres,
> And hearken distant waterfalls, the eilean's music makers. . . .

But I'll sit again on green knoll at Camastianavaig
And watch the curling peat-reek from its brown-thatched shielings rise;
Oh then the waves that tell its name will lead my happy eyes
Across by Braes where, southward, the Coolins cut the skies.

Haste, haste the time when I shall come
Where peace and beauty have their home,
Jewel of that misty isle,
Dear Camastianavaig.

Like every exile of the spirit I often dream of Skye, and in those dreams I wander at will from south to north, going whither my fancy takes me. I can call up remembered sunsets, for if you have seen the sunsets of Skye you will not forget them—the gold and the crimson there are of a depth and beauty that set you dreaming of all the Celtic myths and heroes. I sat once at sunset in Glen Varragill and I made a poem and a story such as the old minstrels might have sung by the fire in the great hall of the Chief of Macleod on a night when inspiration was on him. But, when I tried to set it down on paper, it had gone as the sunset had faded; there was only the memory of that hour of beauty and happiness. But that was something in itself.

It is a great thing to arrive in Skye, at evening, after sailing by Broadford and Raasay. Portree, however busy it may be, has the quietness of all island ports, and, once the busyness of the steamer's arrival is over, it settles down to even more quiet. And it is lovely, late on a summer's night, when you have settled in to your lodging, to go out and just listen, under the stars. If you have chosen the right place to stay you will hear, akin to the silence, the music of falling water, they are in reality "the eilean's music-makers", its essential voice. And, however dark it may be, you will always be conscious of the Coolins, not reflected like ghosts as are the Alps at night on the lakes of Switzerland, but soaring in the mind's eye, real, not actual.

When you leave Skye at the end of a holiday, and are given a good day for your departure, you will understand something of the feeling of the exiles who so often in the old days were driven from their native places by the cruelty of men and circumstance. No wonder that, even in lovely places far away, they sang, as once the exiled Jews by the waters of Babylon. This was their Zion.

From the lone shieling on the misty island
Mountains divide us and the waste of seas,
But still the blood is strong, the heart is highland,
And we in dreams behold the Hebrides.
  Fair these broad meads, these hoary woods are grand,
  But we are exiles from our native land. . . .

There is something of the Celt, I think, in every second Scotsman of the Lowlands, whether we have Highland ancestry or not. This it is that will always unite the majority of us in Scotland. In dreams we behold the Hebrides, their spell is upon us again and again. And that is why we always return in actuality as well as dream.

When our boat has touched again upon the shore of the mainland, as an epilogue to Skye, all around Kyle of Lochalsh there are beauties, and impressive ones at that, which could keep the home-going traveller for many days. Further south there is Loch Hourn, nearer to Lochalsh is Loch Duich and that impressive range, known as the Five Sisters of Kintail, with Ben Attow beyond. If you could cross these mountains easily, you would come to another of Scotland's most famous beauty spots—Affric, glen and loch, but we shall take another way there eventually. You have Eilean Donan Castle, the Falls of Glomach—if you can get to them—indeed, wherever you turn here there is scenery that again is the essence of the Scottish Highlands. Like every part of Scotland that is of this nature this region has its devotees, who will defend its beauties against others. Scotland is like that.

GREAT GLEN

HOW shall we go to Inverness? Perhaps it would be best to find our way back to Fort William, and from there set off up the Great Glen. This is a journey along a series of waterways that, to all intents and purposes, splits Scotland for the second time into two. The first water division is made by the Forth and Clyde Canal, but the difference in scenery along the Caledonian Canal is one of the great differences between south and north Scotland, a difference in nature that, as I have said, extends also to national character and way of life.

It is not only that the journey up the Great Glen is of interest in itself, but on either side there are roads leading off to spots that in beauty and interest will lure the traveller of leisure. Most people now make the journey by road, though the daring will do it by canoe. In time there will again be a steamer service, but for a while that gloriously leisurely mode of journeying—some found it tedious—was in abeyance. There is no doubt that the water journey gave you views and vistas that the road cannot give; yet the road, as a whole, has its pleasures and beauties.

The first break-off is to the south, the road that leads to Spean Bridge, thence by Loch Laggan, with the Cluny country beyond, to Newtonmore, Kingussie, Aviemore into Speyside. Proceeding up the waterway we come next into Loch Lochy, the first of the chain. Away on the left hand is Loch Arkaig and the Dark Mile. The Mile is an avenue of beeches, which were planted by Cameron of Lochiel, the chieftain of Lochaber, before the '45. The coming of the Cameron Clan to Charlie's standard made the difference between the rising taking place or being abandoned. On Loch Lochy we look away to the hills of Glen Garry. That name will remind you of one of our most distinctive pieces of Highland headgear—the Glengarry bonnet, which is used by several Highland regiments and has been copied by milliners for women's head-gear on both sides of the Atlantic. The other Highland headgear is the rather pancake-like Balmoral.

The next loch is the smallest of the chain—Loch Oich—considered by many to be the loveliest of the three. On the roadside by Loch Oich is a curious erection called "The Well of the Heads", in Gaelic "Tobar-nan-Ceann". There is an inscription in Gaelic, English, Latin and French. The inscription tells a rather horrible story of the way in which, once upon a day, justice was meted out by the Chiefs. Here it is:

"As a Memorial of the ample and summary Vengeance which, in the swift course of feudal justice inflicted by the orders of Lord McDonell and Aross, overtook the perpetrators of the foul murder of the Keppoch Family a branch of the powerful and illustrious clan of which his Lordship was the chief, this Monument is erected by Colonel McDonell of Glengarry, XVII. Mac-Mhic-Alaister, His successor and representative, in the year of our Lord, 1812. The heads of the seven murderers were presented at the feet of the noble chief in Glengarry Castle, after having been washed in this spring; and ever since that event, which took place early in the sixteenth century, it has been known by the name of 'Tobar-nan-Ceann' or 'The Well of the Heads'."

What a grim picture is conveyed in the latter part of the inscription. And on the top of the monument you have the seven heads.

Further on is Invergarry Castle and then, just before we come to Fort Augustus, there branches off on the right of the waterway what was once a General Wade road, and one of the most notable. Now it is a track, and a difficult one, leading over the Corrieyairick Pass in the Grampians to Laggan and Newtonmore. It is a favourite with really strenuous walkers.

Fort Augustus, a pleasant but not very distinguished-looking little town—the halfway house, as it were, between Fort William and Inverness, takes its name from one whom Highland and Jacobite Scotland still abhors, the Duke of Cumberland, victor of the '45, and a horrible victor. As one of the chief distinctions of Fort Augustus is a Catholic abbey, the ancient name of the place would be much more appropriate. That was Cille Chumain, for St. Columba probably passed this way on his mission to convert the King of the Picts, Brude, at Inverness. The abbey is one of the most famous in Scotland, but dates only to 1876. Famous names, however, of the church have been associated with it, none more than that of Prior David Hunter Blair, a great churchman and a great Scot. The Order represented here is that of the Benedictines.

From Fort Augustus we are on the way now to Loch Ness, which, for several and especially one reason, is the most famous of the lochs. It is now, of course, known to all the world because of its alleged and elusive "monster". To some people it is, they say, only an advertising "stunt". The monster and the tourist season are apt to arrive together. A certain type of Highlander will believe in the monster's actuality, because lochs have always had their monsters. He will be a clever man who gets, first, a close-up photograph of this rushing, swirling creature or manages to cut a piece off its tail.

Whenever I hear of the monster I think of that friend of other days, who dwelt by the side of Loch Ness and how he taught me to use Mealfourvonie, the mountain that lies between Invermoriston and Drumnadrochit, as a barometer.

Sandy—whom I have already mentioned—his brother, Alistair, and their sister, Elspeth, lived in a large farmhouse in a quiet little glen on the south side of Loch Ness. I used to arrive there just about tea-time. The house was white, beautifully set against its dark tree backing and looked inviting. Once inside, and if you were taken for a tour of inspection, you would find big rooms, furnished with the most solid mid-Victorian mahogany furniture. But those rooms were deserted. I never knew them to be occupied, as, I suppose, they once had been by a happy throng, round about Christmas and New Year time. But the brothers and sister were getting old, and, in the days when I was visiting them, domestic help was not to be had at any price. The girls were off to the towns and cities or preferred to work at forestry and other open-air jobs. And Elspeth was half crippled with rheumatism. Tea-time, therefore, was a surprise to me on my first visit.

We sat in a bare room. There was a good fire. The only furniture were five or six plain wooden chairs, and a table. The table was covered with no cloth of any kind, but with a newspaper. There was bread and cheese in plenty and sometimes an egg for our tea. The tea was not brewed in a pot. Instead, Elspeth ladled into each cup as much tea as would have done for a "masking" for a company twice our size. Then Alistair lifted the kettle from the hob and poured hot water into each cup. And that was how the tea was brewed, black and strong.

When the table had been cleared and the men had lit their pipes, we sat in that bare little room in the gathering twilight, which helped to take away something of its bareness. The talk was quiet and sometimes it would die away altogether. Then you heard the wind among the pines in the valley and a branch tap-tapping at the window. It was a quiet house in a quiet place.

Then Alistair would say to his nephew: "Take down the fiddle, Ian, and give us a tune." I have not yet said that the only decoration on the walls of dark red paper was—what do you think?—a genuine Stradivarius violin. It hung there on a contraption of nails and its bow beside it. Ian would take down the fiddle and, though he was no master, he could bring the Scottish airs to life—some sad, almost like the musical essence of tears, others so gay they set even old toes tapping.

We would get back to conversation, and Sandy was the best talker. After his two years at the university he had come back to his native glen because he was happier there than in a town.

"Aye," he would say with that upward sighing lilt of the voice, "I don't believe in fairies, but I know that there iss mermaids in the sea. I met a man once who told me he saw a mermaid off the coast of Skye."

"And what was she like?" he was asked.

"Well, he just wasnae awful good at his description, and, of course, she didnae bide to let him admire her, but he said she wass awful bonnie, with long fair hair and a tail that splashed as she swam away. Aye, there iss mermaids in the sea. And I'll tell you more, there iss living in Skye today a man who's going to find in Loch Usie the bit of goat's bone through which the Brahan Seer saw the future, and he will get it and tell us what is going to happen in one, two, three hundred years. Yes."

No, Sandy did not believe in fairies, but he would tell you of Torquil who went one summer Saturday night "for the messages" and, as he was coming home from the village, saw in the side of the hill that ran along the road an opening he had never noticed before. Curious, he went and peered in, and then he heard the loveliest music he had ever listened to and there were bonnie craiturs dancing. Torquil could not resist the lure, and he left his messages at the entrance and went in and joined the dance. Then his conscience began to trouble him; he remembered that part of his shopping was medicine for his little year-old son. He ran to the door of the cave, but there were no messages there.

He hurried along the road to his house, and now it was near sundown. When he came to his home, there in the garden was a man of some twenty-five years or so digging. "What are you doing in my garden?" said Torquil. The young man looked at him half in anger, half in amazement. "Since when was it your garden and who are you?" he said. "I am Torquil MacBean, and this was my house and garden before I went for the messages." "Torquil MacBean, is it? He was my father, and it is twenty-five years since he set out one night for the messages and never came back." Would you believe it, Torquil had been dancing for all those years with the fairies and it had seemed like one evening? Aye!

They were great nights. Sandy could keep you fascinated. He would tell you, again, that at the time of the Indian Mutiny above Drumashie Moor were seen in the sky the figures of men and horses, and with guns and swords; they were reflections of the fighting far across the seas in India. I never could quite see the connection between Drumashie Moor and India. But that was Sandy's story, and he stuck to it.

I used to come out into the dark of the glen and walk my miles home, half laughing, half delighted. But seldom have I enjoyed myself as I did at those Highland nights' entertainments.

And oh, the lovely air of the glen, the smell of trees and hayfield, of growing things everywhere! And for music on my journey there was always the sound of a burn and, at one part of the journey, of a little waterfall.

Well, that was on the shores of Loch Ness and almost in the shadow of Meal-fourvonie. Sandy did not live to see the great road they made along the way to

Drumnadrochit. I wonder what he would have thought of it. He was not fond of "improvements". But I think most people would agree that it is one of the loveliest roads in Great Britain. If it can be said that roadmakers are artists, then I think the men who planned and carried out the making of this road were artists. And I have seen one picture that the road inspired an artist to paint. Without having to do more than select, that artist produced a modern painting out of the roadmakers' art.

Like Loch Awe, Loch Ness has its decorative ruin of a castle, Castle Urquhart, standing on its little promontory. Loch Ness is twenty-four miles long and here, near the castle, it is from 600 to 700 feet deep, a fit lair for any evasive monster.

Past Drumnadrochit and down by Dochfour, road and waterway bring us to Inverness, queen and capital of the Highlands.

CASTLE URQUHART, LOCH NESS

STRATH GLASS, INVERNESS–SHIRE

12

INVERNESS

MANY things entitle Inverness to its name of Highland capital, and as many to its position as a queen among towns of Britain. Its history is as old as the history of Scotland. Its setting, its surroundings, its position as a traffic centre—for air as well as rail and road transport—its people and their feeling for tradition and culture, its lovely speech, all these things confer on Inverness a dignity and pleasure for the visitor.

Although it is an important centre, you never feel in Inverness the hectic rush of places such as Glasgow and even smaller centres of the south. Always you feel that life in Inverness goes not to a band, certainly not a brass band, playing at breakneck tempo, but to some lovely melody, played by a little concourse of strings and wood-winds. This may come out of the meeting of many waters, of hills that are not too forbidding. The sea is not far off, the lochs are part of her transport way. Her streets are busy but not noisy. Her people have soft voices and speak an English that, with its burr, is part of the general make-up of the town, or even its essence.

There is only one thing still wanting in Inverness, and that, I am sure, is only a matter of time—a university, the university of the Highlands, the centre and pre-server of Celtic lore, music, art and literature. Scotland needs a fifth university. Inverness is where it should be, and that for reasons practical as well as cultural.

Inverness first came clearly into the Scottish picture with the coming of Christianity to the Highlands. That is between a thousand and fifteen hundred years ago. Scotland was not then the unity she eventually became. This was the land of the Northern Picts, and the first, and perhaps the greatest, figure among that people was the King Brude. To him came that other of Scotland's great men of the time—a greater than Brude, St. Columba. The lives of the saint tell of his mission to Inverness to convert the king. There is a feeling behind the histories that this was a meeting which, if we knew it fully, would be a great story of the determination of the man of God, strong in his belief and in his mission, in his determination for Brude and the Scotland that was to come. Brude was strong, too, and there were those around him who thought the new faith would make for weaklings instead of warriors. If they had considered Columba's character they would have known from the first that here was no weakling, but a warrior among warriors, armed with something against which temporalities and powers could not prevail.

After this first event, Inverness saw centuries of history of an exciting kind, and battle and murder and sudden death made a red-dappled pattern on the city's tapestry.

Brude and Columba began the history. Charles Edward Stuart and the Duke of Cumberland—both men in their middle twenties—helped to write the last red chapter of Inverness and Culloden. But, in between, what a pageant of kings and chieftains haunt this northern site. As in so many towns, history gathers around the castle on its hill—Macbeth, Malcolm Canmore, William Wallace, Robert the Bruce, Mary Queen of Scots. The castle was built, destroyed, rebuilt several times. It was blown up at the orders of Prince Charlie in February 1746. That now seems almost an act of curious significance for the Stuarts. April of that year on the Moor of Culloden finished what had been waiting in history for nearly two centuries.

Today the castle is for the visitor a favourite viewpoint, and from it one can look at vistas that on a fair day give you this part of the country as few other points in the area can. And with you stands another, also looking away out from the castle. That is Flora MacDonald, sculptured, with hand raised to shade her eyes, and, of course, she looks westward, though one could imagine an even more significant airt.

Apart from its history and its setting, Inverness has not a hundred attractions, but it has in in its river, its site, looking either towards sea or hills, something that can keep a visitor interested and quietly happy for quite a while.

Before you go walking or motoring, you should look in at the Town House. There you will find an interesting collection of memorials, pictures and relics. The pictures are both ancient and modern—one of the older artists is Raeburn, one of the more modern Fiddes Watt. The relics are of battles long ago and memorials of wars of our own day. It is a Town House very worthy of the place whose civic centre it is.

The river-side is the favourite walk of both citizens and visitors in the summer months, and it comes to its crown in that pleasance known as The Islands, woods and water. Here is the centre of Inverness's outdoor life in the bright months of the year. It is no place, however, to find one's way through alone in the early hours of a January morning, as I have had to do—determined to save myself the long way round from the house of a friend to that of my host on the Scaniport road. That was really a rather eerie and fearsome exploration. Somewhere in the dark were the roaring waters. I had no torch, and had not only to find my way to the bridges, but often to feel my way. And what a relief when I won through to the road.

I am fond, for sentimental and other reasons, of Scaniport road. It led, as I have already told, to one little paradise of the region, and it led to the beauties of what one foolish person once said to me was "the wrong side of Loch Ness". Silly, when you have Dores and, after, Foyers at the end of your walk or drive.

Few people, I suppose and hope, ever visit Inverness without visiting Culloden Moor. That pretty wide space of country—not now so desolate as it once was—is the site of the most important battle ever fought in Britain, and the last land battle, up to now.

Culloden is five miles from Inverness. Here is the Drumashie, or Drumossie, of which Sandy spoke and which he linked, curiously, with the Indian Mutiny. If, more appropriately, he had described the sunset vision as a re-creation of the battle of April 1746, I could have understood it, for Culloden, like Glenfinnan, seems to me a haunted place. As at Glenfinnan, I have never visited the moor except on a day when few people were about, and, on such a day, one is apt to remember too much all the horrors of that finis to the foolishness of mistaken loyalty and bravery. But that foolishness has always been neutralised and mitigated by the horrible conduct of that young Hanoverian clod, the Duke of Cumberland, a true son of the Germany that produced Nazism. What a contrast was there in the Major Wolfe, who, in the years of his Generalship, was to become the hero of the Heights of Abraham and Quebec. One can understand the difference between such as Cumberland and Wolfe when we remember our school history books and Wolfe's reading of Gray's "Elegy in a Country Churchyard" as he went to the Canadian battle, and his remark: "Gentlemen, I would rather be the author of that poem than take those Heights."

There is a legend that, meeting a wounded man after the battle at Culloden, Cumberland ordered Wolfe to shoot the dying rebel. Wolfe on that occasion said he was a soldier, not an executioner.

The actual battle was a short one, lasting no more than forty minutes—think of it in the light of the battles that have scattered the pages of history since 1746! It was from Inverness that the Jacobites came to Culloden, but that was on the evening of April 14 (old style, new style April 25). There they lay the night. The next day it was proposed that a surprise night attack should be made on the Duke of Cumberland's force, then lying at Nairn. That night-march was the beginning of the disaster; there was no cohesion in what the Jacobite forces did or were trying to do. The neighbourhood of Nairn was not reached until dawn and by that time there was distinct activity in the Hanoverian camp. The Jacobites were ordered to return to Culloden, and that these weary men did, in what order or disorder we can guess. A day of comparative hunger followed. It was a day of differences of opinion and indecision among their leaders. Eventually—led by the Prince, it is said—it was decided to fight on the moor.

The Hanoverian guns opened fire at one o'clock. Those guns both resolved the day to a great extent and caused part of the great slaughter. Once given the order, the Highlandmen charged in face of sleet from heaven and shot from the guns. They managed to break two of the Duke's regiments, and on they went to meet a second hail of shot from muskets and of cold steel. The bodies were found in layers, several feet deep. That charge of the Mackintoshes was perhaps the bravest and most foolhardy work of the day, but the Prince's men carried out other movements, but without avail. The battle was already lost. Then followed horrors among individuals and groups. Hanoverian soldiers set fire to a small building in which wounded Highlanders had taken refuge, and they were burned to death. Officers, wherever they were found, were slaughtered equally with their men. *Noblesse oblige* was a phrase unknown to such as Cumberland.

As for Prince Charlie, he made his way, when it was seen that all was lost, to the west by way of Stratherrick and Invergarry. His five months wandering in Scotland had begun.

There is a huge boulder on the moor, known as the Cumberland Stone. It is, undoubtedly, one of the best viewpoints of the scene of the battle. It is so-called because the Duke is said to have watched the course of the fight from its little eminence. But to stand on it today is to have thoughts very different from those he had. Borne on the wind we seem to hear the names of the clans like a battle roll and remember the men who fought and died for Charlie and now lie under the lonely cairns. Death was more merciful than Cumberland and his men, in its sleep and forgetting. But it is little wonder that, even to this day, Scots have not forgotten Cumberland's name, and its mention can bring a look of dislike to Scottish faces.

As one goes back along the road from the moor to Inverness one cannot help remembering that this was a way of blood and death, almost more than any, for the Highlanders who took it that April day two hundred years ago.

So we come back to Inverness, today a town of peace if any is, and to the Invernessians with their accent, which is supposed to be the result of the conjunction of the Gaelic with the English-speaking Hanoverians, though that is something I cannot quite believe.

From Inverness we can go to so many places of beauty and interest that it is difficult to decide, but I should think that, for a comparatively short excursion, most people would choose one—Glen Affric. Affric, glen and loch, is like the Trossachs, one of the most acknowledged beauty spots of Scotland, probably because so many people have visited it. And yet, I have never seen a crowd in Glen Affric, indeed, no one at all on my first visit. It was a lovely day when we set out from Inverness, and got lovelier all the way, just as did the scenery.

We went by Beauly, past Kilmorack Falls, to Struy. Soon we come to the

CULLODEN

CULLODEN COTTAGE, ON THE BATTLEFIELD

loveliness that is of the essence of Scottish beauty. The way by Eilean Aigas, once the home of the Sobieski Stuarts, is only a prelude to what is to come as we move into Glen Affric, passing Loch Beinn on the way.

In name and actuality Affric is something that has long cast a spell upon the Scots, and that has had something to do with the fuss that was made when the area was marked as part of the hydro-electric scheme that is to bring prosperity and all sorts of good things to Scotland and the Scottish people.

Spend a night in Affric in summer, waken to its beauties early on a summer morning, and you will understand something of Affric's spell. It is like that of the Trossachs, and yet there is something different. The sun here is again on the silver birches climbing up the steeps, but in Affric there is a feeling of remoteness from the world. That may come from your journey to the place, as compared with the road either from Aberfoyle or Callander, or it may be in the contours of Affric as compared with the Trossachs. Whatever it is, there certainly is this difference, subtle but actual. There is a quiet about Affric. There are, of course, no big houses and no turreted hotel—as yet—just loveliness undisturbed. Yes, perhaps that is part of the solution. To wake up in Affric is to wake up in something as near an earthly paradise as I know. And, even as a day goes on, that feeling does not wear away, for every hour of the day brings new pleasure, and as evening comes on this paradise certainly seems to become unearthly.

If we were happy in Affric, and sorry to part with it, we certainly were brought very much to earth as we journeyed back. We had put our car off the road and among the trees by the river. In getting it back on the road again we had "mishapped". The journey was not so bad until we turned from Tomich over the high road that leads from there to Drumnadrochit. That road is very high and there are steep drops. That was a nightmare journey—we had a bent steering-rod and a slow puncture, and always the car seemed to veer towards the side with the steep drop. That is another journey that haunted my dreams, and yet I remember the beauties of the road from Tomich to Drumnadrochit. Never, however, did I love Inverness so much.

7

13

FARTHER NORTH

W E have already been in and out of Ross-shire several times in our recent wanderings, but now we shall stick to that county for a time.

Ross and Cromarty, to give the name which seems to suit the county better, is divided. On the east there is a green belt which stretches from Beauly, along the Black Isle to the Cromarty Firth; crosses that and runs along to Tarbat Ness, with its lighthouse; along the southern shore of the Dornoch Firth; up Strath Oykel until Ross is lost in Sutherlandshire and the green in the finger of the county that points up to Ben More Assynt, just beyond its borders. Green comes again in the edges by Gairloch, Gruinard Bay, Little Loch Broom, past those little places with the lovely name, the Summer Isles, and into Enard Bay, with that curious peak, Suilven, in the offing.

Between east and west lies one of the most mountainous districts in the whole length of Scotland. In its fullest exploration it is the place for only the heftiest of hikers and climbers who can do a long trek towards their goal, a steep climb to it, and all the way back again. Many of the roads, where they exist, are still of the roughest, though there have been improvements in the last seven, eight years, owing to war exigencies. This west coast was a secret hide-out of naval units, and they had to be provided for from land as well as sea.

But let us start at the eastern side of the county. The Black Isle, which is a peninsula and not an island, is, with Easter and Mid-Ross, notable for its farming, both for the produce of the soil and for cattle. There is, in the centre of the Isle, one little range of not very high hills, Ard Mheadhonach, chiefly of note as a viewpoint of the wildness that lies westward beyond. Nearest is Ben Wyvis and then, farther away, you have Sgurr Mor, which, at 3637 feet, is the highest peak north of Inverness. This, on a clear day, is a point from which you can see all that lies north of the Grampians.

If you come by sea, which was the first way in which I ever entered Ross-shire, in happy days long ago, you approach and pass between the Soutars of Cromarty, which guard like bastions, the entrance to the deep firth of the same name. The little town, also called Cromarty, lies on your left. It is a quiet place, but two men have made this white hamlet renowned—Sir Thomas Urquhart, whose translation

ELGIN CATHEDRAL

HUGH MILLER'S COTTAGE, CROMARTY

of Rabelais all the world knows, and Hugh Miller, author and geologist, and a great example of the Scots lad o' pairts, who, from humblest circumstances, rose to eminence and, also, international fame. Monuments to both will be found in their native place. Urquhart lived from 1611 to 1660, and his life was a picaresque romance, his death a tragi-comedy. He was a supporter of the Royalist cause, and he is said to have died owing to too hearty laughter over the restoration that brought Charles the Second back to the throne.

Hugh Miller was of sterner make in every way. He lived from 1802 to 1856, and his span took in the Disruption of the Church in Scotland, and, as might be expected, he was on the side of the "rebels".

These are only two of a long list of notable men whom this county has produced, writers in English, the Scots vernacular and Gaelic, theologians, soldiers, statesmen and diplomatists.

Crossing the firth we come to Invergordon, which was one of the most famous places in the British Isles in the war of 1914–18. Here was established a great naval base, and here a great naval vessel was sunk while a triviality of war-time life was in progress—a children's party.

Behind Invergordon stretches another little ridge of hills, running from Tain to Ardross, where Fyrish stands, the hill that has a curious fascination, I have always found, for the native of Easter Ross. And, certainly, seen at sunset, there is something in this natural landmark to make mind and heart remember it, especially in exile, and it has been in exile that I have heard Ross-men speak so of Fyrish. We are in the Munro country now, and it was a Munro who was responsible for a monument as a crown on Fyrish. This Munro—Sir Hector, who lived from 1726 to 1805—was one of the notable soldiers the county produced. Among his exploits in an Indian career was the capture of Negapatam, and the monument on Fyrish is said to be in the shape of the gate of Negapatam.

By Alness we pass on towards Dingwall. But as we go we step aside to gaze at that curious, narrow gully, the Black Rock, on the River Glass, at Evanton. It is the kind of place that fascinates the mind of youth, and I and my friend of those old days tried to fashion ballads of the lady of Balconie, and her dark fate, bringing in the Rock.

In Dingwall we are reminded of another famous soldier, whose name is too infrequently remembered nowadays. There is on a hill in this county town a monument to one, Sir Hector MacDonald, whose career began in humble obscurity in the Black Isle, in 1852, and ended with a self-fired pistol shot in a Paris hotel in 1903. He was, for the greater part of his life, the *beau idéal* of the Scottish soldier, known to all by his name of "Fighting Mac" and worshipped by the people. He enlisted as a private, fought in the Afghan war. He was promoted from the ranks, and older men will recall what that meant in those days. The Boer war of 1881, the Sudan from 1885, including great work at Omdurman, were fields to his credit. In the second Boer War he commanded the Highland Brigade, and now his popularity and fame reached a peak. After commands in India and Ceylon, and while he was on leave in Europe, there began a campaign of whispering, whispering, whispering. "Mac" scattered it with the pistol shot, but, in the minds of the people he did not die for many a long day. He became a legend. It was said that he was seen in the thickest of the fight in the Russo-Japanese war of 1904. Wherever after that there was fighting, until 1914, he was said to have been there. I have seen his portrait in the homes of veteran soldiers who still worshipped him, and there are soldiers' sons, now well on to middle age, whose Christian names are Hector MacDonald. What truth there was in the scandalmongers' whispers does not matter now; he is remembered as a great man of the people, and Dingwall enshrines his fame.

Just beyond Dingwall is Strathpeffer, the only true spa in Scotland. It was a great place once on a day; it may be again, for it seems on the way to a second round of favouritism. Beautifully set, in the shadow of Ben Wyvis, its waters—not at all superficially attractive, in smell or taste—are regarded as a cure for the rheumatic. To its pump-room in Edwardian days came the well-to-do sufferer and the *bon viveur*, after their London season, on their way to house-parties and stag shooting. The hotel registers had quite a touch of Debrett about them then, and pump-room time was quite a fashion parade. That, of course, may not come again, but we may hear echoes of 'Ansard one of these days during recess of Parliament.

But westward lie the mountains, so thick and so inaccessible in some places, that part of the region may even be *terra incognita*. There are certain places, of course, which are anything but that; Loch Maree, for instance, with its islets and its mountain guardian, Slioch. Kinlochewe and Gairloch are known to many Scots, and, since the war of 1939–45, to how many Englishmen, who, before their service days, may have never seen a mountain and could not even dream of the surroundings in which they found themselves up here. How do they remember them now? According to their temperament, I suppose.

Some writers have seen in this region Scotland's nearest resemblance to Switzerland, but there is the great difference—they are mostly almost regions deserted, except for the wild creatures and those who, to the lover of the lowlands low, seem almost as wild—the ardent mountaineers. Even the names are difficult—one peak for instance is called Liughach by some, by another Liathach, and either name is difficult to pronounce. Ben Dearg, Stac Polly are more than names to a few, and An Teallach seems to others the only companion to the Coolins of Skye.

And now we are into Sutherland, and in its north-east corner more remote than ever. It is not to be wondered that at Ardvreck Castle the great Marquis of Montrose

CASTLE KENNEDY, WIGTOWNSHIRE

CASTLE GIRNIGO, NEAR WICK, CAITHNESS

in 1650 came to the last chapter but one of his romantic and tragic life. Hatred in those days—it might be so, also, in these days, and always may be—will pursue its victim into places that otherwise the pursuers would shun and shudder at. But in 1650 there were, as so often, faults and cruelties on both sides.

In a region that is rich in peaks, one stands out among them all. It has fascinated the painter and the etcher for nearly a generation now, and the great modern romantic among our Scottish artists—Sir D. Y. Cameron—made it known to the connoisseur in art as against the connoisseur in peaks, as such. Others have followed his pioneer trail. This is Suilven, the "Point Aiguille" of Scotland. It has been called "The Sugar-Loaf", from one of its appearances, but it is, seen from another point, a double peak.

Although in one way we are now in remotest Britain—we are over fifty miles from the nearest railway station—we are also in a district which many love, with almost a secret love, because they would have the region and its wild beauties to themselves. We are in Assynt, a name that has fascinated not a few Celto-Scottish poets. But the loch, Ben Assynt Mor and their surroundings are worthy that name.

More and more people are willing to make the journey north of Lochinver and Inchnadamph to the far north-west coast of Scotland. They are oftenest young, they carry tents; they are prepared for any amount of hardship, so long as they can go back to their schools, universities and workshops and say they have been where the ordinary thousands of holidaymakers, travellers and trippers never would dream of attempting to go.

For all that, this north-east corner still remains the haunt of those who will go anywhere for their sport, and the less frequented the better to them the spot. There is a chain of lochs between Lairg and Scourie, beginning with the longest, Loch Shin. But it is a long way, and, given bad weather, can be the weariest. Farther still, you can, if you are determined to, make the journey to Cape Wrath, the uttermost north-west corner, with its lighthouse. You then find your way by Durness, with the Caves of Smoo not far off, Eriboll—whose loch or estuary is in some Royal Navy men's memories—Tongue and Bettyhill and Melvich to the lowland plain of Caithness, and so to Thurso or Wick, where you will find thriving little townships with a good community feeling. Having got as far, of course, you will want to visit John o' Groats—especially if you have come from Land's End. But, like the highest village in Scotland—that is a controversy still—you are not at the northernmost point of Scotland. That is at Dunnet Head.

Having got thus far—which way do you go? South by train to Inverness, down the east coast by Helmsdale, Brora, Golspie, Dornoch and so to Bonar Bridge, where we have completed our northern circuit.

What a journey it has been! How much has been written about this area, and, for all its remoteness, how thoroughly have artist and photographer covered it, and that is the better way. It seems to fascinate them, especially the modern artist and the photographer with the modern camera. But I cannot ever see the region becoming a popular holiday hunting-ground. That will be, for long, it seems to me, prevented by more than difficulty of communications.

On the other hand, on your way down the eastern coast you will pass several places which are favourite holiday resorts with not a few, though never within danger of being overcrowded. All down this coast the milestones almost seem to be castles—the best known, of course, being the seat of the Duke of Sutherland at Dunrobin, and Andrew Carnegie's mansion of Skibo near Dornoch. But Dornoch's chief attraction for certain holiday makers is its golf.

But, supposing you have looked across the Pentland Firth on a fine day. You see, not so very far away, a pillar of stone. That is the Old Man of Hoy, southern guardian of the Orkney Islands. Once again, how many men and women of the Services, in two great wars, know these islands, knew them in some instances, not for months, but for years. To most of these Orkney meant and means only Scapa Flow. But the Orkneys—for long, let us hope—are once more islands of peace and the destiny of travellers interested in far older history and in the lives of a people who consider themselves furth of Scotland, not Scots—be careful about that—but Orcadians.

If you care for the sea you can make the journey to Orkney by boat from either Leith or Aberdeen. If you are air-minded, the air service is there, and regular.

There is one thing I have found about the attitude of a majority of people towards both the Orkney and the Shetland Islands—they are either utter enthusiasts, tiresome at times, or they are almost equally antipathetic. There seems no middle course in the matter. Your Orcadian and Shetlander are, not unnaturally, patriots to a degree, though, incidentally, many of them have a way of leaving the islands to seek fame and fortune elsewhere.

But for those who love islands and the sea, both the Orkneys and Shetlands have their strong fascination. They are rugged rocks with some fertile soil, not so treeless as is often said, but their ruggedness is over and over again as impressive in their coastal way as are the hills and mountains of north-western Scotland. But you must love the sea and the sea-air.

Then there is the history of this ancient stronghold of the Norsemen, for both in speech and in tradition the Norse tradition, even at this far day, still lingers up here. You will find it in the writing of such ardent Orcadians as Eric Linklater, and especially in his book, *Men of Ness*, something of a *tour de force* in style and atmosphere. There you can gather the character and life that shaped long generations of other Orcadians.

THE ISLES OF LOCH MAREE, ROSS-SHIRE

CAITHNESS COAST NEAR DUNNET HEAD

But the Orkneys and the Shetlands are not now so cut off from the life of Scotland, of Britain as once on a day, and there are changes going on. But, as so often happens when old and new meet, there is a great desire on the part of many to preserve the old, not naturally but, almost inevitably, with a touch of artificiality.

For the visitor with such a flair, such a centre in Orkney as its principal town, Kirkwall, presents you with its cathedral, its Earl's and its Bishop's Palaces.

When you go farther north, to the Shetlands, you find the peculiar accent of these islands a bit stronger, you may even consider the rock scenery still more rugged. You may find the climate better, you may think it worse.

I remember asking a young fellow of the Forces what was his chief impression of a Shetland place in which he spent many a day. He said it was the fact that, even on the finest day in summer, you could not sit down with comfort; the wind was always blowing and it was always cold. It may have been that he struck a bad summer, but Shetlanders to whom I have mentioned this have scouted the idea.

There is one thing upon which all who visit the islands in the midsummer dilate, and that is the impressive beauty of the "simmer dim" when the sun scarcely sets and the night knows no real darkness at all. There seems to come with this "dim" a peace, a tranquillity of both place and folk, be they natives or visitors.

There is in Shetland, too, one picturesque survival of the Norse days—the festival of Up-Helly-Aa. This takes place at the end of January. It is a relic of pagan Viking days, and, once again, has to do with the sun. Then the sun came back from his journey southward, the days began to lengthen again; winter was not over but spring was not so far behind. Up-Helly-Aa is also bound up with another old Viking custom. No Norse warrior cared to die in his bed, even if he survived battle, murder or sudden death. That was a "straw death". And so, when it was near his time to make the last journey, to Valhalla, he had his litter carried to his galley. He was left alone, the galley had been set on fire and he went, completely alone, out to sea—a pagan idea and death if ever there were.

The festival of Up-Helly-Aa has become rather a fancy dress affair, but the centre-piece is still the blazing galley. The head man of those who have to do with this part of the festival is the Guiser Jarl, an appointment sought after. He has his squad or crew, all of whom wear an approximation to Viking costume. The galley is drawn in procession through Lerwick to the Market Cross, all the guisers carrying torches, which in the winter's night play tricks of light. There is singing of songs belonging to the festival, and at the Market Cross the whole crowd sings "The Norseman's Home". Down comes the Guiser Jarl from the galley. A bugle blows. Every guiser flings his torch into the model ship. Up she goes in flame, but there is no movement to sea and no lone figure within her, seeking self-immolation.

Yes, I suppose, even today, with all the wanderings, voluntary or compulsory, of her young men, there must be something of the Viking left, for men from these islands are among the best sailors we have, and have proved it in two wars that needed sailors as much as anything. They may never be so needed again, but there are plenty of jobs for them at sea so long as we have peace and ships.

14

TOWARDS ELGIN

HAVING made our way back to Inverness by one or more of the several means of transport, we are here only to leave that delectable town, heading south, either by east or half-west. The road by the coast will take us to Nairn, Elgin and so on to Aberdeen. The road inland will take us to Strathspey. Both are worth our journeying, and they are different in many ways.

Suppose we make an excursion to Strathspey, as I have done so often with pleasure, and, if we desire, find our way back to Inverness before we seek the coast. The way lies by unexciting but picturesque Carr Bridge, and here we come to the Monadliath Mountains. Some people find these hills tame compared with others in other parts, but I have found them not so much tame as, somehow, depressing. A day or two spent in their vicinity, and, more especially when it comes to evening, almost makes me want to flee the district. Yet, look eastward, there are always the Cairngorms, a range of mountains of which, near or far, no one ever seems to tire; they are always beckoning.

Yes, with them and all the lovelinesses that abound, one can be happy at Aviemore, forget the Monadliaths. Summer or early autumn days there can be among the finest of one's open-air experiences. One can walk to the start of the Larig-Ghru, the famous Cairngorm pass which leads from Strathspey to Deeside. One can spend lazy days by Loch-an-Eilean, with its picturesque ruin on its tiny islet.

Grantown-on-Spey is the half-urban centre of the Strath, and with its pines, its Dreggie Hill, its golf course, its comfortable hotels and small modern cinema, there is contrast. But, most of all, at Grantown, give me the River Spey. There are few stretches of this river that have not something to offer those who just want to walk or sit and stare. And, of course, if you are a fisher, you have the double joy, for this is one of the great rivers of Scotland in that way. Yes, Strathspey can offer variety to the holidaymaker, aged nine or ninety, complete leisureliness or ardours and endurances, and always I say goodbye to the strath with regret. I like the places, I like their people. Here the Highlands begin to change from the Celtic to the Sassenach, and I think the people of Strathspey partake of the best of both types.

We need not, unless of necessity or strong desire, return to Inverness. We can take a choice of roads—to Nairn, to Forres or to Elgin. At Nairn we shall find the seaside counterpart of Strathspey, except that there is more leisure than ardour. It is a pleasant township that, long ago, because of its climate, earned the stupid title of "the Brighton of the North". Good heavens, there is as much of Brighton here as there is of Piccadilly or the Strand, and that goes for everything, good and bad, that has made Brighton what it is. Forres is just like Nairn, without the sea; and so, on to Elgin.

Though far from living only in and on its past, Elgin is proud of its history and, more especially, the great relic of the days when Christianity of one denomination expressed itself in the high beauties of architectured stone, and then, with the coming of another denomination, either dung down that beauty, or if, as in the case of Elgin, a barbarian ruined it, never sought to put it to rights again, but despoiled it even further. The Wolf of Badenoch was the Scourge of God in this part of the country, and his work resembled that of Somerset the Protector on the Scottish Borders. But even today, with its ruinous, roofless walls, you can see something of what its beauty must have been, and it still retains something of the ancient peace of such places, though too often there was anything but peace when the despoiler was having his way.

The Elgin area was a great centre of the Old Religion, and there are other places near by where you will find evidences of the man who worshipped God in the holiness of beauty. Most notable, perhaps, is the Priory of Pluscarden. This beautifully set shrine has passed again into the hands of the monks, and, in time, when "luxury building" is again allowed, it is intended to rebuild Pluscarden and bring it back to whatever can be of its loveliness, and to re-establish there the communal religious life.

Elgin has other bits and pieces of ancientry, including a fine market cross and an unusual sample of arcading.

The Royal Burgh of Elgin is the centre of the district known as the Laigh o' Moray. Here is the finest of agricultural land, and one can gather from the climate one of the reasons for the good crops. The climate, in turn, makes the view on a characteristic Morayshire day something, not to take the breath away, but to fill one with satisfaction because of the blending of the colours of earth and sky and sea.

In leaving Elgin for farther south we are saying goodbye to something—to the Rivers Spey and Findhorn—the latter more picturesque than almost any we have passed over in our journey; to many little places that have their own quiet attraction, but little more than that; to lovely bits of wood and lea; to the quiet beauty of the River Lossie just outside Elgin; to the jolly fisher-folk of Lossiemouth; inland, to Craigellachie and Dufftown. And Dufftown reminds me, we are leaving the heart of one of the most important whisky-distilling districts—an industry that helped to make many Scots rich and others poor; an industry that, it has been hoped,

SHETLANDERS

BALMORAL, ABERDEENSHIRE

might help a lot to set Britain on her dollar legs again. The potentiality is there, the methods are wrong.

Scotland has been very badly treated by her English lords and masters. Each succeeding war has been made an excuse for robbing her of one after the other of her native industries, of her own ways of life. If Scotland were left alone to manage her own affairs, in economy, in finance, there is little doubt that she could not only be self-supporting but she could also help the British Exchequer more than she is allowed to do now, and could give reasonable help in many ways to her English neighbours.

We are the land of porridge and milk, and there is not the slightest doubt that that food has, in its day, helped to make the Scots the sturdy race they have been at their best. But our oatmeal was for too long, for all practical purposes, taken away or withheld from us. We are not allowed to produce the milk needed for our porridge or brose. We produce the finest beef in the world—it has to be exported, by order, to feed others. We make the finest whisky in the world, and with its by-product, draff, we could feed the cattle that would produce our so-much-needed milk. But all this has been made part of a vicious circle of bureaucracy that, in the end, gets nowhere, produces little and less and less. So with eggs, so with cloth. All we are left with are heaps of paper-wasting forms. There have been signs of revolt in—of all places—the country districts, where, in a bad winter, in order that bureaucracy's ways may not be interfered with, people are left without their basic food. That has altered the ridiculous oatmeal regulation. The agricultural producers have been told how important they are going to be for the next ten or twenty years. Well, if they are asked to produce, one of the things they are most likely to produce are their terms for production. And, from more than one angle, Morayshire could be leaders in these demands. Morayshire matters.

In the days when bureaucracy began to assert itself—not too badly, and with good results, then—there occurred an incident in a little agricultural town that is still remembered and its rebel is still something of a hero to northern Scottish farmers. The place was the township of Turriff in Aberdeenshire—not so many miles from Moray. The cause was Mr. Lloyd George's Health Insurance scheme. This farmer refused to stamp his employees' cards. The authorities took action. They poinded a white cow belonging to the recalcitrant farmer. That led to extraordinary scenes in the market-place of "Turra"—as Turriff is called in local speech—and to a court case. The neighbouring farmers, when the cow was being sold at the order of the Health Insurance authorities, bought the cow and presented her back to her rebellious owner. The "Turra Coo" became a *cause célèbre*, songs were made of the matter, and other literature—of a kind—appeared and was bought up eagerly. In the north of Scotland the matter of the "Turra Coo" is known to all, old and young. History could repeat itself, and not so light-heartedly.

15

VIA COAST

THERE are two markings on the trains south from Elgin and one of them says "Via Coast". That is the way we shall take.

We go past Fochabers, which is at the beginning of the end of the River Spey. Right round that heaving shoulder of Scotland which, I think, gives part of its character to what is known as the "caul Nor' East", there is a steady series of fishing villages and little towns. There is nothing like it until you come to Fife, and the fishing villages of the north-east have their own particular characteristic. Yet they are linked in certain ways to every fishing village right down to Berwickshire.

One link is the accent, or, rather, the way in which Scots is spoken. You can pick out a person from one of these villages right away by his speech. Even when he has been groomed by success and contact with people of other lands and places, some little touch of speech will give him away. This corresponds, in my idea, to the Glaswegian; for, in this way, as I have told, once a Glaswegian always a Glaswegian. There is something in these speech foundations that sticks like a burr that cannot be detached.

These fishing villages have a character of their own. It begins, outwardly, in architecture. I know of nothing more wearisome and yet amusing as the architecture of their houses—when they have any architecture. Some of them are just dumps of the wickedest of jerry-building—the chief example that comes to my mind is Collieston in Aberdeenshire.

But to take Buckie, in Banffshire, as the last word in fishing communities. Buckie, like most places of its kind and size, is really two little townships. On the high level you have the modern township—a long, very long, main street, ending in a Roman Catholic church with a fine tower and clock faces which are lit by external lighting. One thing has always amused me in Buckie. The central church, Presbyterian, has also a clock which, when I have heard it, chimed the hour five minutes before the hour. That's not a bad idea.

Buckie's high town, of course, is just a convenience—shopping and amusement and so on. The real Buckie, the one on which Buckie's existence depends, is low down, on the sea level. Here you have a higgledy-piggledy collection of small houses, all built on the same plan. Squat, square, with alternate white-faced stones as a decoration, they stand there as symbols of the people who inhabit them, their industry, their little jealousies, their utter community spirit. "If Wullie has a hoose like that, I dinna see foo we shouldna ha'e a hoose like his." That is behind Buckie's architecture. In recent years Buckie and other places have produced a few artists, and it has been good to see that these artists have seen the fun and seriousness of Buckie's architecture and have put it into kindly paint.

There is abundant scope, not only for the artist, but for the littérateur in these villages. It has been done by authors in other countries—France and Belgium, in particular. Why not in Scotland?

I have mentioned the use of speech. That is impossible to convey in print. You need the spoken word to convey its peculiar tang. But I can indicate certain other curious peculiarities, which are beloved by every real Scotsman.

In all these villages there are just a few family names. They repeat themselves over and over again—Fletts and Cowies and Woods, and so on. If you go to such a village and ask for John Flett, you will be met with the query—"Fatna Flett, fat's his tee-name?" To sort out the difficulty there are tee-names, which may indicate the name of John's boat or the name of his grandfather's boat. So you must differentiate between "Rosie" and "Dosie" Flett, "Poopie" and "Po" Cowie, "Shinners" and "Widdie" Wood. Only thus can you find the person you are looking for.

In Buckie you will find a funeral notice displayed in a shop window which says —"Elspeth Flett, 'Rosie'", died on such and such a date, "wife of James Cowie, 'Po', and will be buried . . .", and so it goes on.

The generations, too, matter much in these villages. A person will be indicated by the combination, "Jeannie's Wullie's Jockie". There are three generations in that designation. It's a curious fashion but it's there and goes on and on.

Is it the sea or what is it that makes these usually stolid folk so emotional? Every now and again religious revivals sweep the fishing villages. They are not so frequent as they were. But I will say that any revivalist who wishes to make a success of his job has only to go to these villages, and there fame and fortune await him—sorry to mention money in this connection, but we know that has been the case.

When I was a boy I was brought up in what, in England, would be known as Low Church. But my great friend then was a Methodist. I went quite often with him to his evening service to hear one of the greatest Methodist preachers ever known—the late Rev. Arthur Hoyle; and what a preacher!—as every Methodist in the length and breadth of Britain will agree.

There came to Hoyle's evening services in Aberdeen the fishermen from the north-east villages—their boats were in Aberdeen harbour for the week-end. Usually, the Methodist services were as staid as those of my own Low Church, but when these fishermen were there they were not. The prayers and the sermon were punctuated with "Hallelujahs", "God be praised", "Amen to that, brother". That was the fishermen's way, and the staid middle-class Methodists never blinked an eyelid. They were accustomed to it, and so became I, and loved this fervent expression of real religion. . . .

Many hundreds of years ago the Norsemen came upon Scotland like destroying locusts. Their targets were, mostly, places farther north than the region of Buckie, but I have no doubt that Buckie and its area knew some of their visits. In the war of 1939–45 the Norsemen came again, but as refugees from the tyranny of Hitler. In all sorts of craft they came to Scotland—and, especially, furth of Scotland—the Orkneys, ironic fate! A colony of them was established at Buckie. They lived there, in the finest harmony, with the people of the north-east of Scotland. And they were an example to us. They were given, to start with, a derelict shed and a derelict slipway—Buckie is not what it was, and who can blame it in these days of centralisation?—but what the Norwegians made of their opportunities had to be seen to be believed. When I saw them they had a carpenter's shop, a blacksmith's shop, a pattern-maker's shop and who knows what else, and on the derelict slipway were two ships in repair. All their machinery—which was electrically driven—was devised from what our people had thrown away as of no use. I merely mention this to show what can and could be done in this country by men who were up against it. Buckie today is regarded as—in some ways—a dying town. The young men come back from "the wide" and go away again, because there is nothing for them. This is the fate of ever so many Buckies, ever so many young men. Why cannot we learn from the Norwegians? Buckie's young women, naturally, married young Norwegians—not the first link between Scotland and Norway—but some of them on going home with their husbands have found themselves in a last outpost of Norwegian civilisation, the veritable *ultima Thule*. And so the troubles have begun. Only one Buckie man wished to marry a Norwegian girl! Curious. Why are men so conservative?

I have taken Buckie as the typical fishing place, and because of its size; but along this Moray Firth coast there are many Buckies, large and small. Cullen, Portessie, Portsoy—they are all, more or less, the same. Banff is the peak and the real metropolis. Banff is a lovely town in many ways, and the comic thing is that it divorces itself from its near neighbour Macduff. Macduff is nearer the sea in a way. Banff is more middle-class. It is—or was—a resort of the wealthy. It has a lovely climate, it has a fair amount of history.

To me the most alluring piece of history about Banff is the story of Macpherson, the freebooter. He was due to be hanged, and the authorities were very desirous that he should be. A reprieve was sent, but the town clock was altered so that Macpherson should be hanged, and hanged he was.

All along this Moray coast there has been history from Charles the Second to the first Pretender. But it doesn't worry about these things now, it worries about survival, about having trade that does not consist of taking in one another's washing. Never mind, so long as there is fish in the sea, these places will survive. One of the loveliest sights is the harbour of a north-east fishing village in the off-season or just before the herring fishing, here or in England, is due to begin, with the boats all gathered. As artist or as economist, that is a sight to be looked on and wondered at. All those masts and spars, crowded together, an etcher's dream. And etchers have done it, no one better than James McBey, a great Scotsman, and one of the world's etchers, who was etching only what he had known from boyhood. And McBey has also put into immortality the expanses of the Moray Firth—in its spread and its unusual atmosphere. Of all places on the east coast of Scotland the Moray Firth is the one that can vie with the west—at Morar, for instance—in the beauty of its sunsets.

But heaven help you if you are caught in a storm in the Moray Firth, summer or winter. I have been caught in one Moray Firth summer storm and I never wish to endure another. Even the Bay of Biscay, in which I have been in bad weather, does not seem so bad. Of course, part of the trouble in the Moray Firth is that you are not in ships the size of those in Biscay. A storm in a small ship in the Firth is one of the most alarming and physically upsetting experiences you can come through. The winds seem to blow from every quarter, the waves are house-high, there seems no hope for survival at the height of the storm. It goes on and on and on. I have read only one book that brings home to me the feeling of a Moray Firth storm— Joseph Conrad's *Typhoon*. The difference between the two, to me, is one of extensive- ness and intensity.

Yet our north-east men endure all this, steadily and often. That is what, like the Shetland and Orkney men, makes the Moray Firth men among the finest sailors our country produces, the men who are the backbone of either the Royal Navy or the Mercantile Marine in war-time. God bless them! And as they are good, so are our lifeboat crews. Some of the most wonderful work in this way has been done by men of the north-east lifeboats. The work is there, it has to be done, and they do it, whatever the cost may be.

16

ABERDEEN

A N D so we come to Aberdeen and Aberdeenshire, my native county and my native town—and I am not ashamed to own it, in fact, I am proud. Like so many Scots, I am a mixture of Celt and Sassenach; in me Scotland's differences are united. On the distaff side I have Celtic blood in me and I wear the mother tartan. On my father's side I am sheer, what they call Sassenach. There is a difference. My father was a shrewdly practical man. My mother had both poetry and second-sicht in her. That is why I think that a "double man" in Scotland is a happy man. We say that "a hairy man's a happy man, but a hairy wife's a witch". I say the double man in Scotland is the happy man. He makes the best of both worlds—the ordinary world, and the world of—shall we call it?—faery. To be fey is not so good, but to be half-fey is to enjoy life. The essence of this half-ness was James Matthew Barrie. I am a devotee of Barrie in stage technique—was there ever a technician like him?—but part of his half-ness was, unfortunately, devoted to making fun of Scotland for English delectation? But should we Scots worry about that? He put Scotland on the dramatic map as no one before or since has done, except perhaps James Bridie. On second thought, I think James Bridie has done more for literary Scotland today than any man writing, except Eric Linklater.

This is not a digression, because this is a book about Scotland. James Bridie and Eric Linklater have done more good for Scotland than many men in many generations. James is from the west and Eric is from the north and the east. I would not mention these two, except for the fact that I think they are going to last from generation to generation. They are going to be two of the men in literature who will represent Scotland—the Scotland of our generation—for many years to come. The other man I would add to them is one called Douglas Young, classicist, poet and polemicist—is there such a word? To me, those are three great men in Scotland today.

I believe that Bridie is going to undo all the harm that that master of the charm school, Barrie, did. He represents Scotland, not unvarnished, but still the real Scotland. So does Linklater, in his novels, and especially short stories. I wish that Linklater would write more short stories like "Kind Kitty". Here we have one of the most understanding of Scotsmen (Orcadian? that's a lovable fad; he is a Scot of Scots) as ever has been. Linklater is a link with the Middle Ages, and he would not deny that tribute. He is a descendant of the Scot who went abroad and brought back everything that was worth bringing back, and it would not be matter material. He writes sometimes like an angel, sometimes with a daemon. He is also the descendant of that Scotsman of whom he has spoken so well, Sir Thomas Urquhart, the translator of Rabelais, only he is first-hand where Urquhart was second-hand—but what a second!

Linklater, because of these links, is inclined now and again to—what our professor of English at Aberdeen used to dilate upon—the "style orgulous". But if you know Linklater, then you will know that he lives that style. It is part of his life; he cannot live without it. That is part of his link with grander, greater days in literature. That, as I say, makes him so essentially a Scottish writer. Or, had he lived in the days of Villon, I can see Linklater making for Paris to search out that wonder and making friends with him, literarily. I have seen Linklater play the part of Villon in tha good old-stager, *If I were King*, and I'm sure he enjoyed every moment of that part, stepping in and out of it with gladness and sadness. Why has he never given us a better Villon play to take the old one's place? He was born to write Picaresque comedy. It may come yet. I hope so.

There is another Scottish writer who has something of the same instincts. That is Agnes Mure Mackenzie. She is novelist, poet and historian, and has become most famous as historian—probably to her sorrow; I think she would have loved best to be known as poet and novelist. But it was not to be. Mure MacKenzie is, to my idea, one of the great women writers of our time. She is the finest outcome of a Scottish university, Aberdeen. A Scottish university, as well as Oxford or Cambridge, is linked with the great tradition of learning of those Middle Ages. We do produce certain utility persons who go now more to the laboratories, to the colonies, even to the schoolroom, but every now and again we throw up a Linklater, a MacKenzie, and, if I may introduce a third Aberdeen genius, a Rachel Annand Taylor.

Do you know Annand Taylor? If you are not intensely literary you may not. But Rachel Annand Taylor, to my idea, is another whose name will live. She was one of the products of the new dispensation in British university life—the permission of women to enter academic careers. How ridiculous it all seems now! I know I am anticipating my work in the matter of Aberdeen and its university. But what matter? I am still writing of Scotland. And the roots of these people are in the Hebrides, in the Orkneys, in Scotland.

Agnes Mure MacKenzie is a daughter of Lewis, Eric Linklater a son of the Orkneys, Rachel Annand Taylor a daughter of "braif auld Aiberdeen". The special subject of Dr. Annand Taylor is the Renaissance; and who has written more beautifully, more colourfully of that period than she? She has re-created the time of Leonardo da Vinci as only a Scotswoman can. That is what we Scots can do, to counteract the effect of our grey days and haars.

8

In talking of literature and littérateurs, I am immediately in Aberdeen. It's a strange, unusual town. In other books on Scotland—and you can imagine that in my day I have read a few—I have noticed one curious fact. Most of the writers have taken a flying look at Aberdeen, have said what a lovely city it is, and then have sheered off. Why? I think I know. It is difficult to encompass. It cannot be encompassed except by those who know Aberdeen or have sampled it enough to realise its unusualness, not in Scotland only, but among British and other cities.

One writer and architectural expert, John Betjeman, has in recent times fallen for the allure of Aberdeen. I, personally, am indebted to John Betjeman for awakening me to some of the beauties of Aberdeen which I had never noticed. Familiarity, as you know, is inclined to breed a curious kind of ignorance. How many of us, who are merely visitors to a place such as London, can tell the Londoners things about London that they have never known! And so is it with even such a comparatively small city as Aberdeen.

Most people have heard of Aberdeen and the Aberdonian, but, for every one who has, there are thousands who know nothing of the place from which they and all the mythical tales about them emanate. Like John Betjeman, they cannot believe that Aberdeen exists, or that it is what and where it is—it is too far north, too far from what they think are the centres of civilisation. To come upon Aberdeen, after travelling hundreds of miles towards the North Pole, is to get one of the surprises of your travelling lives, and, I think and hope, a pleasant one. If you come to it by road or rail from the south, and particularly by road, you see the city lying spread out before you, below you as you come to the top of the last hill. It is bounded on the north by a river, on the south by a river, on the east by the sea and backed on the west by woods and hills.

It is built mainly of grey granite and when the sun lights up that unusual building material, it is an unusual sight. And Aberdeen is not like so many places that look alluring from a distance—for instance, those coloured French towns to which we used to march when on active service. Lovely from a mile or two away, how shabby they were when at last you marched into them! Near or at a distance, Aberdeen is a lovely city, and the secret is the granite. Silver grey, it always looks clean, and never, as some are inclined to say, really depressing, not even on the greyest day of winter.

A great English poet, Thomas Hardy, has in a poem, written on what, I suppose, was his only visit to Aberdeen, in 1905, summed up the truth of this first attitude and what comes after to those who seek beyond it:

> I looked; and thought, "She is too gray and cold
> To wake the warm enthusiasms of old!"
> Till a voice passed: "Behind that granite mien
> Lurks the imposing beauty of a Queen."

I looked anew; and saw the radiant form
Of Her who stays in stress, who guides in storm;
On the grave influence of whose eyes sublime
Men count for the stability of time.

Another writer, far from great, but well acquainted with Aberdeen, has given this picture in verse of the city:

Men of the south who do not know its charm
Think of our northern Aberdeen as only
A tent of skies that has its differing shades
Of gray; as a haunt of snow and rain, of winds
Aye snell—little they know who do not live
Upon our seven hills and taste the sweets
Of every season here! No other place
I've known sees autumn come with richer gold,
With lovelier tapestries at dawn and dusk.
Often it seems to me our autumn here
Is only the birth of spring, thoughts of decay
Can never flourish in this seaward place.
The leaves may fall, the fields be bare, but then
The Dee, the Don grow stronger, swiftlier flow
To meet the sea that has no fading time. . . .
Aye, sir, two rivers and the wider wall
Of sea do not enclose this Aberdeen
Without effect on city and on folk. . . .
          How many a night
In winter, when the frost is keen, and comes
The still white flood of moonlight, flowing up
Through street and wynd, it seems—so clearly sounds
The sea through all the town—to be far more
Than light, rather waves' ghostly overflow,
Drowning the city like another lost
Atlantis, deep, deep. . . .

From earliest days Aberdeen has never lacked its poets and writers, its painters and architects.

Much of that which makes Aberdeen what it is in matters material and spiritual comes from the great foundation work of one great man, and he was not an Aberdonian by birth, but became one by adoption and the grace of his love for Aberdeen. This was William Elphinstone, who was Bishop of Aberdeen, at the end of the fifteenth and beginning of the sixteenth centuries. He was a good man as well as great, and he was—besides churchman—statesman and diplomat. He served Scotland as well as Aberdeen, and, had his advice been taken, the defeat of Flodden might never have taken place, and Scottish history been very different.

William Elphinstone was the founder of the University of Aberdeen, "onlie begetter" of that lovely chapel in the old town of Aberdeen which is the spiritual centre of academic life. Against opposition, that of materialists—and, as in every city, today we still have those materialists to contend with—he planned this one of his schemes. What he wrote to the Pope was not very complimentary, but the great work had not yet begun which changed Aberdeen in many ways.

"This college I propose", wrote Elphinstone, "would be especially for the benefit of a remote portion of Scotland cut off from the rest of the kingdom by arms of the sea and very lofty mountains . . . and inhabited by unlettered, ignorant and almost barbarous people. . . . Were a University such as I propose to be founded in the renowned ancient city of Aberdeen, the ignorant would acquire knowledge and the rude erudition."

And Elphinstone had his way and Aberdeen her university. That university has meant a great deal to Aberdeen, and still does. In few places of the kind are Town and Gown so finely linked, so harmonious in their dealings with one another. Edinburgh and Glasgow are too big for their universities to be greatly noticeable in civic life. At St. Andrews the university is inescapable. But Aberdeen seems to be just the right size in this way. It is a curiously compact city, one that you feel could be held in the hollow of a giant hand. It is beginning to sprawl a bit, owing to the mushroom erection of much-needed houses. But the main part of the city remains what it was—there's solidity there. It has its ugly bits—what city has not? The city fathers of a hundred years or so ago allowed industry to spoil the backing of its golden sea beach and also to spoil the last mile or two of the River Dee. When I think what Bedford has made of the Ouse there and look at what was done in Aberdeen, I can rage, and with good cause. But plenty remains.

Yes, Gown and Town and granite have together contrived to make Aberdeen one of the different cities of the kingdom. In Aberdeen, Town and Gown work together for the common good. Education in Aberdeen means more to the ordinary citizen than wealth. Wealth is not despised, far from it—the city would not be characteristic Aberdeen if it were—and it is one of the thriftiest and yet best and most sensibly dressed cities in Britain. But wealth is not enough for the citizen of Aberdeen to evoke true admiration, and even wealthy folk in Aberdeen are anxious that both they and their children shall be well-educated. So comes about the close connection of Town and Gown, and on that I must insist, because it is another essential characteristic of Aberdeen.

Education, up to the highest level, has been made easy for those in Aberdeen who really want it, and you will find at its university the son and daughter of the labourer studying and playing side by side with the son and daughter of the rich man and the laird—few lairds are rich men nowadays. I have mentioned playing—sport, especially golf, has been made as easy for the Aberdonian as education. There's a touch of the Greek about that.

So far as the material side of the university is concerned, it is divided into two or three sections. Elphinstone's college—King's—lies in what is today known as the Aulton or Old Aberdeen. But it is not really oldest Aberdeen, for the site of the original town lies actually in the centre of what is regarded as the new town. But little or nothing remains of that oldest town, nothing that will interest the incomer.

But to Old Aberdeen all visitors are taken or go. There stands the cathedral, the college chapel, and many relics of history. The Aulton, more and more every day, becomes the academic centre of the city. It has always had an atmosphere and a character. The latter is touched with bitter local humour. It is said that, if you are not queer before you go to reside in the academic Aulton, you soon will be. But that is not so different from other academic centres and cathedral precincts. English literature, more than Scottish, is full of examples of the case. But about the Aulton, as about other like centres, there is a peace and a tranquillity that come from both material and mental things.

In summer you could see few lovelier approaches to a cathedral than the Chanonry, with its old walls and its rich foliage. The cathedral is not a thing of exquisite or elaborate beauty. It is also, for instance, the exact opposite of the fussiness of such a cathedral as Lichfield. St. Machar Cathedral is almost symbolic of Aberdeen itself. It is like a rock in a land where rocks are needed, not for contesting weariness, but for practical and oppositional purposes, not excluding the winter weather. Its external unusual feature are twin towers. There was a great central tower once, but, by the depredations of the Roundhead soldiers, that was undermined and fell in 1686, bringing havoc with it.

Between the twin towers is a seven-lighted window that has its own grace, and the other unusual feature, within, a flat ceiling of panelled oak, on which are set the coloured shields of pontiff, emperor, queen, kings and princes, earls and prelates. This interior has the same feeling of solidity, not untouched with the sweetness of strength. And, best of all, the cathedral is neither ruined nor neglected, but in ministration and in music a very busy and well-attended centre of art and religion.

The River Don flows just beyond it, and, if you care to walk a little before you return to the High Street of the Aulton, you will see a historic bridge, a single span across the river at Balgownie. This bridge has its connection with Bruce and with Byron—the latter spent part of his school-days in Aberdeen. Byron was afraid to cross Balgownie brig because of the legend:

> Balgownie brig, wight is your wa',
> Wi' a mither's ae son on a white mear's ae foal
> Doon shall ye fa'.

Byron rode a white mare.

Back in the long, not very wide but fairly straight High Street, we come to King's College. Here again, without and within, is loveliness. The external beauty is a Crown tower, such as surmounts St. Giles in Edinburgh and the cathedral in Newcastle. But to my idea, and I am not alone in this, where experts are concerned, King's Crown—the symbol of their university to arts students of Aberdeen—is finer than its counterparts. The chapel is not large, but, though it has changed several times down the centuries, it is still very lovely within. Part of this beauty is due to some unusual Flemish wood-carving on stalls and the screen that divides chapel and ante-chapel. Here, again, worship and music still have their rightful place. There are two memorials at King's to Bishop Elphinstone the founder—a tomb of modern Italian bronze sculpture, which stands in the open in front of the chapel—and a modern memorial hall, in keeping with the rest of the college architecture.

It is difficult for an Aberdeen arts graduate to pull himself away from dilating upon King's College. As I indicate, King's is the centre of the Arts study. The other college that comprises the university lies a mile or more into the city. This, Marischal College, is now given over to mental and other sciences. In the days when the Reformation shook and divided Scotland, the professors of King's were not enamoured of the new religion. As an academic counterblast an Earl Marischal, the fifth member of one of the great families of north-east Scotland, founded another college or university, where the Reformed tenets would have their sway. That was in the sixteenth century, and it was not till the first quarter of the nine-teenth century that the two colleges were united into one university. The motto of the university is: "Initium sapientiae timor domini"; that of Marischal College an alleged saying of the Earl Marischal: "They say. Quhat say they? Lat yame say." And not a bad motto, either, especially for Aberdeen.

According to your views and taste, Marischal College today is either a monstrosity or one of the most marvellous buildings you have ever seen. I disavow the mon-strosity entirely. It is certainly the most marvellous granite building in the whole world if not, also, the largest. It is built of grey granite, and with its wealth of pinnacles so delicately fashioned, its soaring and, again, delicately fashioned central tower, it keeps the stranger staring and fascinated. It wants to be seen at sunset when the granite becomes flushed, or in moonlight when it takes on a dream-like quality that has haunted many an Aberdeen youth, long after and far away.

There is now a third section of the university—the medical school—where, again, great granite buildings are its house and are set on a height on the outskirts of the city, and part of them forms the Royal Infirmary and Maternity Hospital. Not so famous as the Edinburgh School, perhaps, Aberdeen Medical School yet has a name and fame throughout the world.

That is Gown. Now for something of Town. Town, of course, includes industry, and, chief among the industries are granite, fishing—with its complementary industries of trawler and other shipbuilding—comb-making, engineering, and other lesser but still fairly considerable industries that make Aberdeen Town busy and prosperous. The shipbuilding is not a matter of large vessels and the harbour is hampered from lack of draught, but there is a great tradition in the building of ships, from the famous Aberdeen Clippers—remember the *Cutty Sark*—on, and today Aberdeen shipyards are achieving a new fame throughout the world by the building of super-trawlers.

Fishing is always likely to be a main industry of Aberdeen. It is also the like and dislike of the visitor. Arriving by railway, the visitor's nostrils are often assailed by the odour of fish from the loading bank at the main station. But few visitors fail to go to the Fish Market, and that especially early of a morning. The sight there of thousands of fish laid out ready for auction, the unloading and the auctions themselves draw hundreds daily at the height of the tourist season. And it is one of the sights that visitors remember and dilate upon.

Second in this way are the granite quarries at the western edge of the town. Their deep gullies, their blasting and breaking make a great impression.

I have said that Aberdeen has had painters and architects. You have only to explore a few of the main streets of the city to realise that we have had architects. That main street may not satisfy the architecturally fastidious, as a whole, but every now and again you will stop with an "ah" at a single building or a vista—Aberdeen, I have indicated is built on a series of hills, seven it is said. What has been done with that grey granite undoubtedly sets Aberdeen apart in appearance. Our greatest architect, and the man who taught Aberdeen how to use granite to its greatest effect was one Archibald Simpson, whose centenary was well celebrated in the year 1947. And yet, one of his loveliest triumphs, in Aberdeen, is the exquisite taper of the brick tower crowning the East and Belmont Churches.

As to artists, Aberdeen produced not only the most notable first artist in Scotland, but in Britain. This was George Jamesone, not a great artist in general comparison, perhaps, but in his place in the history of British art—he lived at the end of the sixteenth and the beginning of the seventeenth centuries—and, in certain of his works, quite an important and likeable painter. Samples of his work can be seen in the university and the Art Gallery. Aberdeen has maintained the tradition Jamesone began. The city has one of the finest provincial art galleries in Britain, and it has an art school and a school of living artists whose fame is growing year by year. Both gallery and school stand on the Schoolhill, within a stone's throw of the site of the house where Jamesone lived. Alas, the foolishness of some civic fathers some sixty or seventy years ago allowed this picturesque and historic mansion to be demolished.

There, then, is something of the history and atmosphere of this city of Aberdeen, but the sixth has not been told. I would not, however, like to be accused of un-balancing my general account by an over-zeal of local patriotism. But what a city to write of and to belong to!

The city has one of the longest records of any in Scotland. It was already a place of some importance in the twelfth century, and its first authentic charter for trading belongs to the years before 1185. Some of the men with names that ring, for good or ill, through Scots and English history have their Aberdeen connections—Edward I, William Wallace, Robert the Bruce, among earlier kings and warriors. To the city came James IV, with his bride, Princess Margaret of England, and in their train was one William Dunbar, priest and poet. There were great days of feast and pageantry, and of Aberdeen, Dunbar wrote:

> Blithe Aberdeen, thou beryl of all tounis,
> The lamp of beauty, bounty, and blitheness

and his wish was

> Be blithe and blissful, burgh of Aberdeen.

Aberdeen, however, was ever a place of shows and plays. The motto of the city, "Bon-Accord", which is said to date from Bruce's time, was associated with pageantry—the Lords of Bon-Accord were masters of the revels in the early fifteenth century. Aberdeen is, too, the only town in which we have definite evidence of the performance of a miracle play. This was *The Holy Blood*, and those who know Bruges, the Chapelle du Saint-Sang, and recall the strong trade connection between Aberdeen and Flanders will see the probability of the origin of the play and its performance.

But there was also actual drama in Aberdeen—it is said—during one of the visits of Mary Queen of Scots. On the Castlegate, from the windows of one of the houses there, Mary is supposed to have been compelled to watch the execution of John Gordon, son of the Earl of Huntly. John was supposed to have been in love with Mary, and determined to make her his wife, in spite of the fact that he already had a spouse!

Then in the days of King James, Mary's son, a band of London players certainly visited the town, and were honoured by the magistrates. Among them is supposed to have been one William Shakespeare, and it is thought that on this tour he gathered the matter for *Macbeth*.

In the eighteenth century Doctor Johnson and Burns both left their records of visits to the town. By the time they were here, Aberdeen—which has a fine record in the matter of printing—had already a newspaper, the oldest in Scotland. It began as a news-sheet, a bulletin after the battle of Culloden, and started steady publication on January 5, 1747, two hundred years ago.

For all these things, the fame of Aberdeen will always rest upon its granite and what its architects and citizens have made of that material. Go visit its streets and squares, its crescents and terraces. Walk along that lovely tree-shaded thoroughfare, Albyn Place, to the west end and see what domestic architecture can mean when there is granite to enhance it. One other characteristic of many streets in Aberdeen is that the gardens of the houses are at the front as well as the back. A walk along Queen's Road in spring, summer or autumn is like walking along a long length of a permanent flower show.

And always we come back to the last word—let that mean what you wish—in granite, Marischal College. It is not only without but within that Marischal College has its beauties. Look at the great window above the entrance archway, go into the Mitchell Hall of the college, and look at the great eastern window there. These are the work of Dr. Douglas Strachan, a native of the city, and the re-discoverer of the richest beauty of stained glass work. In size and style these windows are magnificent. Smaller but, perhaps, lovelier are Strachan's windows in King's College Chapel.

In art, in history, in learning, in industry Aberdeen is no mean city.

To sum up the inner meaning of the Granite City let us turn to poetry and the poet who has sung granite as no one else has done—Ronald Campbell Macfie, who was poet, scientist and lover of Marischal College, his *alma mater*. In an ode at the opening of the extension of Marischal College, in 1905, you find this:

> Eternity is throned upon thy spires:
> Upon Eternity thy towers rest:
> Thou wert conceived in the eternal fires
> Of the sun's womb: upon the sun's white breast
> Wert carried ere the souls of men were made—
> Nay, in the nebula the seed was sown
> Of every stone,
> And by the stars were thy foundations laid.
> The fire-mist held thee, ere the sun it bore;
> The sun had presage of thee ere she hurled
> From her wild heart the world;
> And the hot world enwrapped thee at its core,
> In lava and in lightning to await
> The slow fastidious finishing of Fate. . . .
>   in man's magnificent desires
> And high imaginations, wilful, warm,
> Thy polished pinnacles, and frosty spires,
> Took shape and form,
> Till all this growth of granite towers,
> And pediments and columns round,
> Like spikelets of colossal flowers,
> Came burning through the ground. . . .

Yes, granite and Marischal College evoked this ode of which these are part of the opening stanza. There must be something to them.

17

ABERDEENSHIRE

ABERDEENSHIRE is a county of contrasts, of history—prehistoric and known —and of beauty in variety. Towards the coast it is bare and almost as treeless as the Orkneys and Shetlands. It is a county that has a dialect, almost a language, of its own. Like Fife, it has often been called, not exactly a part of Scotland; not, like Fife, exactly a kingdom; but just different. The accent of Aberdeen is strong, but it is entirely apart from the dialect of Aberdeenshire. That is something that only the interested native or the expert can understand. If the Aberdeen accent is anything, it is debased Aberdeenshire. What amuses the incomer in Aberdeen is the use of the most curious diminutives and variations of the diminutives. Your Aberdonian speaks of an "aul' wifie" when other places in Scotland talk just of an "auld wife". A loon—meaning a boy, is a "loonie", a quean (or quine) is a "quinie". And so on. Another peculiarity of Aberdeen and Aberdeenshire is the substitution of "f" for "wh". "Fit" for "whit", "why" is "foo", and "who" is "fa".

I remember when I returned after an absence of some years from Scotland, standing listening to a group of natives, and thinking—I, who had known the language or dialect, from my infancy—that I had never realised what a curious concatenation of sounds the dialect of this north-east corner presented. What could the incomer make of this foreign language? And that is what does happen. But, fortunately, more and more the people of Aberdeen and Aberdeenshire have become more and more bilingual. They speak one dialect among themselves, but to the stranger they will speak as much of an approximation to English as possible.

One afternoon a small boy came to the door of the inn where I reside. I went to find out what he wanted. We have a doo'cot and a large flock of doves. He said— "Hiv ye ony young doos te sell?" Perhaps a little sharply I said "What?" In perfect English the youngster, who seemed to think I did not understand his accent, asked again—"Have you any young doves to sell?" And, let me say, that when a north-east Scot sets out to speak as good English as he can accomplish, he speaks what I consider the best English in the world. Not the English of a Glaswegian, not the related dialects of the Cockney or the Mayfair "wah-wah", but English as it is written. I think—or hope—George Bernard Shaw would agree with me in this.

But still, as I say, there is the greatest difference between the Aberdonian of the city of Aberdeen and the Aberdonian of the county, except that Aberdeen nowadays is full of people who have migrated from country to town, and the migrated county man's accent blows like a breath of country air through the debased accent of the city. Like most other cities and their debased speech, the chief trouble is a complete disregard of consonants, a slovenly use of words.

But, no matter where you go in Aberdeenshire, whenever you cross the city boundary you come into a new place, even a mile or two from the city. The city ceases to matter; it is—as I have said—merely a convenience, for shopping, as an alien amusement centre. There begins everywhere a feeling of a series of communities. That, of course, is partly because there are no satellite towns for Aberdeen, only little towns, here and there, every fourteen or fifteen miles. The accent, as I have told, is different, the character changes.

Aberdeenshire is, *par excellence*, in stock and the produce of the ground, one of the greatest agricultural counties in Scotland, but more, perhaps, in stock.

Suppose, then, we take our way along the eastern part of the county, and first along the coast-line. Beginning at the River Dee and crossing the River Don at the northern edge of the city you have miles and miles of golden sand. Reverting to the city for a moment, there is one of its pleasures, either as native or visitor. From almost any part of it, you need only a ten minutes' tram or bus ride and you are on these golden sands, at the edge of the sea, not the sea of the west, but something more invigorating, with a breeze that takes away every thought of the city. But Aberdeen is never at any time a stuffy city. There is always the sea air.

Golf courses line the first few miles from the city along the coast, but, apart from these, all you will find are sea-salmon fishers' bothies, for neither in Aberdeen nor for many a mile northwards do you find houses built on the sea front.

Your first break after the River Don on these miles of sand is at the estuary of the River Ythan. This is a great bird sanctuary, but on this estuary you will also find a lazy little port, Newburgh. Here are wharves and a warehouse or two that seem as if they had been built and then forgotten.

You cross the Ythan and then you are again on miles of sand, the Sands of Forvie, which are kin to the Culbin Sands in Morayshire. The finest use of these places, to my idea, would be for British cinema companies to use them as substitutes in making desert pictures. The Forvie sands have the usual legends about them, though many people are sceptical. It is said, of course, that during a great storm—when, is a date never mentioned—the sand blew over fields and covered a village. Of course, again, on stormy nights there can be heard the ghostly chimes of the church bell. In time, I have no doubt, at Forvie, as at Culbin, there will be attempts at reclamation.

But soon we are past both Forvie and sand, and the rocks begin. I have mentioned already the rough little fishing village of Collieston, which lies in its little cove. Collieston now, more than anything else, is a tiny summer resort for happy families. Year by year the fisher-folk tend to disappear. The place was, and to a certain extent still is, noted for a kind of little dried fish called "speldins". Twenty-five years ago it was a happy hunting-ground of my own. That was before the crowds invaded it —cars and buses were few and far between then. I loved the old fisher-folk and spent happy hours in their company. Two things, characteristic of what I have said of fishing communities, remain in my mind. My last sojourn coincided with the coming of the first Sunday picnic parties. They were very innocent affairs, family affairs as always. I stood on the point with an old fisherman on the Sunday afternoon. Fathers and youngsters on the little strip of sand, were enjoying a game of rounders. My old fisher friend gazed at them with solemn eyes. Then he turned to me and, with a heavy sigh, said, more in sorrow than in anger: "There ye are, the new dispensation—juist Sodom and Gomorrah all over again." Rounders!

And what used to amuse me, also, was that the fishers would work on all through Saturday evening, preparing the speldins, setting them out to dry. They would work until nearly midnight in the midsummer light. But—as soon as it came to midnight —they ceased. But they sold the speldins to the Sunday visitors!

Beyond Collieston, and still heading north, we come eventually to another golf course, one that has had its ups and downs of fame and something near neglect. This is at Cruden Bay and, beyond Cruden Bay, we come again to the cliffs, this time to some of the most picturesque on the whole of the east coast. Here are the famous Bullers o' Buchan; nothing so grand as, say, Fingal's Cave, but, in their own way, and especially in rough weather, something to remain in the mind.

We are also on a coast now that is, in its season and weather, a terror to shipping. In some winters of the past there have been wrecks here that had, in the stories told by survivors or rescuers, with elements that have distressed the whole nation. It is a wicked coast, and not only the rocky part of it.

One of the most distressing things for a landlubber—and I have experienced it on this east coast—is to watch a ship go down, almost within hailing distance, and to know that neither you nor anyone can lift a hand to help the men whose plight you know so well. You stand, as the wind roars and the waves heave mountain-high, and watch the lanterns on the doomed ship wave to and fro in an agony of beseeching. Every now and again those lights go out for a moment, as the waves wash over. Then the lights begin to go higher, as the men climb up the rigging for a safety that, we guess—while they hope not—is useless. The lights wave more and more wildly, then—all of a sudden—they all go out and are never seen again. The men on that ship have dree'd their weird; the sea which lured them has claimed them. That is not an uncommon story of this coast.

So we move on to Peterhead and Fraserburgh. These two towns, within eighteen miles of one another, are the twin towns of this area that is known as Buchan, a name that also belongs to the speech spoken in the district. They are, with the exception of Aberdeen itself, the largest centres of the herring fishing on the east coast. Fishing is their mainstay, and almost all else in the way of industry in them is ancillary or incomer. Of the two towns, talking superficially, I prefer Fraserburgh. Both have a certain amount of history. At Peterhead landed the Old Pretender to make the first of the ill-fated attempts of the Stuarts to wrest the Crown of Britain from the Hanoverians; and Peterhead was also, in its day, a whaling port. Today business and golf, with a little touch of literature, are the sum-up of its life.

Fraserburgh's chief bit of history is very recent. It was the most-bombed town of its size in the British Isles during the war of 1939–45. That was because it was the first landfall the German bombers encountered on their trips from Norway. The damage was not very extensive, but the bombing was sometimes intensive. The people were brave almost to carelessness.

Fraserburgh's rather unusual piece of older history is retained in the name of one of its streets—College Bounds. At the time when the Reformers were determined to have their own college to defeat the anti-Reform professors in Aberdeen, there was an attempt to establish a university in Fraserburgh. It did not last.

Both Peterhead and Fraserburgh have industries of fair size and importance, the one preserving-works and the other tool-works. But their foundation is fishing. At Fraserburgh there is what seems to me a most picturesque harbour front, and it is time some of our Scottish artists found this out and made a change from the eternal painting of the Fife fishing villages.

When we go inland in this Buchan area we come to what many consider the dreichest part of Aberdeenshire. Buchan is bare, all but treeless, with only an inconsiderable hill here and there. Yet there are places and times at which I can love the comparative austerity of Buchan; and I certainly love its people. There are great vistas to the west in these lowlands of Aberdeenshire; here it is a rolling shire, and I know, as I look across them to the Fujiyama of the shire, that central hill known as Bennachie, that I am looking on acres that, in produce and stock, are worth, in time, not thousands, but millions, both to their owners and the country.

Here are the lands and here the men who produce the famous herds of Aberdeen-Angus and Shorthorn cattle, stock that has linked these bare acres with the Argentine and with the United States and Canada. A year or two ago an Aberdeenshire Shorthorn was sold to an American breeder for the record price of £15,225. There is no doubt about it, Aberdeenshire is one of the great farming counties of Britain, and not the least part of the county is this Buchan.

As for the people, they are slow and tough, rugged in speech and difficult of apprehension by the outsider, but, if you know their dialect, you will enjoy every moment of your stay with them, for they have a native wit that comes out of their character, and they can sum up things in their own dialect in a way that is hardly possible in any other of our dialects, except those, perhaps, of Lancashire or Yorkshire. The "townie"—or "toonser", as he is known here—may be amused at the yokel—"Country Geordie" or "Buchan hummlie" as he is called—but, except where your confidence trickster, "spiv" or "smart Alec" is concerned—the Buchan man has the town folk pretty well sized-up. He still remains, in essentials, a Buchan hummlie, but days and ways are changing. Easy communication not only makes the Geordie quicker in the uptak' of certain matters of urban life, but, alas, also corrupts something of the old country life. But, for all their easy in-and-out of the city, the countrymen who stick to their soil and native places are still, in most matters that count, the essential countrymen. Long may it be so!

As we go westward in Aberdeenshire we come into another division of the county. This is known as Formartin and is not very easily divided in any way from Buchan. It is not so treeless, perhaps, not so flat; agriculture is still as good and the character still as rich as the speech. And then we come to another division known as the Garioch—pronounced "Geeree". Here we are approaching a part of Aberdeenshire that is rich in history, much of it national.

The Garioch is dominated by the hill I have already mentioned—Bennachie— which I take to mean the hill of the mist—Ben-na-cheo. It is a little range, actually, ending in a little peak called the Mither Tap. As I have said, Bennachie and, especially, the Mither Tap are visible all over certain parts of Aberdeenshire, and seem to centralise a certain differentiation of character and speech. The people of the regions with which I have been dealing are different from most other Scots in not a few ways. They have something of the granite in them, they pride themselves—some of them, at any rate—in being not Highland, though they would object to being dubbed Sassenachs. That, for them, is the name for the folk farther south. They are just Aberdeenshire, and that is enough. It is difficult to analyse what has set these folk apart. Some say they are the true descendants of the Pictish folk, and there is plenty of archaeological remainder to back that up. Others say it is the admixture of Scandinavian blood that has done it, and you will find plenty of Scandinavian-sounding names among them—Anderson, Henderson, Mann, for three—to back that up. Or is it just the nature of the country and their once-upon-a-day isolation that makes them still what they are?

One thing, however, they have, and to this day create: that is, a literature that stands by itself in Scotland. It is written in their own strong dialect, can sound as strange as Anglo-Saxon or German or Dutch or Scandinavian to outside ears. But it is a literature, be it prose or poetry, that is rich in life and character, full of native wit, and pithy. We are also in the country of some of our ballad literature and that jolly degradation of the ballad, the cornkister, which is a ballad without the touch of poetry. From Buchan come such famous and still-sung cornkisters as Mormond Braes, the tale of a lass who lost her lad, with its famous quatrain:

> There's mony a horse has knappert and fa'en
>   And risen again fu' rarely,
> There's mony a lass has lost her lad,
>   And gotten anither richt early.

Anywhere in Aberdeenshire they will sing you the refrain of this ballad:

> Sae fare ye weel, ye Mormond Braes,
>   Where aften I've been cheery,
> Fare ye weel, ye Mormond Braes,
>   For it's there I lost my dearie.

Not only the words of these cornkisters, but their tunes, which are equally, if not artistically, more important, have a tang which is not found elsewhere in Scotland. They are the very essence of folk-song. They tell, mostly, of domestic tragedies and of farm work and all its joys and draggledom.

When we rise to the ballads we find one of them dealing with one of the famous historic events of the Garioch—the Battle of Harlaw, which was fought, near the capital of the Garioch, Inverurie, in 1411. It was a fight between the Highlandmen and the men of these Lowlands. It begins:

> As I cam' in the Garioch lands
>   An' doon by Netherha',
> I saw sixty thoosand Hielanmen
>   A' marchin' to Harlaw.

It is all, probably, an exaggeration of what today would be regarded as little more than a fracas. But the ballad presents us with the story of the battle in the same way, though not with such artistry as, for instance, Uccello's famous painting gives in its early presentation of a battle. The battle, according to the ballad, lasted a week. And the ending is that of all battles, ancient and modern:

> Gin onybody spier at ye
>   O' them they took awa',
> Ye can tell them plain, and very plain,
>   They're sleepin' at Harlaw.

The battlefield of Harlaw is well-marked and has its monument, though a still greater one is the height of Bennachie, which overlooks the field from a distance, like an eternal battle-cairn.

At Inverurie we are on the River Ury and on the way to the greater River Don and Strathdon. There is great rivalry in Aberdeenshire between Strathdon and what is known as Deeside. I say there is no need for any rivalry. Both have their characteristics; they are not rivals but complementary.

Before we come to Strathdon, however, we have the Howe, the Vale, of Alford. This is a part of Donside that has achieved not one but several fames. It is a great agricultural countryside, but, unlike Buchan, it has a less stern beauty; it is a gateway to the hills; it is the haunt of fishers, and it produced one of the most famous of modern Scottish poets, Charles Murray, known to many by the name of his first volume of verse, *Hamewith*. This naming is typical of his countryside and of Aberdeenshire, generally. A farmer is always attached by name to his farm. If that farm is Westside of Such-and-Such, then the farmer is "Westie"; if Eastside, "Eastie"; and the farmer of Mains of This, That or the Other is "Mains". It was a last touch of love for Charles Murray that gave him the name of "Hamewith". And how well he deserved it! Few poets have ever found their way into Scottish hearts, and, especially, north-eastern hearts. He is and will continue to be the laureate of the north-east, though his poems are known all through Scotland and wherever Scotsmen gather abroad. Every school child in Scotland, I should say, whether he can speak the Aberdeenshire dialect or not, knows "The Whistle". Its opening is as famous in its way as is the opening of Aberdeenshire's prose classic, "Johnny Gibb of Gushetneuk". The opening of "Johnny Gibb" is "Heely, heely, Tam, ye glaiket stirk", a marvellous opening. Of "The Whistle":

> He cut a sappy sucker from the muckle rodden-tree,
> He trimmed it, an' he wet it, an' he thumped it on his knee;
> He never heard the teuchat when the harrow broke her eggs,
> He missed the craggit heron nabbin' puddocks in the seggs.

Charles Murray was born and brought up in the Vale of Alford. That was part of the making of him as a poet. Later in life he went to South Africa, where he had a notable official career. That exile was the second part of the making of him as a poet. Nostalgia has a wonderful effect upon poets. It may be nostalgia for a dream world that can never be realised, but it can also be nostalgia for the scenes of home when they are far away. That kind of nostalgia is all through Scottish verse, sometimes to the point of heart-break, and yet Scotsmen will roam. What Hamewith did in his poems was to gather up in word and atmosphere—and he was the master of illuminating phrase—the life and work and loveliness, the character and custom of Aberdeenshire. Now if, as I maintain, Aberdeenshire is the essence of non-Celtic Scotland, then he was the essence of that essence, and that is what will make his work live when more pretentious work has been long forgotten. Apart from the poems of the great ones, such as Shakespeare and Wordsworth, who took the particular to the universal, the only way for a poet to live is to delve deep into the heart of his native ground and native folk. Hamewith did that. Here is a poem that collects all Scotland, by means of hills and mountains, and then lays it at the foot of his native peak, Bennachie.

> There's Tap o' Noth, the Buck, the Newe,
>   Lonach, Benrinnes, Lochnagar,
> Mount Keen, an' mony a Cairn I trow
>   That's smoored in mist beyond Braemar.
> Bauld Ben Muich Dui towers, until
>   Ben Nevis looms the laird o' a';
> But Bennachie! Faith, yon's the hill
>   Rugs at the hairt when ye're awa'.
>
> Schiehallion ay, I've heard the name—
>   Ben More, the Ochils, Arthur's Seat,
> Tak' them an' a' your hills o' fame
>   Wi' lochans leamin' at their feet;
> But set me doon by Gadie side,
>   Or whaur the Glenton lies by Don—
> The muircock an' the whaup for guide,
>   Up Bennachie I'm rivin' on.
>
> Syne on the Mither Tap sae far
>   Win'-cairdet clouds drift by abeen,
> An' wast owre Keig stands Callievar
>   Wi' a' the warl' to me atween.
> There's braver mountains owre the sea;
>   An' fairer haughs I've kent, but still
> The Vale o' Alford! Bennachie!
>   Yon is the howe, an' this the Hill.

In its lesser and localised way that poem to me seems to compare with a piece of music, the work of a great genius and a mystic—which Charles Murray was not—the second movement, at least, of Elgar's Violin Concerto, which gathers up the lush loveliness of Worcestershire.

From Alford we begin to move into Strathdon, and we are moving in the footsteps of many cavalcades from the time of Robert the Bruce onwards. We are also moving into ballad-dom.

Other parts of Scotland, other parts of Aberdeenshire have produced their ballads, but whether they be of the best brand, such as "Edom o' Gordon", or of the cornkister type, such as "The Guise o' Tough", Donside has enriched Scots folk literature as few other places have done. It is something to be considered and analysed. The question is, why? What is there, what was there about this countryside to evoke such literature? Life was rough and rude, and men had little care for life or lives. Yet, behind it all was this feeling that survives in such ballads as "Edom o' Gordon"

9

That still today can move people as few things move them. The drama of today is ridiculous compared with this ballad. It is not great poetry, it is good drama, but there is something—the spirit—behind it, that endures. There is a lesson for us all, literary or not literary—the spirit is that which endures through the generations and the centuries.

What was this business of Edom o' Gordon, which makes Strathdon remembered when other things are forgotten? It was only one of many incidents of the time, but folk literature has made this one immortal.

In November, 1571, Margaret Forbes of Towie and her family were at Corgarff Castle, in Strathdon. Along came a party of the Gordons, demanding the surrender of the castle—the head of the Forbeses was away from home. Margaret Forbes refused to surrender, so the attacking party set fire to the castle. The ballad tells the story in a way that could put many a modern journalist to shame. You can conjure up the scene—the smoke, the fire, and the young children. The children make the tragedy of the ballad.

> O then bespake her youngest son,
>   Sat on the nurse's knee,
> "Dear mother, gie owre your house," he says,
>   "For the reek it smithers me."
>
> "I winna gie up my house, my dear,
>   To nae sic traitor as he;
> Come weil, come wae, my jewels fair,
>   Ye maun tak share wi' me."
>
> O then bespake her dochter dear,
>   She was baith jimp and sma';
> "O row me in a pair o' sheets,
>   And tow me owre the wa'."
>
> They row'd her in a pair of sheets,
>   And tow'd her owre the wa',
> But on the point of Edom's spear
>   She got a deadly fa'.
>
> O bonnie, bonnie was her mouth,
>   And cherry were her cheeks,
> And clear, clear was her yellow hair,
>   Whereon the reid bluid dreeps.
>
> Then wi' his spear he turned her owre;
>   O gin her face was wan!
> He said, "You are the first that e'er
>   I wished alive again."

SAILORS' WALK, KIRKCALDY

KILDRUMMIE CASTLE

He turned her owre and owre again;
O gin her skin was white!
He said, "I might hae spared thy life
To been some man's delight."

Of course, you can go up Donside, if your interests are shootin' and fishin' and
have the time of your life, and never know a single thing about all this of which I
write. But the man or woman who goes up Donside and knows its history is the man
or woman who enjoys Donside to the full. There are certain districts in Scotland, or
any other country in the world, which cannot be enjoyed to the full unless, even
apart from their natural beauty, you know their history. For what do you go to
Italy, to certain parts of France and Belgium? You cannot help it, you are influenced
by the past. We are all influenced by the past. We cannot help it. The past shapes
us, shapes our lives. The future is all in the past, for good or ill, according to what
we choose from the past. That choice is most important, and most important as to
who chooses it. Think of Hitler, think of Stalin.

But—to Strathdon. The place seems littered with storied and ruined castles.
Today it is just beauty and agriculture, but in days long gone what history, what
stuff for song and story! Kildrummy, Glenbuchat and, going back a bit and away,
Balfluig, Terpersie, Craigievar, Corse—all these had their day and their history.
Craigievar, the home of the Sempills, still survives, and will as long as D. Y.
Cameron's famous painting of it exists. Craigievar is something in Scottish architecture—and I have largely kept off architecture in this book, because I think
architecture has been overdone in books on Scotland; in these days of "pre-fabs" we
don't live on our architecture—Craigievar is something to see and wonder at. It
has only one door, it is a tall, almost dreamlike, tower, something that might have
come out of a play by Maurice Maeterlinck. It is still very much inhabited. It is
still one of the dreamlike things of Scottish architecture.

The Don winds its way to its source; how few people have ever seen the source
of the Don!—the Dee, yes, but not the Don. I have, because I love the Don and I
love the people who live along its course. They are not a curious people, but—
that adjective which I use so frequently in this book—different. They are tough,
they are successful, and I think they come out of history. Here, if anywhere in
Scotland, we have the mingling of the Gael and the Sassenach. You find it in their
dialect. You find it in their character. Softness and hardness meet here. The hills
and the river. What beauty there is here of the hills and the river. That is Strathdon.
Hills and river, all the way to the top of the strath.

And then, at the top, you come to something English. Yes, you come to the
Lecht. The Lecht is a road, a most unusual road, that goes from Strathdon to Tomintoul. Queen Victoria used to think Tomintoul was the highest village in Scotland.

But Queen Victoria was wrong—as she so often was!—Leadhills on the Borders is the highest village in Scotland.

When you reach the top of Strathdon, your head filled with the beauty of river and tree, you come to a place called the Cock Brig. This is one of the most famous spots in Aberdeenshire, and my friend, Fenton Wyness, one of the most learned archaeologists and architects in Scotland today, has told me the origin of the name. After the '45, when the Hanoverians were in possession, there was an inn here which had as its sign a muir-cock. Hence the name, which is known to motorists and hikers throughout the length and breadth of Britain.

After a corkscrew climb, not very long or difficult, you come to the Lecht. It is an open, wild road. The Cairngorms are your companions here. It was built in 1754, a military road—what the English military did for Scotland in that way!—and rises to a height of 2114 feet, between Sgor Damh and Corr Riabhach. It is the joy of the man with a good car, the sorrow of the man with a "relic". But there is no doubt of the beauty of the view from the Lecht.

Now, having pursued Strathdon in my way from the start to the finish, let us cut across to Deeside. The way we go is the Royal way; do not forget Deeside is the Royal part of Scotland. Deeside and Donside both end in the Cairngorms, and yet, Deeside compared with Donside is soft and lovely. I think that is the great difference between those two rivals. It is also the difference in character. Deeside has its ballads, but nothing like "Edom o' Gordon". You have the Deeside ballads of the Earl of Aboyne and the Laird o' Drum. But these are of love; the Donside ballads are of fighting and death. Have I solved a problem?

Queen Victoria started something when she chose Balmoral as her Highland home. It was not the first Royal connection with Deeside. Do not forget that the Royal standard was first raised at Braemar in 1715!

In September 1840 Queen Victoria arrived at Balmoral and changed the history of this lovely place. The old castle of Balmoral was demolished and the foundation stone of the present castle laid in 1858. Stone and lime matter nothing in this, it is the *cachet* that, to this very democratic day, belongs to Royalty. Politics may change, as they have done, very violently, even in this Britain of ours, but the love for the Royal family remains, and every August, September and October thousands flock on every possible occasion, and especially on Sundays, to see the King and Queen and their family go to quiet Crathie Kirk.

The Dee rises in the Cairngorms and flows leisurely down its lovely miles. Its source is probably better known than that of any other river in the kingdom, because the Cairngorms are the climbing ground of thousands of young, and not so young, men and women. They have the most peculiar fascination of any group of hills in Britain. Why it should be I cannot say, but that fascination is undoubtedly there.

The fascination gripped me in my younger days, but I still cannot explain it. The Larig Grhu, the Lui Beg, Glen Derry, they are names that at once unite men and women wherever they meet, at home or overseas. In nature, as the name of Robbie Burns is in literature, the Cairngorms are the great uniter.

Of course, they are lovely. Of course, they are there to be conquered, and they do not need a great deal of conquering, just a stout heart to a stey brae, but what joy in the ascent and in the accomplishment! They are not a paradise for trippers. Is that part of their attraction? You have to pad it for miles and miles before you even begin to ascend—but what miles! To my idea, the loveliest time to look at or ascend the Cairngorms is in early spring or early autumn. I have only once been on the Cairngorms in snow, and I never want to be again; up to the waist in it—ardours and endurances!

What does remain in my mind is the outline of those peaks on an April or an October evening. The pale sky of spring—sometimes blue, sometimes with a tinge of green in it, cold but beautiful, and the lines of the Cairngorms against that sky, clear, sharp and darkish, the very essence of a D. Y. Cameron painting. Most of all I remember one April day when, with a companion, I climbed Ben Macdhui. We set out from Inverey, near Braemar, just a little too late for climbing. We achieved what we wanted to do, but when we got back to Derry Lodge it was dark. Our last few miles were more good luck than knowledge of the way. Then the moon came up, and, as we crossed the Derry moor and looked back on those hills, something rose in me, something I have never forgotten through all the years, something that made me so happy to be a Scotsman, to think those hills were mine and part of me, part of my life.

So we come down from the Cairngorms, and I have mentioned Inverey. But, before we reach that clachan we have crossed the Linn o' Dee, the farthest the trippers go towards the Cairngorms. It is not so fascinating—to me—as the Black Rock at Evanton, but it has its attraction.

At Inverey today there is something missing. The thousands who have climbed the Cairngorms within the last twenty-five years will know what I mean. Maggie Gruer has gone, one of the most wonderful characters Scotland has ever known or ever will know. Just as the Cairngorms unite people all over the world, so does Maggie. Thistle Cottage, Inverey, had a visitors' book, and to go through that book was to meet the names of some of the most famous in the world today. They were not so when they stayed with Maggie, who charged an absurd sum for your night's lodging. Of all the elastic dwellings I have ever come across in my life, I think Thistle Cottage, Inverey, beat the band. Six or eight would have filled the house comfortably, but Maggie would see anything up to twenty housed before she would say "nay" to any mountain-bound traveller. Life and living were simple and rough at Maggie's, but mountaineers are accustomed to these conditions. What mattered was good fellowship and character. She died in September 1938, and, since then, for many, something has gone out of the place and the hills. Nothing can quite take her place. She was an adjunct to the Cairngorms.

And so to Braemar, a lovely place in itself and in its associations. It is a quiet place except for one day in the year, a day in September, when the Braemar Gathering takes place. That day is the peak of the Royal Deeside season. From all over Scotland, from the United States, from all over the British Empire and many a foreign land, people gather in their thousands to this little hollow of the hills. For myself, I have never found it anything except boring, and mostly it has rained while I have been there.

The day begins with a march of the Highlanders, a picturesque survival only, and rather ironic when one remembers for whom and against whom the Highlanders used to march once upon a day. The pipes drool on through the earlier part of the day, you will see some dancing, some athletics. But people really begin to waken after lunch-time. There is a bustle and expectancy. The scene then becomes animated. In the circle of that hill hollow are thousands and thousands of people. You hear a far-off cheering, that grows louder and louder as it comes nearer. Into the circle drive the Royal party—the cheer is now a roar. The Gathering has really begun. The dancers become more animated; the pipers blaw better; the athletes put an extra spurt into it. On a fine September day, when the sun lights up hill and haugh, given plenty of tartan and gay dresses, the scene has quite a lot to it; but the Gathering goes on too long, and the place takes a long time to get rid of towards evening.

Apart from this day, Braemar is a lovely, leisurely place, with plenty of outlets for the young and arduous. It saw curious sights during the war, for here the commandos and mountain artillery of more than one country went through their training. A hope came out of that that this part of the Highlands might become a summer and a winter sports centre. As yet, little or nothing has been achieved. But there is not the slightest doubt that the possibility is there. But how slow Britons are to appreciate their own possibilities! Think of aviation in the years after 1919, and the cinema. Hardship and our economic imprisonment, if these last a matter of years, may alter things in such places as Braemar.

Braemar has one interesting link with literature. You will find the news of it on the inscription above a modest cottage door near the centre of the village. Here Robert Louis Stevenson began the writing of the tale that, in boys' and men's literature, stands on the shelf of immortality alongside *Robinson Crusoe*. The book was *Treasure Island*.

The road from Braemar passes by the castle of that name, another of those austere towers, and for many of the miles the Dee, flowing beneath the Balmoral hills, keeps you company. You pass the lovely span of the old Bridge of Invercauld, surely one of the most photographed and painted bridges in the world. You will, in time, get a glimpse of the turrets of Balmoral Castle, but little more. This is Royalty's best holiday home.

Whether by accident or by choice, the castle is so set that the road that runs from Ballater to Braemar has practically no counterpart on the other side of the river. For miles and miles the folk of Balmoral can go without meeting any but estate workers or a short-cutting and adventurous climber. And here is pursued, has been pursued through generations, the tradition begun by Queen Victoria—the contact between the laird and lady of Balmoral.

I have had the privilege of being present at more than one of these meetings between the laird and the lady and their folk, and anything more happy, more informal, can hardly be imagined. It would not be surprising if, from generation to generation, the Royal holidaymakers who come here were, as Queen Victoria put into writing, so very, very sorry when the time comes each year for leaving Balmoral. And the time of year when they leave Balmoral is one of the loveliest in the whole round of the calendar. Spring is lovely, in delicacy; summer becomes lush and rich in purple; but autumn is to move in a world of reds and golds in earth and sky, that would defeat the greatest painter with the world's richest palette.

Upper Deeside has its loveliness, but when we pass down the river, past Ballater with its tree-covered guardian hill, Craigendarroch, Deeside as essential Deeside begins to change. The hills recede, they are not so high or steep or frowning; the Cairngorms are far off; and "the steep frowning glories of dark Lochnagar" become something enjoyed from the distance.

One of the most beautiful of the lesser sights of Deeside, for me, is the way by the river at Cambus o' May, towards the end of August and on a sunny day. Here the green of the silver birches, the purple of the heather and the blue of the river combine to make as delicate a symphony as any colourist could wish. Another sight in this area is the Moor of Dinnet in heather time, more especially when it is a great wine-red stretch, summing up—and some sneer at it because of this—every popular picture of Scotland. They forget only one thing—that such scenes are copies of actuality, that Scotland is like that.

For the best of two vistas of Deeside you must turn off at Dinnet, along the road that leads to the Burn o' Vat—quite near the Deeside road, and that also leads to Tarland. At Burn o' Vat, climb the height above the burn and look eastwards. The lower Dee valley stretches in front of you in miles of sylvan beauty; on a clear day you have the feeling that you could pick out and count every tree in all those miles. The days here towards autumn can have a crystal clearness that goes to the head like chilled wine. On a midsummer day the whole landscape seems to slumber in brooding beauty. I know only one other landscape that has something of the same effect, and that is when you stand on some high spot in Malvern and look away across that great orchard of Worcestershire, that lies between the Liffey Hills and the Cotswolds.

For a view that, however, has no English counterpart you must go beyond Tarland and take the road to Aberdeen. There, at a spot called Tillylodge, there is another of these famous "Queen's Views"—the Queen, of course, is Victoria. The landscape dips down rapidly into a great bowl, and beyond the hollow are miles and miles of hills and mountains, ending, of course, in Lochnagar and the Cairngorms. It is not a breath-taking view; it is rather something that brings a great satisfaction and a curious peace. You will gaze long at this landscape and come back again and again, to gaze again. It has that kind of fascination.

So we return to essential Deeside, and by way of the lovely village of Aboyne set our faces towards the city. Aboyne is, to some extent, Braemar's rival in the matter of its annual gathering—though the name here is Aboyne Games. The gatherings take place on two successive days.

At Aboyne there is no Royal procession or visit, but it has always been said that at Aboyne the athletics are better, and so with the piping and dancing. Braemar has its Gathering; Aboyne its Games, and there is one more event of the kind in the area—the Lonach Gathering, which is the highlight of the Donside season.

There was a feeling at one time that these gatherings which occur north, east, west and south in Scotland, were on the wane. The very opposite has been the case. I have said something of the Border gatherings. The years since the end of the 1939–1945 war have seen a new spirit in these folk-meets; not only have old gatherings been revived in glory, but district after district has started new ones. And everywhere you will find the crowds, in hundreds, in thousands. The kilt, the pipes, the brawn of the men, the neat nimbleness of dancing lassies and laddies make an afternoon and evening that seem to delight the Scottish heart. Of course, they are, in some instances, great places for meeting; but you must hear also the talk, the argument that goes around this and that athlete's prowess; this and that tug o' war team; and the talk goes back through the records of generations of athletes.

Aboyne has a lovely setting for its games. The village green lies, once more, in a hollow of the hills and just beyond the green is the castle of the Chief of the Games, the Marquess of Huntly, the premier marquess of Scotland, with his famous sobriquet, "The Cock o' the North".

There are still not a few miles beyond Aboyne towards Aberdeen, of quiet beauty, but we have seen the essence of Deeside.

One of my most memorable journeys and views of this essence occurred on a summer morning. We set out from Aberdeen in the half-dark. As the miles between us and the city mounted up, the landscape began to take on a curious, almost sub-terranean light; hills and woods and river became lit by a gathering glow. The strange light changed to the rose-red of day, so soft, so—what should one call it?—heavenly, a hymn come true? When the day was fully come we stopped our car and looked on a scene that was half-way between a great glorious enamel and a page from a missal. Yes, Deeside is like that at its best.

18

THE MEARNS

YOU leave Aberdeen and cross the River Dee. You are in Kincardineshire, known to people of the north-east, unofficially, as The Mearns.

As the railway runs by the sea you will notice that you have changed the golden sands that run north from Aberdeen to a rocky shore. There are glimpses that, especially in winter, make the comfort of, say, a dining-car, a curious contrast to what you are looking out upon. You pass by the edge of deep gullies into which the sea may be roaring and the waves throwing spume high into the air. But in summer this rocky shore is one of the happy playgrounds of the Aberdonian asking a change from his gold—of sand, I mean. Here is the haunt of the rock fisher, of the climbing boys—with every now and again their tragedy of death or disablement.

You will also pass near to a few fishing villages, but, as in the case of Collieston, the heydays of these little places as fishing portlets are gone. One of them, however, has given its name to the eating world. That is Findon. The local pronunciation is "Fin'on", and so you have the further corruption into "Finnan" and, join that to the haddock, and you know. From this tiny hamlet by the sea came this famous "haddie"; it was the peculiar way of smoking or curing it that brought this haddock into favour. But your "finnan haddie" today is not quite the haddie that made Findon famous.

The capital of Kincardineshire, Stonehaven, stands on the sea-shore, some fifteen miles from Aberdeen. It is bounded south and north by rocks, but the town occupies a rising crescent, a break in the rocks. On a miniature scale it will remind you of Oban, even of Genoa. Stonehaven is a pleasant and even enterprising little town, one of whose chief sources of existence is the holiday-maker. It provides golf, it provides a swimming-pool, a cinema and cafés, dancing and concerts—and yet, for all of these venallurements for the incomer, it retains its own identity. Although fishing has again largely departed, there is a fishing community in their own fairly quaint old town. They have all the characteristics and speech of the fisher-folk of the east coast, though, unlike their neighbours down the coast, Gourdon and Johnshaven, the latest generation tends to become merged with the ordinary folk of the Mearns.

OLD MAR BRIDGE AND LOCHNAGAR, ABERDEENSHIRE

DUNNOTTAR CASTLE, KINCARDINESHIRE

Two roads lead south from Stonehaven, one inland, the other still more or less by the sea. On the sea road, not very far from the town you will, if you know, turn off to visit what has always been for me one of the most curiously atmospheric relics of the past, Dunnottar Castle. I am not alone in thinking there are few places of its kind quite like Dunnottar, and you can spend a day or an afternoon letting the past—and the fine sea air—seep into you.

The setting of the castle is magnificent. You first descend into a grassy gully, which, although without water, separates the castle from the mainland like a dry moat. You then make your way to the little entrance door—where you must ring the bell and pay your sixpence entry fee. This door immediately brings the centuries back to you. You can be either conspirator, friend, fugitive seeking sanctuary, or victim doomed, for Dunnottar has seen all these types in its day. The atmosphere increases when the door is opened and you proceed into the cobbled alley-way into the castle. Even in daylight you can see the sky suddenly blacked out, and you expect men with torches or lanterns, and hear the clatter of arms.

But you come out into the daylight, and proceed either to take the air in the grassy court that is the centre of the castle or to explore and again re-create history. Not only because of this, but because, on a pleasant summer day, you can look out to sea, as, no doubt others did long ago when life in the castle was good. But your exploration will bring you to the Whigs' Vault. That is not so happy. At the time of the Covenanters—in 1685—Dunnottar was used as a prison. Into this black hole of Dunnottar were crammed between one hundred and fifty and two hundred men and women, packed like herring. They tried, some of them, to escape, and if you look at the way by which they were to get down to the shore, you will understand how desperate they were. But anything was better than that hell, and it was a hot hell for the weather was thunderously warm. Some died, others were recaptured and brought back to torture. All this in the cause of so-called religion.

But there have been ironic incidents in the history of Dunnottar. At the end of an eight months' siege, when the Cromwellians thought they had pinned in a big force, and that the Scottish Crown Regalia was in their hands once the castle fell —out marched less than two score men and the regalia was not with them.

That is Dunnottar, dark and light. Today it is an adjunct to an Aberdeen or Stonehaven holiday, an intelligent outing.

The castle is best seen slightly to the south of the rock on which it stands—160 feet above the sea, a curious and romantic-looking outline it has.

Leaving the sea for a time, let us turn inland. We shall now be in the long Howe of the Mearns, a great agricultural land. The shire takes a curious back leap and bites a chunk out of Aberdeenshire that includes the favourite village of Banchory and such show places in historic architecture as Crathes Castle. There are natives of the shire who, except for their birth certificates, would never realise that they are not natives of Aberdeenshire. One reason for that, of course, is that in speech and character the man of the Mearns and the Aberdeenshire man are closely allied. It is not until farther south, near and beyond the Angus border, that speech and, to some extent, characteristics begin to change.

The hinterland of the Mearns is closed in by hills which include some of the most favourite walking spots in eastern Scotland. If there is a road to the isles, there are roads to the Cairngorms, and among them are the Mearns and Angus glens—Isla, Clova, Esk and Prosen. One of the lower peaks between Kincardineshire and Aberdeenshire is a landmark for many a mile. That is Clochnaben. A great lump sticks out of the side of it like a carbuncle. The legend goes that the devil was pursuing an old wife whom he wanted to catch. But she eluded him, so the devil seized this great stone—you can see it for miles and miles—and threw it at the eluder, and it stuck in this hill. So, Clochnaben—the hill of the stone.

Below the hills lie the great stretches of agricultural lands, with no townships to speak of and very few villages. Great fields of cereals ripen and are cut and dealt with by the last word in up-to-date machinery. Here are almost miniature prairies. We are also coming towards and into the potato country, and again there are, in farms here and there, herds of the finest pedigree cattle.

One change a stranger might notice in the land, before he noticed anything in the people, is that the loam begins to redden.

The change which I myself always notice is that as the loam changes, the people of this countryside begin to become, not exactly pagan—I would not go so far as that—but they seem more and more of the soil. They have not the hardness of the men of Buchan, which seems to raise them above the soil somewhat, they have the softness of their land, and yet there is also a ruggedness which becomes most notice-able in their speech.

Was it partly out of this that, by ancestry, Robert Burns became the poet he was? His ancestors, his father, in fact, belonged to the Mearns. Also, out of the Mearns, to some extent, came one who has come to be regarded as the most notable modern Scottish novelist, he who called himself Lewis Grassic Gibbon, author of *Cloud Howe*, *Grey Granite* and *Sunset Song*. In a mixture such as I have described of softness and ruggedness, poetry and realism, both pretty intense, Gibbon seems to me to have extracted, in certain parts of his novels, the very essence of the Mearns border, that part which begins almost to be Angus.

So, with Burns, I feel that there was more than Ayrshire in his poetry. No doubt, in Ayrshire in his day and, especially, in some of the sets in which he delighted, there were "tough enough guys", but is there not in some of his satire the rough edge of the north-eastern tongue, and when he set to writing of nature, rather than the lasses—we shall give him the Ayrshire lasses, though the Mearns and Angus can do quite well in that way, too—he had this nearness to the soil, to its rough and its smooth.

We have wandered back to Laurencekirk, one of the centres of the farming region of the Mearns, with its mile-long single street, and from Laurencekirk to Bervie, with its old cross and love for a touch of pageantry now and again. Before we leave the Mearns we can wave one hand to the hills and another to the fishing villages low down on the seashore—Johnshaven and Gourdon, among the most truly-true fishing villages still left on the east coast of Scotland, great little communities in the veins of whose people the sea seems to course and beat.

All the superstitions of the sea-folk are here. A teacher in one of the schools there told me that, in class, whenever she mentioned the word "pig", all the little fingers were crossed. The pig is an unlucky animal to these fisher-folk. I have been told that if, by any chance, the men of a fishing vessel in these communities were to meet a pig on their way when they set out to sea, they would turn back and would not go fishing that day.

For many things, as you can see, I like the Howe o' the Mearns, and the people of its coast as well.

19

ANGUS AND DUNDEE

I do not forget Forfar, Brechin, Arbroath or even Dundee, but, for me, Angus largely means Montrose. I think it is one of the loveliest little towns in Scotland.

One writer on Scotland has said Montrose is "of little interest except to golfers". That is the view of one who does a whirlwind literary tour round the countryside, boring his nose into a guide-book to see where the next ruin is situated and annoying people by asking if they can explore their private dwelling because "it's such a fine specimen". This type also haunts graveyards, churches, for the wrong reason, and will say the most ridiculous things about a town which they have never tried to understand. One ruin one lunch is their ideal of a day's visit to anywhere.

Of course, we all care for storied antiquity, but it is not the first and last thing in a country. And I can say, from experience, that such writing has driven away, especially from Scotland, more people than it has attracted. These ordinary men and women come to see life and live it, not to spend their days among non-existent dead, and I mean non-existent dead.

Montrose may not be everyone's taste. It may not be clamorous with industry and palled with smoke, but it has enough industry to keep its inhabitants going. It is a bonnie town and a clean town, and it has one of the most remarkable main streets. That street is unusually wide, and reminds me almost equally of the *grande place* in some French town or of an English market town. The domestic architecture that borders the top end of this wide street, towards the church that stands as a centre-piece in this place, is both quaint and interesting, some of it standing with gables to the street. The church has a tower that is a landmark for many miles round.

The sea-front of Montrose is pleasant, and behind the town lies an estuary that, unfortunately, is sometimes emptied by the tide, but—on a fine day, when the tide is in and reflecting the blue sky and dappling white clouds in itself and its vista into the Forfarshire landscape—has a loveliness all its own.

Domestically, in house and people, Montrose is a model of quiet aliveness. The people are friendly and intelligent; the latter can be judged by the way in which they set forth the town's attractions to the visitor. It is a place of good and friendly hotels, and the people you meet in them make them even more so, because they are happy and content. At one time I had the idea that every man in Montrose was either a potato-grower or worked for one; I've discovered that that is not so, but there are lots of them.

I never visit Montrose without paying, also, a visit to Ferryden, the little fishing village that lies on the sea-point just south of the town. I like the long walk that leads down that other fine open street of the town, towards the rail and road bridges that cross the South Esk. And so to Ferryden.

One of my reasons for liking Ferryden is because I have been led to it by the work of that distinguished Scottish sculptor and native of Montrose, William Lamb, R.S.A. He has devoted a great part of his sculptor's life to depicting the Ferryden fisherman, who, of course, is also the typical Scottish fisherman, and, in his rhythm, his angle of approach, has caught the tang of the sea. In works suggesting storm and calm, Lamb's Ferryden folk give us a whole little world of experience. Montrose has also been depicted by another native and resident artist, Edward Baird, who has as personal an approach as Mr. Lamb. I quite understand that Montrose is a place that should produce artists and also keep them from going away from it.

Leaving Montrose, if we go west, we shall in less than ten miles come to Brechin. Brechin, in streets, is the opposite of Montrose. In this way it has its own picturesqueness. It has also a cathedral of the Decorated type, and, adjoining it, a curiosity, a round tower such as we might expect in Ireland, but not in Scotland. It is one of three in this country, built by Irish priests—one as far north as Orkney at Egilsay. The third is at Abernethy.

If we had gone south, along the coast, from Montrose we should have passed the lovely sands of Lunan Bay, with the Red Castle, standing behind and above them— a lovely stretch of sand—and so to Arbroath. Arbroath always strikes me as a curious mixture of a sea and inland town. If you come to it from inland you are surprised to find the sea. When you leave the sea you are surprised how soon you seem to get away from all feeling of it. I like the curious streets, in which you go through pends and round corners. Motorists find it a trying place in which to find their way. Arbroath is another little centre of Scottish art, for, at the mansion of Hospitalfield, there has for some time now been established a school of art, endowed. The students who have come from this school in recent years have been making their mark. That, in part, has been due to the tutelage and guidance of one of the most notable minds and fancies in Scottish art of the last generation—and a half—shall we say?—James Cowie, R.S.A. This is all part of the Scottish renaissance.

Cutting back inland on our tracks, we come to Forfar, and it is not very different from these other little Angus towns, perhaps even a little less interesting. Its chief natural charm is the loch on its outskirts, a haunt of the pursuer of wildfowl, and its landmark is a tower on a hill to the east of the town. This tower has its counterpart on an answering distant eminence.

There is one thing in Forfar that everyone ought to see, and how few, I find, even know of it. It has greatly to do with a certain aspect of Scottish art. In the Lowson Memorial Church, on the comparative outskirts of the town, there is a window by one whom I have already mentioned—Scotland's most famous stained glass artist, Dr. Douglas Strachan—the name is usually pronounced Straan. This is an Apocalyptic window, and, if you ask at the manse, you will get a key to the themes and lights. As with other windows of his which Scotland possesses, there is not only metaphysic, but, it seems to me, more than a touch of mysticism. That is the great thing about Strachan. There is not only the surface beauty of his glass, but he has the high seriousness, the depth and burning fervour of the true artist's vision. This window, I think, represents him at his all-round best. So few seem to know of it and, so often, of Douglas Strachan, apart from the windows of which I have told you—the Scottish War Shrine at Edinburgh Castle—and at such places as King's and Marischal Colleges, Aberdeen.

Not a few people who go to Forfar are, of course, making their way to Kirriemuir, or "Thrums", as it has been known since James Matthew Barrie immortalised it. The road from Forfar to "Kirrie"—which is the other pet name of this famous little town—is unlike most Angus roads. It is bare, whereas one of the joys of travelling by road in Angus is the constant light and shade of so many miles of its tree-bordered highways. Most of these parts of the roads are part of the many arboreal estates which the county contains.

And so we come to Kirrie on its height. The way climbs up a steep street, and, when you have reached the centre of the town, it is difficult to know which way to go for this or that. This is one of the quaintest centres of a town that I know. It puzzles and fascinates, and, in that way, is rather like the character, literary and otherwise, of its most famous son, the man who has made part of the town's fortune—if it has any—James Barrie.

If you ask the way, you are answered in what I would call a thick but rich accent, rather inclined to the guttural. But it is an attractive accent to me; you feel in it both the rugged independence, and yet, at the same time, the kindliness of the Angus folk, for here, in Kirrie, I think we have, almost more than in most Angus places, the meeting of the country and the town, and the influence of the not-so-far-off hills is added.

If all these influences went to the making of J. M. Barrie, then it explains a lot. There was the vigour with which he pursued his career in its earlier days—he was too elusive for a new edition of Smiles's *Self-Help*, but he had that spirit in him. There was the sly or pawky humour, and the Kirrie folk still have that. And there was the touch of faery. That, I think, came from the not-so-far-off-hills, for Kirrie is the gateway to more than one of those lovely, but not too wild, glens that are part of the Angus hinterland. From there, I think, came, *The Little Minister* and, better still, "Farewell, Miss Julie Logan". When the latter was written I know not for sure, but I remember when I first read it in a *Times*, at Christmas, thinking it must be a winter sunset song or a harking back to something of a sunrise. It is no noonday story.

But there is no doubt that Kirrie is haunted, and not only for visitors, by the people of *A Window in Thrums*, not so much by the folk of "Auld Licht Idylls". They were prototypes of people you will still find in Kirrie today. Folk in such places as this do not change so rapidly as all that; character stays.

When I went to the Barrie house, that humble little place, I was most interested of all in the wash-house that was the scene of Barrie's earliest exploits in the stuff of the theatre. That was because I had had exactly the same sort of experience myself, with one whom, I think, if he had not died so young, might have been another J. M. B. It was this experience that made me understand a great deal.

Our theatre was in an attic, and it was only a little contrivance, as were all the characters who walked its stage, one of the most magical I have ever known in half a century of theatre-going. The theatre was candle-lit, and in the dark beyond the candles I used to sit while my mate contrived half a dozen voices. The plays were melodramas of the most violent type, the more picaresque of them the result of voracious reading of *Jack Harkaway*, or some such periodical. Apart from the theatre, there were the magazines which we "printed", by pencil, and exchanged. This other Barrie had the greatest ideas. Although he and I saw one another almost daily, we wrote secret notes, and we used to contrive to hide them behind a loose stone at the corner of a ruined wall. I never pass the spot, even nowadays, nearly fifty years after, but I smile and remember. That I think was distinctly Barrie-ish. And that was what has held me in that backyard in Thrums when other places of greater import historically have got only a glance and away.

From Thrums—and what a change—to Dundee. My favourite way is by the bus that takes you along by the walls of Glamis and on to backlands behind Dundee that I find so few people who do not belong to Dundee do not know—the countryside of the Sidlaw hills. When one thinks how near Juteopolis is, one cannot but appreciate more the comparative remoteness of this pleasant countryside.

Dundee is another place that seems to scare the scouting literary traveller in Scotland. They mutter something about it having few or no features of interest, and then they run to the nearest ruin or into the hills. On the surface, Dundee is not a very attractive town; but you must get beneath the surface for the best of almost any place. I will say that Dundee is, perhaps, best seen at a distance; say from

10

the other side of the Tay on a fine day, or at evening when the city, climbing up its hills, and ending at the Law, sends up its lazy smoke. But Dundee has been, as it is today, always an important place in Scotland, and, with one thing more it will, in my idea, take a very important part in the future development of Scotland, and will itself become a new place in certain ways.

Dundee must have a road bridge over the Tay. The projected road bridge over the Forth will, of course, be complementary, but, I think, a bridge over the Tay is even more needed. At present, because of this lack, Dundee is something of a dead end. Either the ferry or the train or the detour by Perth must take you south from Dundee. This, I think, has had an effect not only on the industrial aspect of Dundee, but, curious as it may seem, on its cultural side. Dundee, culturally, stands far higher than it did some years ago, but it could be better still. And Dundee has among it men and women who have the push and go to get what they want and what Dundee needs.

Dundee is not exactly looked upon as a Royal city, but it has always been; and today, it should be remembered, it is the city that is the capital of the shire to which her Majesty the Queen belongs, and almost always when she is at Glamis she finds one reason or another for slipping into Dundee for some piece of good work.

There, on occasion, you would find the father of the Queen, the late Earl of Strathmore. I remember meeting him at a certain luncheon there. It was given to recognise the good work of one who had done much for Dundee. I sat next the Earl of Strathmore and, as the praises were being poured out on this good citizen, I was amazed to see that the object of the praise kept smiling and nodding his head, as if in complete accord with all that was being said. I said to Lord Strathmore that the good citizen seemed to be rather lapping it up. "Not he," said the Earl quietly, behind his hand. "He's stone deaf; doesn't know a word that's being said."

Dundee's connection with Royalty began, it is thought, as far back as Malcolm Canmore, and through many centuries that Royal connection has continued. The pity is that almost every material link with Royalty through these centuries has gone. All the Stewart kings paid several visits to the town, and important work was done there by several of them. One of the kings who seemed to have a fancy for the place was James V, and from childhood to his death he was a frequent visitor, often staying for quite long periods. His daughter, Mary of Scots, shared her father's fancy, and gave to the city the orchard of the Franciscan monastery, now the Howff of Dundee. Here James VI held fierce altercation on religious matters with an eminent churchman, Andrew Melville. Charles II was in Dundee on several important occasions, and the Old Chevalier, James VIII—we are in Scotland—here was given public proofs of loyalty. And then, for quite a long time, Royal visits ceased, the Hanoverians had other things to do. Scotland was only a remote province to them.

Before she found and took up residence at Balmoral, Queen Victoria made Dundee her landing-place after the sea voyage from London. That was in September 1844. She came in the yacht *Victoria and Albert*, along with Prince Albert and the Princess Royal. That was, perhaps, Dundee's most ceremonial Royal visit, and though it is not the original arch, there is an archway still to be seen at the harbour that was an outcome of this visit. When next Victoria came it was to make use for travelling south of the ill-fated Tay bridge. That was in June 1879. The bridge had been opened in May 1878.

On December 28, in the same year as the queen's visit, occurred the disaster, and it is an event that still can make Scotland shudder. When you come across the Tay by the new bridge, especially on a stormy night, you can hardly help thinking of that terrible December night. The lights of the train gleam on the water that seems very near to the rails on which your carriage moves along. And, always, whether you can see them or not, you are aware of those piers of the first bridge, which stand there like a memorial to the victims of what still must rank as Scotland's worst railway disaster.

No one really saw what happened on that dark and stormy night, but there was terrible fear among those who were watching and could almost guess the worst. Dr. A. M. Millar in his book, *Haunted Dundee*, tells of a party in a house in Magdalen Green, who dimmed the light of the room in which they were sitting, after they had heard a crash. They saw what they took to be the lights of the train coming from Fife. There was an unusual gust of wind and "three separate streams of fire" descended from the height of the bridge and disappeared in the water. Brave work was done by railway officials—who made their way from the Dundee side, along the bridge (think of the conditions) until they saw that some of the girders had definitely disappeared—and by those on board the ferry boat, *Dundee*, which ventured out to look for survivors. None was found; the tale is still incomplete.

It was estimated that some eighty people lost their lives, and those of an older generation always added the touch of pathos as they told you what they knew of the story—a bride and bridegroom returning from their honeymoon were among those lost.

One curious aftermath Dr. Millar relates. The engine of the train was twice fished up from the waters of the Tay and twice sank. After a third raising it was finally beached, put on the rails and towed to Glasgow. For nearly a quarter of a century after it continued in commission. How many would know the history of the locomotive that was drawing them!

There is one other curious connection between Dundee and storm and bravery that few people remember now. The ship to which Grace Darling and her father rowed on their errand of mercy, in September 1838, was the Dundee-built *Forfarshire*, sailing from Dundee to Hull. They saved nine. Dundee acknowledged the work of the Darlings by a public subscription, and a portrait of the heroine—commissioned at the time—hangs in Dundee's art gallery. She died four years after her famous act, at the age of twenty-six.

Mention of Dundee's art gallery reminds us that that gallery has been improving year by year, and from the Dundee area are emanating some of the more distinguished Scottish artists of today. In the arts, Dundee for a time languished sadly in the matter of the theatre, but that, too, has improved. Where music is concerned Dundee, in its huge Caird Hall, hears some of the greatest orchestras and solo musicians of the world.

Dundee is half a university town; it houses the college that is attached to the University of St. Andrews. Economics as a serious study also find a place in Dundee.

It has been said that part of the trouble with Dundee—whose main industrial stay was, and still is, the jute and linen trade—was that there was no middle class. There were only the jute nabobs and their workers. That is not the case now. There is a happy medium.

If Dundee has no great urban features—there is the auld steeple or, more officially, the tower of St. Mary, which is likely to have been built towards the close of the fifteenth century—it has, just beyond its western fringe, one of the loveliest outlooks in lowland Scotland. This is the famous Carse of Gowrie, which is also the course of the Tay on its first way from, or its last way to, the sea. The Carse takes everyone's fancy, and even the passer-by, as he crosses the Tay bridge on his way to the north, looks—in summer or winter, and, particularly, in spring and autumn, and towards the close of a day—to see how the Carse is looking. He is seldom unrewarded. There is vista, there is colour. But there is more to the Carse than just that. It is a great piece of agricultural country, and its inhabitants not only know the beauty and usefulness of their home, but can express their views on them. In the Carse is some of the best character in central Scotland. Almost, it would seem, they are a people by themselves. And yet, I have found them allied to those farther north in this varied county we have just passed through.

Angus has passed into Scottish literature through the work of one of Scotland's poetesses—Violet Jacob—in something of the same way in which Aberdeenshire has done through Charles Murray. There are, again, poems of Violet Jacob which are household poems. Every man, woman and child knows them, and many by heart. There's "Tam i' the Kirk":

> Oh, Jean, my Jean, when the bell ca's the congregation
>   Owre valley an' hill wi' the ding frae its iron mou',
> When a'body's thochts is set on his ain salvation,
>   Mine's set on you.

Most Scots will recite that to you. It's almost too well known. For me, I find in some of the vignettes that occur in her poems real glints of Angus. Such as this from "The Neep-fields by the Sea":

> The lang lift lies abune the warld,
> On ilka windless day
> The ships creep doon the ocean line
> Sma on the band o' grey;
> An' the lang sigh heaved upon the sand
> Comes pechin' up to me
> And speils the cliffs tae whaur ye stand
> I' the neep-fields by the sea.

And as we cross the Tay bridge to Fife, we look, not only up the Carse of Gowrie, but down towards the mouth of the Tay. Angus ends in sand, as Fife begins with it. The Tay divides them, and so do other matters, but, already, in Dundee, in its running up the scale, the speech of Dundee has anticipated something of the accent of the Kingdom. At any rate, "Ae think so", as the Dundonian would say in one of his most characteristic utterances.

20

THE KINGDOM

"TAK' awa' Fife," said a Fifer to me, "an' whit's left? Juist Scotland."

It was said with a twinkle, but I think there was a touch of seriousness behind the utterance. Fife believes in its particular difference. The Kingdom of Fife, it is always called, and if I were to judge from train and bus journeys, from meals in hotels and drinks in bars, if this kingdom has a king, his name is Agriculture. This is not unusual in Scotland, but in Fife they seem to eat, smoke, drink and even practise agriculture. They have a village whose name suggest a queen for their king—Ceres. But, of course, that is not all there is in Fife. They can provide diamonds for their queen—black ones—coal. They can provide silver for her—fish. And gold? The Fifers know what to do with that.

Fifeshire is a broad peninsula. It shares, with Angus, the Tay as far as Magdrum; it shares the Forth to just beyond Kincardine, but has the stretch of the North Sea between Fifeness and Tayport to itself. On its western border it has hills, some of which it shares, some of which it does not. Between the hills and the sea lies a great, fertile and, in parts, industrial plain.

Fifeshire has had several histories—geological, folk, royal, religious, agricultural and industrial. There is no gainsaying the interest of the Kingdom. The name of Kingdom may, in very great ancientry, have been derived from the fact that the region was one of the kingdoms of the Picts. The probability of this would be, in part, due to its peninsular form, and its cutting off by its western hill border. It has changed its boundary shape several times. At one time Kinross was part of Fife; at another, part of Fife was transferred to Kinross; while, at yet another, part of Perthshire was transferred to Fife and vice versa.

Industrially, also, Fifeshire has known its changes. These have already been hinted at. Before the Clyde and the West became important, through trade with America and other lands across the Atlantic, Fifeshire had an importance it lost but has slightly regained. Our trade then was with Scandinavia, with Germany and the Lowlands low.

Fifeshire was also a "Kingdom" before Midlothian, and Dunfermline was the Royal capital before Edinburgh. But even after Dunedin became the dwelling place of kings there was much traffic across the Forth between Edinburgh and Fife. It is the cradle of the history of united Scotland; it saw the start of Scottish academic history —at St. Andrews; and Scottish architecture and Scottish literature have strong and lovely roots in Fifeshire. And, last as well as first, there is agriculture—cereals and stock.

Pleasant but not very remarkable is the journey from Newburgh towards St. Andrews, but as we pass through Leuchars, let us stop a moment to look at that Norman apse of the church. You will not find much else in Leuchars and, except that we know that at Guardbridge its mill is providing employment—and, of course, paper—we are soon at St. Andrews. This Scottish Oxford is so many other things besides, that it is almost difficult to sort them out. You cannot, however, escape the university. If you are there in term time the red gowns—here, unlike Aberdeen, compulsory wear for classes—flit like scarlet butterflies about the grey streets and crowd the teashops, bookshops and along the ways by the sea. Yes, I suppose the university and all that goes along with it are really St. Andrews.

Not everyone would agree, for St. Andrews in these days has several strata of population. Some will tell you, as they have told me, that the university and every-thing connected with it are "just a nuisance". These are the "residents", those who belong to St. Andrews, and those who have come to live there, mostly, one suspects, because of the golf. For its size St. Andrews is about the least industrial town in Scotland. In that way it is almost unique in Scotland, though there are quite a few like it over the Border. It is more and more becoming a residential town. I do not much like many of them, but I rather envy them. But, if the residents do not like the university and its denizens, what do they think of the summer visitors? For St. Andrews is quite a resort nowadays. It has its bathing, it has its little—very little— theatre and it has its concert party. Not all its visitors, however, come there for the golf and the summer fun. I have met not a few who have come there because of the history that cannot be dismissed from the mind in this town. Its very stones breathe history, and it is not St. Andrews—but national, Scottish—history and, at its ugliest, religious history.

In a certain way the Reformation in Scotland began in St. Andrews. It is even claimed that a certain aspect of Scottish nationality began here. You will see a tower in the town, that of St. Regulus or Rule. Legend had it—though not so much now—that this tower was built somewhere about the fourth century by this St. Regulus, who came from the east and bore with him the relics of St. Andrew, Scotland's patron saint. Then this settlement was known as Kilrymont.

As to the Reformation, the chapel of the Black Friars, not much of a relic, was part of a monastery in which there dwelt a monk of dark renown. He it was who acted as accuser of Patrick Hamilton, a Reformation pioneer. On that accusation

Hamilton, in the year 1528, was burned at the stake. More than the faggots were set aflame that day, and St. Andrews was to see a great deal of the Reformation's evil side, and to hear its great protagonist, John Knox, at his preaching best—and worst.

The cathedral, the castle and St. Mary's College, with St. Salvator's and the Town Church, are the repositories of much of St. Andrews history.

The cathedral is a "poor remains". That, in part, was due to the zeal of the Reformers—we have in Scotland so many remains of this kind, and for the same reason. But the cathedral must have been a glorious place in its day, and kings and queens came there for their orisons.

The castle is the place which has the chief tales of blood and fire, tales that have never yet been fully exploited by Scottish writers. It is a curious fact that the part of the castle that remains is the one which saw the episodes that stand out in Scottish religious history. In March 1545 was burned there George Wishart, who, had he been of the Old Religion, would most certainly have been canonised. This austere yet likable zealot was a man who won Knox's admiration as few did, and yet, it is possible that in St. Andrews there was a scene between Knox and Wishart that repeated the scene when, in the High Priest's hall, the cock crew thrice and Peter went out and wept bitterly. Peter founded his church, and Knox, too, was to all intents and purposes the founder of another.

Cardinal Beaton it was who ordered the death of Wishart, and three months after the burning, from the window through which he had watched Wishart's death, the Cardinal's mutilated body was hung for the delectation of people who loved him not. There could have been no greater contrast between two men than that between austerity Wishart and the luxurious and sensual Beaton.

Most people who go to the castle go also to the bottle-dungeon, a companion to the chamber at Dunnottar. It used to be quite one of the grim amusements of St. Andrews to listen to the guide, who, as he swung a lantern mechanically round and round the dungeon, as mechanically but cheerfully repeated the story of the dungeon's evil days.

St. Andrews, almost more than any other place except Edinburgh, is haunted by the memory, not the spirit, of John Knox. Here in the parish church he would deliver one of his thundering sermons. The pulpit of that day and the hour-glass— how often was it turned during one sermon?—are preserved in the college church. From St. Andrews Knox was sent for those long weary months to the French galleys—how his opponents must have wished it had been to the gallows! He tells how, once, the galleys came so near that he could see St. Andrews plain. That must have been a moment that nearly broke that stout, bitter heart.

There is one other grim tale that has its centre in St. Andrews. In May 1679 Archbishop Sharp, who has been called "the betrayer", was murdered on Magus

Moor, just outside St. Andrews. It was a ghastly deed, whatever Sharp may have been, and performed in view of his daughter.

Although the university means so much in St. Andrews—it is the oldest of the Scottish universities—there is not so much that is notable about its material aspect; pleasant, yes, but not so notable.

Yet it is the university atmosphere, coupled with the general atmosphere and the setting of the town, that has evoked in so many a student a feeling of the strongest nostalgia. Every student after he has gone down speaks of "St. A." in a way that can make those who never were students there almost wish they had been. Two men have said their say in verse on the matter and the place. Wrote Robert Fuller Murray:

> O dear St. Andrew's Bay,
>   Winter or Spring,
> Gives not nor takes away
>   Memories that cling
>
> All round thy girdling reefs,
>   That walk my shore,
> Memories of joys and griefs
>   Ours evermore.

And W. Keith Leask:

> One has said that, if his heart
> Could like the Queen's that Calais bore,
> Bear one loved name, that could but part
>   From him with life and not before;
>   A name that only brought the more
> The years within the old grey town,
>   The Castle, Links, the sea and shore—
>   The City of the Scarlet Gown,
> Then on his heart that name should be
> St. Andrews by the Northern Sea.

Yes, I am afraid that, after all, it is not the residents who make St. Andrews what it is. It is the scarlet gown, the wide and lovely North and South Streets, the little touches of antiquity of, say, the Priory arch down at the Pends, and the history. That is unless, of course, St. Andrews means to you a good hotel and a good game of golf on one of the three courses, or an exciting golf championship meeting. Which is to say, that St. Andrews can be many things to many men, a lucky state for any town to be in.

So we go up and out of St. Andrews and on around Fife Ness, and there we come to a series of seaside places that have won fame with and through the artists and as summer haunts. Crail, Anstruther, Pittenweem, St. Monance. They are all picturesque places and their houses are well preserved. Crail is the best haunt, perhaps, of the lover of unimportant but taking antiquity. It has a fine tolbooth and a church with details of interest. So with the houses. Few parts of the coast and its villages have been so often transferred to canvas or cartridge paper. In fact, as I have suggested in connection with Fraserburgh, they have been a little overdone, and a change would do no harm.

Elie passed, we come to Largo, a pleasant little place, one of whose chief claims to fame is that it was the birthplace of Alexander Selkirk, the rover on whom was founded the immortal Robinson Crusoe. Largo is not forgetful of that fact, and you will find an inn of the name and, in a niche on its wall, a figure of Robinson in the coat of his island garb, holding a musket and looking, looking, like Sister Anne, to see if there is anyone coming.

By Leven, Buckhaven—"Buckein"—Wemyss, Dysart of the carls and of interest to the antiquarian in its crooked streets and buildings, to Kirkcaldy. Kirkcaldy is, as it were, the Glasgow of Fifeshire. It has not, like St. Andrews or Dunfermline, much to offer the historian or the antiquarian, but it is a busy industrial centre. One of its main industries is linoleum, and the visitor is aware of this as soon as he enters the town—just as you become aware when you enter Aberdeen station that fish is a main industry there—by the all-pervading smell of size. The inhabitants are un-aware of this aroma, and soon the visitor becomes like the native. The linoleum industry was one hundred years old in 1947. But if Kirkcaldy has no great matter of architecture to offer the mind of that type, it has a pleasant lot of folk, and I have met not a few of them in visits over a long number of years. It is a very old settlement, with traditions going back, says one of its historians, to Columba's time. This long straggling town—its high street is reputed to be four miles in length—borders on the Forth, and a walk along its front on a fine day is a relaxation from its, not exactly drabness, but some lack of distinction.

Kirkcaldy can also boast a name or two. Here Adam Smith, the author of *Wealth of Nations* and founder of the science of political economy was born; here Thomas Carlyle spent part of his teaching days. And—a tender attachment—in the town's graveyard is a little grave with a little white cross. Here lies "Pet Marjorie", Marjorie Fleming, that most adorable of child prodigies, friend of Sir Walter Scott. She is enshrined for ever in Dr. John Brown's essay upon her, and in her own work that brings both tears and laughter as you read it.

Before we take the Forthside way to the crossing at Queensferry, let us go inland for a visit or two. Up to now we have held rather closely to the coast. There is Cupar, the county town, to be visited. It is a pleasant town, pleasantly set in char-acteristic Fife scenery of the milder kind. It has long been a seat of justice, and still is, and from that comes the Fife proverb, with a sting in it: "He that will to Cupar, maun to Cupar". Like Aberdeen, Cupar has a history of mystery and morality plays. It is an old place and still today a busy one. Nearer the Fife border is a small town, set in fertile country and, like Cupar, "rale busy", whose name, with its gutturals is one of the speech teasers given to Englishmen—Auchtermuchty. At the foot of the East Lomond Hill stands Falkland Palace, for long a seat of Scottish kings—James V died there, soon after he had heard of the birth of that daughter who was to stir the world for centuries, Mary Queen of Scots. The palace has been restored. It is a piece of rather fine renaissance work, attached as in other buildings of its type, to a sterner gate-house.

We could slip across the border into Kinross for an hour or two, there to visit Loch Leven, with its island and its castle. Here was enacted one of the most romantic dramas of the many which made up the life of Mary Queen of Scots. Here she was imprisoned. From here, by the good graces and clever, daring work of men who loved her enough to risk all for her sake, she escaped. It is another tale that still waits its best telling, not in the confines of history, but in the imaginative freedom of drama or the novel.

So we come to one of the most storied towns in Scotland, one that still wears its past with something of an air, even if it does not make the most of its modern good fortune—the town of Dunfermline. But before we pass on to pearls and rubies, let us remember black diamonds. We have not visited the mining centres of Fife, important as they may be, because, they are, like mining places everywhere, of interest only to those who live in them, and, alas, so often, not even to them. When, O when, will the men who—along with their greatest industrial compeers, the men of agriculture—matter most, be given a decent deal in housing and amenities? We demand so much from them. In return, we give so little that will make their lives worth living above ground and away from the ground. Slag heaps will never be as beautiful as the Cairngorms, no matter how high they grow, nor will middens, as middens, ever blossom like the rose.

Why all this out of black diamonds and Dunfermline? Because in Dunfermline was started Scotland's coal industry, as far away as 1391. It was a matter of monks and their monastery, and remained so for long. Even when coal was freed from the religious ban, as it were, it was long before the country took to it as fuel. This country—and England—must be naturally very conservative. One remembers how long it was after its introduction before the country took to that now staple food, the potato.

But coal was a minor matter in Dunfermline's early history, in comparison to what it eventually became in that of Fife; yet it is interesting.

The first line of the famous ballad of Sir Patrick Spens always seems to me to epitomise the Dunfermline of Royal and colourful days. "The king sits in Dunfermline toun sipping the bluid-red wine." There is magic in that line. In the first place, it begins the ballad with a snap that the modern journalist might envy and would do well to emulate. There is next the picture of royalty at ease and in luxury. Then, thirdly, there is the epithet "bluid-red". That introduces what is, perhaps, the central magic of the line—the rich touch of colour, a colour that accords with Royalty and its surroundings in those days—the days of cramasie in opposition to the white of linen, and in linen you have again Dunfermline.

The first off-go of Dunfermline's days of royal history seems to me like a blend of tapestry and missal. Malcolm Canmore, the king, is in himself comparatively a shadowy figure compared with that of his queen, that royal lady who was eventually canonised and deserved the sainthood more than the husband for whom, legend says, her bones and spirit cried out aloud. It was a great day for Scotland as well as Dunfermline when Malcolm—son of that Duncan whom, we can take it, Macbeth slew—was wed to Margaret. It is likely that Malcolm, then a man of forty, was more warrior than scholar, if he was the latter at all. Margaret was then only into her twenties, and there is little doubt, in spite of the admiration with which her historian, Bishop Turgot, described her life—just as Adamnan did in the case of St. Columba—that she had beauty of person as well as of mind and spirit. But she had her pride in the royal state as well as her ideas of what was fit for the worship of God, and so was begun the building of the Abbey of Dunfermline, which came in time to be a place of splendour as well as of sanctity.

That was in keeping with Margaret as queen and saint. The court of Malcolm and Margaret was a truly royal court. Margaret herself dressed magnificently, and she saw to it that those around her did the same. Palace as well as abbey had their gold and silver, vessels in the one and all the paraphernalia of the Mass in the other. And besides precious metals there were all the precious stones that could be gathered. Added to religion there was what there could be of learning as well, something that could not be lost, whatever happened.

> Matters of might and venery
> Go out upon their tides,
> But beauty born of mind and soul
> When these are sped abides.

The loveliness and dignity and high moral of the court of Margaret and Malcolm endured for some twenty and more years. Then the warrior Malcolm set out for a battle that was of his own desire, at Alnwick in Northumberland. Margaret at this time was at Edinburgh. At Alnwick, in 1093, Malcolm and his eldest son, Edward, were killed. The queen was ill. The news had to be broken to her. This task was entrusted to the youngest of her six sons, Ethelred, a mere boy. The scene is one of intense and tragic drama. The boy hesitated, but Margaret knew, and knew also that her life was ended. And so she died. While she was dying, Malcolm's brother,

Donalbain, was besieging the castle in which she lay. After her death her body was lowered down that fiercesome rock. Mist hid the act from Donalbain and his men. She was taken back to Dunfermline and there, before the altar of the abbey, she was buried. The body of Malcolm and that of his son Edward were brought from Northumberland for burial in the same place.

One hundred and fifty-seven years later, from Rome came the order for Margaret's canonisation. She had for long won the adoration of the faithful, and this order was merely official confirmation of what already existed.

Then comes the penultimate drama—according to legend—in Margaret's history. This drama had gone on after death. It was decided to remove her body to a resting place, in the abbey, considered more fitting. What remained of that body was enclosed in a silver casket, made richer, as she would have desired, with gold and precious stones. But re-burial was more easily ordered than done. The bearers of the casket stopped in their procession. The casket had become too heavy for them to carry. Even with extra help it could not be borne. Suddenly a voice cried out: "The Queen will not stir till equal honours are performed to her husband". The grave of Malcolm was opened, his bones laid in the casket with those of the queen and saint. The double burden lightened, and the two, reunited long after death, were buried in the choir of the abbey. An epilogue to this was the canonisation of Malcolm some months after, which seems to have been less a desert than a curious tribute to his queen, faithful in life and after death.

But even that was not the end. Mary of Scots feared what, in the zealous desecration of the Reformation, might happen to the relics of one so worshipped by the faithful of the Old Religion. In 1560 the casket was taken to Edinburgh, where it remained for seven years. In 1567 it was returned to Dunfermline. In 1597 it was removed again, this time to Belgium, and later to France. At the time of the French Revolution the casket went wandering and was lost. Some relics of her remains and is venerated, not least in the yearly celebration of her festival at Dunfermline.

After the death of Malcolm and Margaret the glory of Dunfermline did not die. But, in 1292, Edward I, who hated the Scots as much as they did him, set fire to the royal palace. This act was part of the debt that was recovered at Bannockburn. Robert the Bruce, Edward's conqueror, also found burial in Dunfermline, but he was, otherwise, never associated with the town as were Malcolm and Margaret.

It is not possible here to follow all the windings and workings of Scottish royal history which are associated with Dunfermline. But we must say something of two poets, one of whom was a king. The king was James I, who was born at Dunfermline in 1394. All the world knows the story of his being sent into captivity in England as a boy of eleven. There he remained for eighteen years until, in 1424, he came back to Scotland, bringing with him, as wife, Lady Joan Beaufort, whose beauty, seen from the window of his prison, turned him into a poet, evoked the lines that today still ring fresh and lovely with love.

The scene is set with simple but colourful touches, like a vignette from an old master:

> Now there was maid fast by the touris wall
> A garden fair, and in the corneris set
> Ane herebere grene with wandis long and small,
> Railit about, and so with treis set
> Was all the place, and hawthorn heis knet,
> That lyf was non walking there forbye
> That mycht within scarce any wight aspy.

Then comes the revelation and the love at first sight:

> And there-with kest I doun mine eye again,
> Where as I saw, walking under the tower,
> Full secretly new comen her to pleyne,
> The fairest or the freshest yonge flower
> That ever I saw, me thought, before that hour,
> For which sudden abate, anon stert
> The blude of all my body to my heart.

> And though I stude abasit tho a lite,
> No wonder was; for-why my wittis all
> Were so ourcome with plesance and delight,
> Only throw latting of mine eyen fall,
> That suddenly my heart became her thrall
> For ever, of free will; for of menace
> There was no token in her swete face.

That was the beginning; and we all know the end—in 1437—not in Dunfermline, but in Perth, when James was murdered by the men he had roused against him by acts which were not really part of his true nature—the poet, but part of the policy he was forced to pursue as a king.

But James was not the only poet connected with Dunfermline in this century. I have never yet walked the pleasance of Pittencrieff but I have felt the presence or influence of Maister Robert Henryson. In the poem by that greater poet, William Dunbar, "Lament for the Makaris", Henryson's name is linked with Dunfermline —and death:

> In Dunfermline he has done roune
> With Maister Robert Henryson. . . .

But it is not of the dead Henryson one thinks in Pittencrieff, but of a gentle, scholarly figure walking the paths beneath the trees, his mind busy with the making of his verses. He united in his personality the best of the time—the sweetness of rhyme and the seriousness of pure religion. I think he must have been one of the most likely to be loved and admired men of his own or any time. It comes out in his poetry; there is an adumbration of it in the poem by Dunbar. Of many, Dunfermline has no lovelier ghost than that of Robert Henryson. He was a moralist—but not odiously so—and even when he talked of Dunfermline toun it was to point a moral, and at any time—no doubt—even the people of Dunfermline could do with something of that, especially when so gently and sweetly said.

Waiting for us behind all this history—and, once again, the whole of that history cannot be told here—is the Abbey, which still retains in its interior an atmosphere that can set you apart from the ordinary life of today. This begins in its architecture, which combines Gothic and Anglo-Norman, and continues in the history of which we cannot be unaware. Here, as in Iona, we cannot forget the royal dust that, no matter how ideas and attitudes change, still has an effect upon our minds and imaginations. This finds a kind of culmination in the tomb of Bruce. Incidentally, in this abbey again is a lovely example in stained-glass of the colour-genius of Douglas Strachan. Outside, as you take your way about, you will find such lovely corners —ruins though they be—as the Abbey Gatehouse and Refectory.

And as you take your way farther about, you will come upon, in one of the streets of small houses in Dunfermline, a little corner house. It stands between Moodie Street and Priory Lane. Here was born one, Andrew Carnegie. He was, appropriately enough for so devoted a son of Dunfermline, the child of a weaver. His mother was as true a Scot as ever walked and breathed. Like so many famous men, Scots especially, Carnegie was his mother's son. Barrie in one way, Carnegie in another, both were that. Carnegie went to the United States and amassed a millionaire fortune. That, however, was not the important thing: so many men have amassed millionaire fortunes and have never been heard of, except to their bankers and stockbrokers and, of course, lawyers. It was what Carnegie did with those millions that mattered and has made him a name in Scotland and far beyond. Had it not been for the academic benefactions of Andrew Carnegie, there are many Scotsmen, high in office, who would never have been able to do what they have done for the country and the Empire, for learning and for religion. So, too, apart from the universities, Carnegie money has endowed Scottish libraries and set many young minds upon roads they might not otherwise have travelled.

It is understandable that especially did he endow Dunfermline. A technical school, a school of music, baths and gymnasium, the policies of Pittencrieff—there is no end, it would seem, to what Carnegie did for Dunfermline. The question is—has Dunfermline responded as it should? There are few towns so endowed. Here can be heard the finest music and musicians at a minimum cost. Do the people of Dunfermline flock to hear them?

In its many outlets and aids the Carnegie Trust has been of value, not only to Scotland, but to the world. In the realm of music alone there are works being performed today which might never have known the light of day otherwise. There are matters of science which might never have been developed. All this was not just the outcome of a rich man's *largesse*, it was part of the philosophy of a man who could not help becoming rich and who thought inordinate riches, not used in the best way and to the advantage of the most, a sin against the Holy Ghost. This tribute, which is personal as well as general, is part of my return for what the Carnegie Trust has done for me. But for its aid I might have stood at the gates of my university, a different version of "Love Locked Out"—love of learning, I mean. And I am only one of many thousands.

The ancient Dunfermline merges gradually into the modern Rosyth, one of Britain's great naval dockyards, and every now and again a matter of grave controversy for Scotland and Forthside. We shall leave it at that.

We have come back to Kirkcaldy and the Forth. In happy days, when Kirkcaldy was one of my hunting grounds, I was never happier there than when, in the sunshine, I set off down the way by Kinghorn, Burntisland and Inverkeithing to Queensferry. As a person thirled to romance and history it was a journey that filled my head with pictures and thoughts. The way, today, is not all lovely, but when I had the Forth as near companion, that was enough. It was not only all that belonged to this historic water-way that entranced me, but the sight of the Forth itself. I have looked at it and been on it in all weathers. A bad sailor and a choppy Forth are a wretched pair. A fine day and a good ship make a day's delight. In appearance, too, the Forth has its pleasures. There are days when even its slate-grey waters bring thoughts of doul and woe that were. There are, however, plenty of days when the Forth seems like a pavement of violets, fit for some lovely queen to tread upon. And always there are its distances. In these are its islands—from the Isle of May, and its lighthouse, at the neuk; Inchkeith and, most historic, Inchcolm with its ruined abbey. Always, upon the farther shore, is the Lothians outline that includes Auld Reekie, and from that distance never better named.

Down the Forthside then we go, remembering that at Kinghorn is King Alexander's Crag, over which one dark night in 1286 went King Alexander III and his horse. Burntisland is busy, Aberdour has its sands and summer visitors—how many of them, I wonder, remember Sir Patrick Spens?—and Inverkeithing is usually haunted by sailor men going on or coming from leave—it is the "port" for Rosyth.

But, before leaving Fife, we must go beyond Queensferry for a visit to one of the most interesting repositories—shall I call it—of ancient architecture, now in good hands and well cared for. This is Culross. A very ancient little town, Culross is now known to archaeologists and architects, it is safe to say, the world over. It is amusing to think that this lovely backwater has its connection with roaring Glasgow, if only by legend. To Culross, it is told, in very far-off days came the *currach* in which Loth, an ancient king, set his daughter adrift because she preferred a Christian swineherd instead of a noble but pagan suitor. With the Princess Thenew was her new-born baby boy. He was given the name that is now known as Kentigern, and Serf, the saint into whose care they fell, gave him the pet name of Mungo, which, in its original, meant "dearest friend". The boy became a gospeller on Clyde-side and today is Glasgow's patron saint.

James VI seemed fond of Culross and from his time dates Culross's architectural treasures. The most notable of these is the Palace and the Study, but there are other lesser buildings—ordinary houses which have their charm, and protection, and Culross in itself has, in its older parts, something to waylay and keep the lover of old and good things.

And so to Queensferry and the great bridge across the Firth of Forth. From a distance and on it this great piece of engineering, with more than a touch of artistry, impresses as few of its kind can do. To cross it is an experience to which every young Scot looks forward. And all of them know the tradition, that, for luck, you must on your first crossing throw a penny into the waters of the Forth. There must be something like a fortune lying in the waters below the bridge. You know that famous railway-side advertisement that pursues you all down the east-coast railway in England. For some similarity, I can never cross the Forth Bridge without looking for those indefatigable men, the painters, who spend their whole year painting the bridge. That is no mere matter of aesthetic, but of preservation. I think that if ever, by chance, I met a man and having asked his occupation he answered that he painted the Forth Bridge, I should gaze upon him with something like awe, solemnly shake his hand and solemnly ask—"What's yours?" I should consider it my duty.

When I am crossing the Forth Bridge, however, my thoughts also wander to the history of the water-way. When I look towards Rosyth and see the warships lying there, sometimes big enough to look like lazy leviathans, or sometimes small enough and quick enough to look like darting water gnats, I remember the day when the German fleet came up the Forth after the war of 1914–18, a day when we thought that this was the end of a war to end wars. There has been no repetition of that degraded armada. That procession of the conquered rouses thoughts that, in a way, have nothing and yet something to do with Scotland. For Scotland with its fishermen and its men of the sea has a good deal to do with the Royal Navy. There was something in Kaiser Wilhelm that had to do with his British ancestry— (by the way, was ever a bogy-man so forgotten as he is now? Will Hitler in time share the same fate?)—that made him love the sea and all connected with it. Was there ever such a landlubber as Hitler, a man who could not go on a ferry-crossing

11

but he was sick? Hitler, because he did not love the sea, forgot his navy. When he did remember it, it was for evil that has nothing to do with the tradition of navies. But then, Germany broke all traditions of clean fighting. If there must be fighting, and the biological inevitability of war seems more and more instead of less and less evident, let it be clean fighting. These are such thoughts as the westward-looking eye engenders on the Forth.

But look east from the bridge and you see, first, Inchcolm and its abbey. Look to the coast of Fife, and you remember the ancient water pageantry of this firth. If only some imaginative author would set out upon that historical pageant, what he could write! Think of all the comings and goings on this water, from the *currach* of Thenew, through all the years when, in beauty, in triumph and in the most extreme agony, men and women of royal and lesser blood crossed and re-crossed the Forth. Edinburgh to Fife, Fife to Edinburgh, think of the history of Scotland that has been written upon this water! It came almost to a peak in the reign of Mary of Scots, and yet, even after that troubled period, there was still picturesque history.

Well, here we are at South Queensferry, and, on our way to Edinburgh and the south, we pass Dalmeny. There, if you step aside, you will find in its church, undoubtedly, one of the loveliest buildings of its kind in Scotland. This Norman edifice, although edifice seems the wrong word for something so exquisite as Dalmeny, is a joy in the past and a reproach to the present. What have we lost? It is something of the spirit.

And so, at long last, goodbye to Fife, a county that, nothing great in itself though worthy of every respect, is, in retrospect, one of the glories of Scotland.

DUNFERMLINE ABBEY

CULROSS PALACE

21

SOUTH TO BERWICK

EDINBURGH, with regret, we now by-pass, but it must be done. And yet, lovely and romantic as Edinburgh is, it is, for many people, an even lovelier city because of its surroundings, its hills and its history, whether you go inland or along the coast-line. And it is good to think that none loves the outskirts and surroundings of Edinburgh like an Edinburgh native. Meet them, and after you have exhausted Edinburgh, they will start on its environs. This is not a matter of golf, or any kindred pastime, but of love of place and history. But then, it is so with their "oppos" of the rival city, Glasgow, or with the folk of Aberdeen. Is this or is it not unusual? Are Scots in this way also different? Maybe not; are they just more intense in the matter?

In the immediate outskirts of Edinburgh there are one or two places which are associated with one who was, perhaps, more essentially Edinburgh than any author down the ages—not excluding Walter Scott, who divided his love between the Borders and the capital. I mean, of course, Robert Louis Stevenson. Mention Colinton, mention Swanston, mention even more the Pentlands and you think of R. L. S. One of the great lovers of Scotland, who also has happened to have the gift to write about it, Dr. Ratcliffe Barnett, has a flashing phrase in one of his books: "A Scotsman never thinks of hills but he hears a whaup". And then he goes on to speak of Stevenson, because you never think of a whaup but you think of Stevenson. This is one of the most un-vicious circles ever known. The Pentlands are Edinburgh's background as well as Stevenson's, and they are his because he was so essentially Edinburgh. The Pentlands are riddled with memories of the Covenanters, and Stevenson, who really was as far from the Covenanters as Paris is from Rullion Green, could not get away from his romantic obsession. It did him no harm, perhaps good, but it was merely a romantic obsession, except that he had the Covenanting characteristic of being unable to write for long without a bit of preaching. He also wrote prayers, a terribly un-Covenanting thing to do. But the Pentlands have their own un-historied and un-literary attraction. They are, in their way, the ideal wandering place on a summer's day, or even at most seasons of the year, for those who do not ask for heights and difficult ones at that. But, just as in other parts of Scotland, you cannot get away from their associations so, in the Pentlands, you cannot get away

163

from those Covenanters. On those hills in November 1666 took place one of the most pitiful yet bloody and cruel little battles ever fought on Scottish soil. As an army the Covenanting men were a rag-tag and bob-tail crew, but their spirit was as dour as their religion. They were nine hundred, miserably armed, against three thousand Government troops with plenty of arms and ammunition. The distant combat was hopeless, but in the hand-to-hand encounters it was a fierce and terrible affair. There could never be any doubt as to the outcome. How many battles and even campaigns have there been of this kind in the long history of Scotland! It is not that Scotland is always the home of lost causes, it is more that it needs a great deal to convince a Scot that he has not won and cannot win, that he must change his opinion, that he is on a losing side. That, of course, is an attitude that has been so often so useful to Britain and the Empire in the last hundred years and more. It is not foolishness or pig-headedness so much as honest belief, and goes through many matters of life and living.

If Rullion Green was a grim battle, over the border of Midlothian, in Haddington-shire, there was a battle fought in the famous year 1745 that still can make Scotsmen laugh, and that inspired a song which every Scotsman knows, and the tune of which has put life into the feet of how many Scotsmen, marching to or from greater, grimmer fights? That was the Battle of Prestonpans, when Prince Charles, aided by the knowledge of the ground on the part of one of his local supporters, was able to surprise the Hanoverian leader, Sir John Cope, at dawn and make him and most of his men take to their heels. Adam Skirving's song is not only fine in its irony, few songs in Scots literature have drum-beats in it like this one:

> Hey, Johnnie Cope, are ye waukin' yet
> Or are your drums a-beatin' yet?
> If ye were waukin' I wad wait
>   To gang to the coals i' the mornin'.

> Fy now, Johnnie, get up an' rin;
> The Highland bagpipes mak a din;
> It's best to sleep in a hale skin,
>   For 'twill be a bluidy mornin'.

The substitution in the metre is really as masterly as was the manœuvre that made the battle a subject for Skirving's pen.

It is not surprising that, with the proximity of Edinburgh, the Lothians were for long the ground of history of many kinds, and we can wander here and wander there, inland or on the coast, and find something of note almost everywhere. If, still near Edinburgh, we take a walk along the Esk we come to a house on a height above the river, lying amid trees. This is Hawthornden, the home of William

Drummond, the poet of Elizabethan and Jacobean days. Here to visit him came Ben Jonson, Shakespeare's rival dramatist, and Jonson's report of their conversations makes most lively reading in parts. They even ventured into the problem of Queen Elizabeth's spinsterhood!

Straying again, towards the south, we come upon Haddington, the town, and here in this haunt of modern as well as ancient peace, broken only by the business and talk of agriculture in its Corn Exchange, there are figures of history to haunt us again. The first, for me, is that of George Wishart whom we saw die at the stake in St. Andrews. It was from Haddington that he began his last journey. The nets of Cardinal Beaton were ready to close. Wishart knew that intuitively, and it seemed to take away some of his outward power and action. But he felt himself doomed, and all that John Knox—who may or may not have been a native of this quiet town—could do, could not dissuade Wishart from what he thought was his path, wherever and to whatever it might lead. There you see the same spirit as that of Rullion Green. In the great church at Haddington Wishart preached one of his last sermons, and in that sermon, like some of the ancient men of God in Biblical days, he warned Haddington of the dreadful fate that would come to it if its men and women did not seek the light, the light that Wishart saw, the light of the Reformation, and follow it.

From Haddington and its area have come many men whose names are famous in one aspect or another of Scottish history. And there is one woman whose name is linked with one of the greatest names in nineteenth-century British literature, Jane Welsh. To Haddington, to the house of Dr. Welsh, Thomas Carlyle came as tutor. Jane's tutors seemed to have had the habit of falling in love with their pupil. She married Carlyle, but the story of that tragic union does not affect us here, except that Jane Welsh Carlyle came back to Haddington forty years after to be buried there. Haddington could have watched her heart-broken widower kiss her tombstone— the curious, strange, incalculable Thomas!

Now, to the coast, eventually haudin' south, on the last stages of our journey round and through territorial Scotland. Behind us we leave some of the loveliest and most productive lands in the country, we shall touch the hills at their seaward fringes, the Lammermuirs down by Cockburnspath, but our way is mainly by the sea.

A last look up the Forth towards Granton and its trawlers, Newhaven and its fisherwives—who are known throughout Scotland by their addiction to the old and picturesque dress and their singing—and we set out by two places with names that might belong anywhere except Scotland—Portobello and Joppa—just as on the other side of Scotland we have Alexandria. But a few miles on we come to "honest" Musselburgh, whose name has the tang of Scotland and the sea, and whose sobriquet

is derived from the town's motto—"Honestas". To most people the name Musselburgh means races, just as, again, Hamilton in the west means the same thing. But
Scotland is not strong in this matter, and not a great deal of money, comparatively,
is lost or won on Scottish racing events. Somehow racing does not seem in keeping
with the traditional Scottish character, although today betting has as strong a hold
on the Scots as it has anywhere else.

Once upon a day you would have been told that drink was the curse of Scotland,
and especially the mixing of whisky and beer. The pint of beer and the nip or the
"wee hauf" have been given to strangers as the excuse for the, allegedly, greater
number of "drunks" seen on the streets of Scottish cities after closing-time. Others
blame the shorter opening hours, others the poor class of our public-houses. They
say they are places to which Scotsmen go only to throw liquor down their throats
as fast as they can, and then stagger out. That may have been so, generally, once
upon a day; it may be so in some places now; but today the public-house has become
more and more what it should be—the poor man's club. In public-houses and inns
in town and country you will see men gather on most nights of the week—not
always the same men—not to drink steadily or quickly, but to play darts and
dominoes and such-like games. In an hour or two not more than two pints will be
consumed by these players; the game's the thing.

Drinking in Scotland has always struck me as one of the most curious things in
the land. There is plenty of drinking, but among a great number of the people it is
either frowned upon or engaged in with stealth. If you wish to make money in the
Scottish licensed trade you should, apart from buying a fashionable lounge restaurant,
set yourself up in a public-house in a quiet by-street or in one that has a back door
giving on to such a street. In every such public-house in Scottish towns and cities,
you will meet citizens of substance and some of important positions taking a harm-
less drink, but afraid to let it be known. It's a foolish attitude; either be open or let
the stuff alone. Furtiveness in anything is bad.

This stealth, of course, is something new in Scottish habit. Once upon a day that
man was the exception who did not go to his "howff". Scotland took its liquor just
as the Frenchman takes his. Most churchmen did not then look upon liquor in
moderation as a heinous sin. Today in the church that is becoming more and more
the attitude, especially in the Presbyterian churches. In one church, of which I have
heard, the minister went so far as to refuse church membership to anyone connected
with the liquor trade or to baptise that man's children. So ends this dissertation.

We have now, at Musselburgh, come into a land of golf, and for quite a long
stretch around this coast we shall come upon places which consist today, whatever
their past history may have been, of hotels and golf courses. There is no poor man's
golf here; it is all very expensive and rather exclusive. Like Strathpeffer in the old

THE FORTH BRIDGE

THE BASS ROCK—A TRANQUIL EVENING

days, the hotel registers and the names attached to the houses are like pages out of Debrett, and some of the names are even more exclusive than that. But there are also people in this area digging the earth in a different way, not with a mashie or a spoon, and the earth they delve is redder than almost anything we have yet seen. These latter delvers belong more than the other delvers to this corner of the coast, and to its crown, the castle of Tantallon. Although not cut off from the landward side by a dry ditch, Tantallon has something of the setting of Dunnottar in Kincardineshire, but it is more of a ruin and not quite so picturesque. The other landmark here is at sea, the Bass Rock, once again like its counterpart across the firth May Island, complete with lighthouse. The Bass Rock had not always its lighthouse; instead it was a dreaded prison rock, a Devil's Island of Scotland; for, although so near the mainland, Covenanting prisoners going to it knew there was very little likelihood that they would ever again see home and kindred. North Berwick and Tantallon had their connection in the old days, when Tantallon's lords, it was a Douglas stronghold, ruled their land.

On past North Berwick and we come to Dunbar, at least twice a battleground— in 1296, when Edward I fought and subdued, and again, in 1650, when Cromwell was fighting the Scots, and, once more, the Scots were defeated. The castle has not pretty memories of Mary of Scots. Here she came with Darnley after he had contrived the murder of David Rizzio, and here she came with Bothwell after the murder of Darnley.

But some eight or so miles from Dunbar—which today is a very happy holiday haunt—we come to Cockburnspath and thoughts of art. This lovely little place—a haunt of the "Glasgow School"—has for many years seen the painter at his easel. There is one other little place in the area which has produced no less than three artists, all of whose names have meant much in Scottish and British art—John Pettie, Arthur Melville, Martin Hardie were all born at East Linton.

There is one last architectural bastion between us and Berwick, and it is a notable one in several ways. That is Fast Castle, seven miles from Cockburnspath. Even today it stands lonely, beyond quicksands, on a high rocky shore, rock on three sides and the moorland behind it, an impregnable place. It is supposed that there was no way to it except from the sea. It was a fit place for plots and stratagems, and here the Gowrie conspirators plotted against James VI in 1601.

Down the coast now by St. Abbs' Head, where the last rocks of Scotland tower and the North Sea dashes against them and its lighthouse. But at St. Abbs there is, too, a little village on the sands, just to give the variety that is the essence of Scottish scenery on the coast and inland.

And so to Berwick, which is and is not Scotland. Here the river, the Tweed, becomes not only a county but a national border, though not with any great matter of seriousness. There are no customs, no passports, no barriers. Berwick is not the county town of the shire of that name. That is Duns, and a place more remote from the busy world I think I have seldom visited. True, I was there on a Saturday afternoon, but I cannot imagine it much more lively than it was that day. At one time the county town was Greenlaw, and that place has still a relic of its old importance, its court house.

It is very tempting to go on to the slopes of the Lammermuirs and from there to look across once more to the Eildon hills and the Borders proper, at which we entered Scotland and the pages of this book. But Berwick is here, no-man's land, and with a quick walk round its walls, a stroll along its pleasant-enough streets, we come to the River Tweed. We can get across, nothing easier. There are two bridges. At the sixth span of the older one, we are in Northumberland and, so, in England.

But, nay, even having come thus far, I turn back. I am quite content, meantime, with and to be in Scotland.

II

THE ARTS IN SCOTLAND

LITERATURE

THE controversy as to whether Scotland has ever produced a major poet will be ended only when a Scottish major poet marches into England preceded by a piper playing "The Cock o' the North".

In common with most countries in the world, Scotland may or may not regret that it has not produced a Shakespeare, but only one of the greatest of his plays—*Macbeth*. Scotland has not produced a Milton—any regrets?—has produced a near-Chaucer, no Wordsworth, though Wordsworth at one time nearly adopted Scotland and Burns.

But Scotland's poetic greatness does not depend upon one or two major poets, but upon the accumulation of the work of a host of minor poets, known and un-known, that, in its accumulation, is more than equal in effect and in relation to the people than almost a dozen major poets. Scotland is a natural democracy, and dictatorship or totalitarianism in literature is as unnatural in this as in any other aspect of her national existence.

No one would be foolish enough to disdain the national wealth of a major poet. Think what Dante has been to Italy—but Italy for long was the producer of major geniuses in painting—just as Germany and Austria were the producers of musical geniuses such as the world has never seen in number or quality. Up to now Scotland has never been like that. But there is the future, and incidence in such matters has, undoubtedly, changed. So has Scotland.

With one or two exceptions, literature in Scotland, so far as the world in general is concerned, has always meant—the work of her poets. Scottish literature began with poets and, it may be, and I hope so, that her latest period will continue with them, and—if it must be—produce that major poet.

Every anthology of Scottish literature, poetic or otherwise, begins:

A! Fredome is a noble thing!

Far through the time of our literature come also the words that every school-boy knows, the words of one who, though never a great poet, had that within him which, behind his prose and rhetoric, had, at any rate, the elements of poetry:

> Breathes there the man with soul so dead,
> Who never to himself hath said,
>   This is my own, my native land!

In between Barbour and Walter Scott there lies a wealth of Scottish poetry that breathes, in a variety of aspects, all that is involved in the expressions of those two quotations.

One of the first things I should like to say about Scottish poetry is that it has an interesting, if not unusual, consistency and continuity. The seeds of later work is in the work of the pioneers. Henryson, Dunbar, Allan Ramsay, Fergusson, Burns, the Ballads, James I, James Hogg, Walter Scott, Robert Louis Stevenson, Charles Murray, Violet Jacob, Ronald Campbell Macfie, Rachel Annand Taylor, Hugh MacDiarmid, Edwin Muir, William Souter, Douglas Young and his associates— they are all linked across and through the ages.

In another part of this book I have already spoken of Robert Henryson, in his relation to Dunfermline, but there is still something more to be said of and for him. In his version of the tale of Cressida he was not the equal of Chaucer; none would claim that; and he was, of course, not in competition with Shakespeare. But when we come to such jewels as "Robene and Makyn" we have something that is Henryson's own, we have also something that is pioneer work in British as well as Scottish poetry. And it must be remembered that the language of Henryson was not then essentially Scottish, nor was it vernacular. It was what then was the equivalent of British. The break, the division came later. It is a pity that language has so changed that only scholars and those who take the trouble can appreciate the work of Henryson and the early poets. It is useless, or all but, to attempt a modernisation of such work—as has been done with Chaucer—virtue goes out with such transmogrification. But with a glossary it is far from difficult to read and appreciate these early poets. After all, we struggle with Anglo-Saxon, with French, with German, with Spanish, why not with early Scots?

The lovely pastoral of "Robene and Makyn" begins beautifully, with a gentle sound that in words is as lovely as an oboe in music:

> Robene sat on a gude green hill
> Keepand a flock of fe:
> Merry Makyne said him till
> "Robene thou rue on me;
> I haif thee lovit loud and still,
> Thir yearis two or three;
> My dule in dern bot gif thou dill,
> Doubtless but dreid I die."

How simply, how exquisitely the world-old situation of the doleful suitor and the merry lass is set forth. If it does not seem, to the intense, a degradation, I would remind you that here, in ancient days and with different air, we have the same situation as you get in Gilbert's lyric in "Patience":

> Prithee, pretty maiden, will you marry me?
> (Hey, but I'm doleful, willow, willow, waly.)

And it is another coincidence between the old and the new that nothing's concluded in either lyric.

Robene pleads with Makyne to come with him to the woods and her answer is that of the French chanson—"Non, non, je n'irais pas au bois", but how beautifully expressed:

> Robene, that warld is all away
> And quite brocht till ane end,
> And never again thereto, perfay,
> Sall it be as thou wend;
> For of my pain thou made it play,
> And all in vain I spend;
> As thou has done, sa sall I say,
> Murne on, I think to mend.

But the gentle Maister Henryson was also a character-drawer and a psychologist. Listen to the last verse of this, almost, mock pastoral—and that in those days!

> Makyne went hame blyth eneuch,
> Attour the holtis hair;
> Robene murnit, Makyne leuch;
> Scho sang, he sichit sair;
> And so left him, baith wo and wreuch,
> In dolour and in care,
> Keepand his herd under a heuch,
> Amang the holtis hair.

So the poem ends as it began with a touch of the open air. Henryson was a genius of his own kind. By the way, this poem which I have chosen to represent Henryson has its modern counterpart in the work of a living poet, a Scot writing in English. I mean Eric Linklater's "Faithless Shepherdess".

The next poet in Scotland after Henryson was of a very different poetic and psychological hue. This was William Dunbar. Some would have that he is Scotland's greatest poet. I think that is a futile controversy; there is so much that is different to consider between him, and, for instance and I suppose that is always the instance, Robert Burns. I always think of Dunbar as dark and saturnine, with a smile on his countenance that is not exactly a leer, but the variation of a leer. He saw his world very clearly, but he was also a courtier as well as a cleric and he had to write to order. But when he wrote for himself he wrote darkly, because he saw that world and life in a glass darkly, not vague but with Rembrandtesque chiaroscuro. In poetry I set Dunbar, in a way, with John Donne. He is the dark genius of Scotland, and has his modern prose rather than poetic compeers—George Douglas Brown and Lewis Grassic Gibbon. Both were the children of the Dunbar tradition.

Perhaps the most famous, if not the best, of Dunbar's poems is that great elegy "Lament for the Makaris"—that is, lament for the poets. It is largely a catalogue of names, and yet it has the most extraordinary effect. That, of course, is largely due to the refrain which comes at the end of each stanza, like the tolling of a funeral bell —"*Timor mortis conturbat me*". What a tribute to Latin!

Here is the dark conclusion and, after, what he had said at the beginning:

> Our plesance here is all vain-glory,
> This false warld is bot transitory,
> The flesh is brukill, the Fiend is sle;
> *Timor mortis conturbat me. . . .*

> Sen for the dede remead is none,
> Best is that we for dede dispone,
> Eftir our dede that lif may we;
> *Timor mortis conturbat me.*

And just one example of his catalogue:

> He has Blind Harry and Sandy Traill
> Slain with his shot of mortal hail,
> Whilk Patrick Johnstoun micht nocht flee;
> *Timor mortis conturbat me.*

And yet I would not be surprised if Dunbar did not live as happy a life as it was possible in the times, and enjoyed it. But the dark was there, in contrast, artistic contrast. You will find lovely and gracious tributes to women, to cities, but always the cleric broke in. Of course, the thought of death and dreams of a heaven of beauty and warmth were part of the medieval make-up and came out of the conditions of life. That is why it is often so incongruous that we, with all our domestic advantages in these days—houses with good walls and central heating, and the same applies to churches—sing hymns that have become outmoded because of the difference in our ways of life. But there was one theme that pervaded poetry for a century or two, and nowhere more than in Scotland—and that was winter:

> When that the nicht dois lenthen houris,
> With wind, with hail and heavy shouris,
> My dule spreit dois lurk for schoir
> My hairt for languor dois forloir,
> For lack of simmer with his flouris.

TANTALLON CASTLE

FAST CASTLE

So, when we come to another poet, contemporary with Dunbar, Gavin Douglas, we find the presence of winter brings out some of the best of his work:

> The frosty ringis of the year . . .
> Riveris ran reid on spate with water broun,
> And burnis hurlis all their bankis doun. . . .

We are no better today in the open. What was written in the fifteenth or sixteenth century still rings true. We find it again in Shakespeare—what is so marvellous in atmosphere as the battlement scenes in *Hamlet*? And there is that perfect winter lyric, "When icicles hang by the wall".

I have said that Scottish poetry is an accumulation of the work of a host of minor poets. Some of these poets we know by name and can place their dates, but there is that great host of unknowns in that fine, if unequal, body of Scottish poetry—the ballads. Ballads, of course, are not peculiar to Scotland or to Britain, for that matter, but there was in Scotland a curious flowering of the ballad, and Scottish ballads have about them an atmosphere and a statement that sets them apart. It may be that life in the remoter parts of Scotland was grimmer than in the more civilised areas of this island, among those nearer the court and what comparatively large centres there were of population. The Borders was one area in which the ballad reached a certain height of accomplishment and the hill regions of Aberdeenshire another. But there were other areas of Scotland which produced some work that competes with those other two. Ballads have given rise to many years of academic controversy, many many years of research and analysis. And, again, nothing's concluded. But the ballads themselves remain to be enjoyed for themselves. There are those who think the ballads to be the work of, originally, one author, and that they were sometimes enriched, and sometimes degraded as they were handed down through the generations by word o' mou'. There are others who think that, in the lowlands and the hill country, just as in the islands of the west, this folk-literature was the outcome of concerted effort, group composition as it were. We know how many Hebridean songs, especially the songs of labour, were begun by one person, added to by another and another until the song had taken shape. It may be so with the ballads, but my own idea inclines to the single original authorship. I have been present in rural companies when a song was made in the group way—not, of course, of the quality of the ballads—and I have been in others where the single author began and the group acted as "improvers". But in these modern instances I have always found that the one original authorship produced the best work. And why should not there have been, as ballad authors, men, or women, of some poetic flair, even though we do not know their names, and their work has been bandied into a shape and sometimes into shapelessness? But the ballads remain—a body of work of which any country might be proud.

The ballads have certain characteristics that are common to many of them. They are not perjink, either in rhyme or rhythm, and they have a curious vagueness, hiatuses and jumpiness in the telling of their tales. This, for some people, is part of their attraction, and you will find, when later and more sophisticated authors have taken to the writing of ballads, that these are the qualities so often imitated. William Morris was a case in point.

Besides the ballads there is a certain body of lyrical poetry written by poets without a name, such as "Christis' Kirk of the Green" and "Peblis to the Play", though there are those who would give to these an author. They are the equivalent in Scots verse of the paintings of Pieter Breughel: lively work; and they have undoubtedly had their effect upon Scottish poetry, which, as I have said, is consistent and continuous. Of the anonymous non-ballad works, there is one that should be quoted, it is so very typical of a certain rough Scots attitude:

> Wha has gude malt and makis ill drink,
>   Wa mot be her weird!
> I pray to God scho rot and stink,
>   Seven year aboon the erd;
> About her bier na bell to clink,
>   Nor clerk sing, lewed nor lear'd.

Of the ballads, I have already mentioned three—"Sir Patrick Spens", "Edom o' Gordon" and "The Battle of Harlaw". But though they rank high, they are far from exhausting the gems of Scottish ballad literature. Famous and known are such as "Edward" again with a fine opening:

> Why dois your brand sae drap wi' bluid,
>   Edward, Edward?

—and "Marie Hamilton". This latter is known mainly by three or four verses and is among the most frequently sung by Scots singers. In the song version it is known as "Yestreen the Queen had four Maries", and I think that, coupled with its tune, it is as near heartbreak in its effect as any piece of Scots or English literature of its kind. There are likenesses among several of them: for instance, "Clerk Saunders" and "Sweet William", and such a ballad as "The Twa Corbies" has almost created a class of its own. Then there are ballads such as "Binnorie" with its refrain:

> There was twa sisters in a bower,
>   *Binnorie, O Binnorie,*
> There came a knight to be their wooer,
>   *By the bonnie mill-dams o' Binnorie.*

This matter of the refrain attracted the sophisticated balladist of the nineteenth century, who so overdid it that it is no wonder such a humorist as Calverley pricked the bubble in his parody, in which he used "Butter and eggs and a pound of cheese" as his refrain.

Dates and periods are difficult, but there is little doubt of the ancientry of some of the ballads, and of their authenticity as folk-stuff. Later the ballad gave way to the song, and with these I shall deal later, as they mean almost more to the generality of the people of Scotland than the ballad properly. Unfortunately, too many of the ballads are now becoming only a literary possession, but seventy and a hundred years ago they were almost as well known as the words of the music-hall songs are today. Unlike most music-hall songs, however, they have a way of lasting more than a month or a week or two.

When we come towards the seventeenth century the style and language of Scots poetry underwent a southern change. Poets such as Drummond of Hawthornden might be Scots by birth, but Scotland has little to do with their poetry. It might just as well have been written by a Londoner. So with Ayton, the Earl of Stirling, the Marquis of Montrose and others. In fact, if it had not been for the body of song I have mentioned, Scots poetry for almost a century seemed to go underground. There were no Henrysons, no Dunbars. That body of song saved us from sterility. And what a body it is!

I often wonder if young or old, as they sing what is sentimentally known as "the auld Scots sangs", realise how far down the years many of them belong. Again, dates are difficult. You find them lumped together in anthologies, although a century or more may separate them. These songs seem, unlike the ballads, to have come mainly out of the south countree. Yarrow has been the airt of several of them; the original version of "Annie Laurie", with its verse:

> She's backit like the peacock,
>   She's breastit like the swan,
> She's jimp about the middle,
>   Her waist ye weel micht span;
> Her waist ye weel micht span,
>   And she has a rolling eye;
> And for bonnie Annie Laurie
>   I'd lay me down and die.

belongs to Dumfriesshire; and the lively "Maggie Lauder" belongs to Fife.

In some collections you will find such a song as "The Bonnie Banks o' Loch Lomond" set along with songs that may belong to the sixteenth and seventeenth centuries. The information I have about this, one of the most popular of all Scottish songs—popular with Scots and English alike—is that it was taken down from lips of a street singer in Aberdeen by the father of the famous actor Sir Johnston Forbes-Robertson. Also, the lines, "Ye'll tak' the high road, An' I'll tak' the low road",

12

have a deeper meaning than they suggest. The song, I have been told, belongs to the days after the '45, and is the song of a prisoner in Carlisle Castle. This prisoner is condemned to death, his companion will go free. The condemned man says "he'll tak' the low road", the quicker way of the spirit to Scotland and home.

There is variety in these songs. Some people are inclined to think that most of the old songs and ballads deal only with love that went astray and sudden death. Of course, there is "Helen of Kirkconnel", in which hate and revenge are marvellously expressed in a stanza:

> I lichtit doun, my sword did draw,
> Stern was the fight on Kirtleshaw,
> I hewed him doun in pieces sma',
>   For her sake that died for me.

If ever clenched teeth and a gripped voice were in any verse, they are there!

But, on the other hand, you have the jovial and the gay, which are just as much part of Scots minstrelsy as doul and woe. There are such songs as "Tibbie Fowler", "Get Up and Bar the Door" and "Todlen Butt and Todlen Ben". Married life has a great share in many of these songs. You have the man who either fears his wife or is determined that she shall not rule him. On the other hand, where will you find a trigger song and where will you find the love of the wife for her man who has been long at sea so well expressed than in one famous and well-loved song, with its equally good companion melody? It is sometimes called "The Sailor's Wife". You know how the excited wife gives all her orders about the tidying of the house, the cleading of the bairns, all in a kind of poetic breathlessness; and she does not forget that she must be, herself, in and at her best to meet her spouse. And then the last verse:

> And will I see his face again?
> And will I hear him speak?
> I'm downright dizzy with the joy;
>   In troth I'm like to greet. . . .
>   There's nae luck aboot the house,
>   There's nae luck at a',
>   There's little pleasure in the house,
>   When our gudeman's awa'.

How often that situation must have arisen in the days of the two great wars. The whole atmosphere of the poem is finest *genre*, such as we meet in the Dutch and French painters. The author had, at least, some moments of genius.

And we cannot go from these unknowns without mention of one of the simplest, but most touching of Scottish songs. It always seems to me to sum up a certain aspect of county character, that which is as far opposed as can be to sophistication, and yet has no mawkishness. It is "Logie o' Buchan", and I need not say to which airt it belongs. It is the story of the lass who loves the lad on whom mother and father frown. So, in the end, the lassie sings:

> I sit on my creepie and spin at my wheel,
> And think on the laddie that lo'ed me sae weel;
> He had but ae saxpence and brak it in twa,
> And gi'ed me the ha'f o't, when he gaed awa'.
> Then haste ye back, Jamie, and bide na awa'.
> Then haste ye back, Jamie, and bide na awa'.
> Summer is comin', cauld winter's awa',
> And ye'll come and see me in spite o' them a'.

The picture is perfect, in every way, and, once more, the tune is the perfect complement. Of course, that fitting of melody and verse is what has been the making and keeping of so much Scottish minstrelsy.

Towards the end of the seventeenth century there were born some singing birds —of both sexes—who brought to Scottish lyricism a number of songs that today are unforgotten and certainly not unsung. Among them were Lady Grizel Baillie —"Were na my heart light I wad die"; Robert Crawford—"Doun the burn, Davie"; Alexander Ross—"Woo'd and married an' a'"; and, last but most in fame and output, there was Allan Ramsay. His pastoral operetta, *The Gentle Shepherd*, cannot be set with, for instance, Gay's *The Beggar's Opera*, but it has qualities of its own and some of its lyrics are part of the Scottish book of memorable words.

Then the eighteenth century and English got hold of Scottish poetry, and so we have James Thomson and Beattie *The Minstrel*. They are now names rather than fames or favourites. These twain, however, were offset by lesser but intenser lights such as Skirving—"Johnnie Cope"; Jane Elliot—the better version of "The Flowers of the Forest"; Dougal Graham, author of one of the first skits on the English-speaking Highlander; John Ewen—"The Boatie Rows"; Alexander, Duke of Gordon —"Cauld kail in Aberdeen"; Hector MacNeill—"Come under my plaidie" and "I lo'e ne'er a laddie but ane". The stuff of Scotland is in these songs, and so they have kept their place on the lips and in the hearts of Scottish people when other more pretentious work has had the dust of years accumulating upon it. There is a lesson in this for those who would write for more than the vogue of the moment. These songs are basic. The intellect must reach the highest flights, otherwise it and its product are merely Icarian.

In this century there were two Scottish poets, and both were from Aberdeenshire. One was the Rev. John Skinner of Linshart, an Episcopal clergyman who suffered for his faith, but kept the sense of humour in his life that he put into his songs and so won through, and Robert Fergusson, whose folk belonged to the central Aberdeenshire village of Insch. Skinner was born in 1721 and lived until 1807, Fergusson was born in 1750 and died in 1774. Their lives were very, very different, and, to some extent, that is mirrored in the span of them. Both, however, had this in common, that their works were of the essence of Scots poesy of the lively and living kind. It has been said that, had Fergusson not written, there might have been no Robert Burns as we know him. I do not believe that for a moment. There would have been a Robert Burns—what had Fergusson's work to do with the genius of Burns? The form in which Burns wrote might have been different; he might have stumbled longer before he reached that which Fergusson helped him to more quickly. But there were other exemplars besides Fergusson, and Burns was Scots from the beginning; his English strayings were only temporary and weak aberrations.

Skinner, like Murray, who came long after, is known by the name of his best-known song—"Tullochgorum". Anything more unlike "The Seasons" or "The Castle of Indolence" of Thomson or Beattie's *Minstrel* can hardly be produced. Tullochgorum is a Scottish reel, and to its rhythm the poem is written. Skinner sees in the reel a means of uniting political opposites, praises it above "dull Italian lays". The opening gives its tang:

> Come, gi'e's a sang, Montgomery cry'd,
> And lay your disputes a' aside;
> What signifies't for folks to chide
>   For what was done before them?
> Let Whig and Tory a' agree,
>   Whig and Tory, Whig and Tory,
>   Whig and Tory a' agree
>   To drop their whigmagorum;
> Let Whig and Tory a' agree
> To spend this night wi' mirth and glee,
> And cheerfu' sing, alang wi' me,
>   The Reel o' Tullochgorum.

When Burns visited Aberdeen and met "Tullochgorum's" son, who became Episcopal Bishop of Aberdeen, he expressed his admiration of Linshart's poems. If Burns admired "Tullochgorum's" poems, he did far more where Fergusson's were concerned. He learnt from them, he founded some parts of his own immortality upon them. Has it been the case that this has tended to obscure Fergusson? Anyway, in recent years there has been an attempt by most admirable folk to get a hearing for Fergusson. They will succeed in time; Fergusson is essential Scots, and his place in Scottish literary history entitles him to respect and admiration. His personal history is soon told—it is almost as short as his years. He went to the High School of Dundee—a lad o' pairts—and then to St. Andrews University. His father's death broke his university career, he came back to Edinburgh and, like so many of his kind, went into clerkships in first one and then another legal office. He was a social soul, and the clubs and the pubs knew him, and, like Burns, his convivial verses led to other conviviality. But the body was not equal to the spirits, and so the body broke first and then the spirit, and Fergusson died in a mental hospital, twenty-four years of age. Think, he was never even on the verge of middle age; think and read, little more than a boy. But a prodigy, one who changed Scottish literature, a literary John the Baptist, and that's not blasphemy. Behind all his riotousness, behind all his lightsome attitude to life and literature, there was a spirit of humanity rather than anything transcendental. It was not given to him to achieve Burns's second life—attachment to the land and his ability to link the plough and the stars. Fergusson was a "townser" by birth if not by descent, and his nature poems are what I call "tripper poetry", elegant but empty. Whenever he touches the town he touches something very like genius. In his town poems we have, what has so often been pictured, but not always so finely as this—Auld Reekie. That town has never lacked in delineators, in prose and poetry. Fergusson is among the best.

> *Auld Reikie*! thou'rt the canty hole,
> A bield for mony caldrife soul,
> Wha snugly at thine ingle loll,
>   Baith warm and couth;
> While round they gar the bicker roll
>   To weet their mouth.

So do we, in verse and phrase, hear the fore-echo of Burns. In the same poem—"The Daft Days"—we also hear an echo of "Tullochgorum":

> Fiddlers, your pins in temper fix,
> And roset weel your fiddle-sticks,
> And banish vile Italian tricks
>   From out your quorum;
> Nor *fortes* wi' *pianos* mix,
>   Gie's *Tulloch Gorum*.

Fergusson met and saw all that made the motley Scots population of Edinburgh. He gives us the Highlander, he talks of "Buchan bodies", who through the beach "Their bunch of Findrums cry":

> An' skirl out baul', in Norland speech,
>   "Gueed speldings, fa will buy?
> An', by my Saul, they're nae wrang gear
>   To gust a stirrah's mow;
> Weel staw'd wi' them, he'll never spear
>   The price o' being fu'
>   Wi' drink that day."

The accents of the native shire of his father and mother come again in "Hallow-Fair":

> Here Sawny cries, frae Aberdeen,
>   "Come ye to me fa need:

> The brawest *shanks* that e'er were seen
> I'll sell ye cheap an' guid.
> I wight they are as protty hose
> As come frae *weyr* or *leem*:
> Here tak' a rug, an' shaws yer pose:
> Forseth, my ain's but teem
> An' Light this day."

This differentiation of the airts of Scotland in speech was something new in Scottish verse, and it was a long time again before it returned. Fergusson was a pioneer as well as a revivalist in many ways. But what he remains most of all in general is that verse equivalent of the Dutch or Flemish painters, of Rowlandson and Hogarth in London. He stands apart. The time is coming when he will have his vogue and his fuller due. And, remember, he died when he was twenty-four.

If you look at any reasonably sized anthology of Scots poetry, even though you are a Scot and fairly well acquainted with the sangschaw of your native land, you will, I think, get a surprise when you see the work of one period collected. In the second half of the eighteenth century Scotland was a nest of singing birds, if ever it was. They were not nightingales—those are not native to Scotland—but they were the next best thing—mavises, and even the humble sparrows—sporgies, as we call them—can, in choir, make a sound that has its effect and value. Once again, I say that it is in the accumulation of minor poets that Scotland, with so few exceptions, has found her poetic fame.

In this half-century were made such songs as Lady Anne Lindsay's "Auld Robin Gray"—the gentry as well as the man in the pub and at the loom, and the female as well as the male were in this Scottish aviary; Mrs. Grant of Laggan's "O where, tell me where, is your Highland laddie gone?"; Jean Glover's "Owre the muir amang the heather"; Joanna Baillie's "Saw ye Johnnie comin'?"; and, to give names only—Sir Alexander Boswell, Robert Jamieson, William Laidlaw, Alexander Rodger and Hew Ainslie. These are men and women known now, perhaps, by only a single song or by two or three, and there were, again, not a few of the unknowns, who have left songs that refuse to die or remain unknown like their writers.

I have mentioned Hew Ainslie—born in the last ten years of the century, and he lived until 1878—and one cannot help quoting the lines from "Mary" that, somehow, sing in the ears after we have read them, in something of the same way that does Tennyson's "Tear, idle tears".

> It's dowie in the hint o' hairst
> At the wa'gang o' the swallow,
> When the winds grow cauld, when the burns grow bauld,
> An' the woods are hingin' yellow;

> But, O! it's dowier far to see
> The wa'gang o' her the heart gangs wi'—
> The dead-set o' a shinin' e'e
> That darkens the weary warl' on thee.

And it must be remembered that, while I have been telling of the minor, and sometimes very minor, members of the choir, at this time there were also the mavises. There was Robert Burns—of whom no more need be said here; there was Lady Nairne, in her songs as famous as any singer, greater or smaller in her day and after; Walter Scott, the scop of the period; James Hogg, shepherd of Ettrick and singer of faery. To close the list we must mention Robert Tannahill, whose gentle muse has left half a dozen or more songs, many of which the Scot knows from childhood and treasures until old age.

The nineteenth century came, and though years and verse merged so easily for a time that the new century and its verse were hardly noticeable, there did come a difference.

One poet who stands out as linking the old and the new that was to come was William Thom, the weaver poet of Inverurie. He is beginning to be rediscovered because the year 1948 was the centenary of his death, but with those who really care for Scottish poetry certain of his poems have never been forgotten. His output was unequal, and the circumstances of his life helped towards this—he was petted and he was left alone. In "The Blind Boy's Pranks"—the blind boy being Cupid—is something with a tinge of newness in Scots poetry; the nearest in English would be, I should say, George Darley. The poem is in Scots and it is set in Thom's native region, but there is a delicate colour about it that was only in Thom's own imagination:

> Men grew sae cauld, maids sae unkind,
>   Love kentna whaur to stay;
> Wi' fient an arrow, bow or string—
> Wi' droopin' heart an' drizzled wing,
>   He fought his lonely way. . . .
>
> He launched a leaf o' jessamine,
>   On whilk he dared to swim,
> An' pillowed his head on a wee rose-bud;
> Syne slighted love away did scud
>   Down Ury's waefu' stream.

From start to finish the delicacy is mixed with a native strength of expression that gives the poem its curious attraction.

Men like Robert Gilfillan, Henry Scott Riddell, John Park—especially in his song of "Gadie rins"—and Lady John Scott added to the real Scots wallet; but by the middle of the century, except for work that has only a local fame, Scots had given place to English in the work of the poets, even when their themes were Scottish. Walter Scott instead of Robert Burns had, for a time, won the day in influence. So we have Walter C. Smith, George MacDonald, Alexander Smith, James Thomson, Robert Buchanan—and who reads them now?

But, here and there, the Scots tongue found some utterance, and there was a looking-back and some looking-forward to what was to come. Robert Louis Stevenson's Scots poems are as admired among Scots as any he wrote. There was a railwayman called Alexander Anderson ("Surfaceman") who was beloved of thousands for his simple lays such as "Bairnie cuddle doon". Near Stevenson and Charles Murray and Violet Jacob stands Logie Robertson. Take his "Ochil Farmer":

> Abune the braes I see him stand,
> The tapmost corner o' his land,
> An' scan wi' care, owre hill an' plain,
> A prospect he may ca' his ain.
>
> His yowes ayont the hillocks feed,
> Weel herdit in by wakefu' Tweed;
> An' canny thro the bent his kye
> Gang creepin' to the byre doun-by.
>
> His hayfields lie fu' smoothly shorn,
> An' ripenin' rise his rigs o' corn;
> A simmer's evenin' glory fa's
> Upon his hamestead's sober wa's.
>
> A stately figure there he stands
> An' rests upon his staff his hands;
> Maist like some patriarch of eld,
> In sic an evenin's calm beheld.
>
> A fermer he of Ochilside,
> For worth respectit far an' wide;
> A friend of justice and of truth,
> A favourite wi' age and youth.
>
> There's no' a bairn but kens him weel,
> And ilka collie's at his heel;
> Nor beast nor body e'er had ocht
> To wyte him wi', in deed or thocht.
>
> Fu' mony a gloamin' may he stand
> Abune the brae to bless the land!
> Fu' mony a simmer rise an' fa'
> In beauty owre his couthy ha'!

For peacefu' aye, as simmer's air,
The kindly hearts that kindle there;
Whase friendship, sure an' aye the same,
For me mak's Ochilside a hame.

I have not been able to resist quoting this poem in full, for several reasons. One is the poem itself, which seems to me to sum its object and its atmosphere not, perhaps, greatly, but in its own way, perfectly. The spirit of the poem is genuine. And both subject and poem belonged to something that was passing away. It was not the deepest twilight of the little gods of Scottish poetry, but the twilight had begun. As I say, there was still the work of Charles Murray, Violet Jacob and one or two others to come to full fruition and popularity.

The war of 1914–18, of course, brought out Scots elegiac verse in great quantities, good and bad, but nothing, for instance, to compare with Rupert Brooke in English. Much of it, if not all of it, is now practically forgotten, except that which "Hamewith" wrote in "Sough o' War" and now appears in his collected works. It is an interesting fact that the last poem of any importance which "Hamewith" wrote, "There's aye a something", sold out the paper in which it appeared and every extra copy that was printed; sold out a repetition of it in another periodical form, and today it is constantly asked for; copies go all over the world in typescript. Whatever the new young men may say, Charles Murray has a vogue and an appeal that must be recognised, even by them.

The years between 1919 and the rise of the new men in Scottish poetry, near the beginning of the 1939–45 war, present a problem. It is not that there was any hiatus; men and women kept on singing; but not only in the matter of Scots and English, but in the matter of shape and form, they fell between two stools. Scots was not yet a vogue for the more highbrow poets—except one—and most of those who wrote in Scots, or with a Scottish tang, harked back to older days and ways. One or two names might be mentioned. There was Pittendrigh MacGillivray, sculptor as well as verse-maker, who is kept in memory, though he never had a vogue; John Ferguson was something of a ferlie with his sonnets; Helen Cruickshank is almost a one-poem woman, and so was Muriel Stuart; Alexander Gray was better known as an economist than as poet, Lewis Spence as a dealer, in poetry and prose, in archaeology; Andrew Young's fame has come late, and has not very much in connection with pure Scottishry; and there was one maker of humorous verse, some of whose songs will last as long as convivial gatherings in Scotland, Dr. David Rorie. "The Lum Hat Wantin' a Croon" and "The Pawky Duke" are part of every students' repertory of jolly song, and they are heard on the concert platform as well. But, in words, they can stand by themselves. All these writers belonged, in birth, to the seventies and eighties of the nineteenth century.

Two others stand apart, one of whom belongs to the 'eighties, the other to the early 'nineties, who must be mentioned. They are of importance in their work and in their relation to the Scottish renaissance. These are Edwin Muir and Hugh Mac-Diarmid, the latter the name chosen for his literary work by Christopher M. Grieve. It is interesting that neither is a product of any university—Muir was at one time a clerk and MacDiarmid a journalist, yet the universities—the intelligentsia of the student bodies, I mean—the universities officially do not seem to recognise littérateurs until they are decrepit or dead—have adopted both.

Muir is critic and poet, and one of the finest translators in Britain. There is nothing very Scottish about much of his poetry, except, perhaps, a certain austerity and granitic quality. Like so many poets in recent days his affinities are with the Continent of Europe, Holderlin and Rilke. He has come to his full stature and his fame is beyond Scotland.

MacDiarmid is a Scot if ever there was one, but an intellectual Scot, whose political affinities are very definitely with the present regime in Russia. One of his bigger works is the "Hymn to Lenin". He is one of the begetters and leaders of the literary side of the Scottish renaissance. The young men sit at his feet, and some of them, unfortunately, copy his worst mannerisms. There is no doubt that MacDiarmid in verse, like Grassic Gibbon—his friend and literary ally in prose—was the reviver of Scots, hard, real Scots. Let me give two examples of his short poems, they are well known to the connoisseur, but not, perhaps, otherwise.

Here is "Milk-Wort and Bog-Cotton":

> Cwa' een like milk-wort and bog-cotton hair!
> I love you, earth, in this mood best o' a'
> When the shy spirit like a laich wind moves
> And frae the lift nae shadow can fa'
> Since there's nocht left to thraw a shadow there
> Owre een like milk-wort and milk-white cotton hair.
>
> Wad that nae leaf upon anither wheeled
> A shadow either and nae root need dern
> In sacrifice to let sic beauty be!
> But deep surroundin' darkness I discern
> Is aye the price o' licht. Wad licht revealed
> Naething but you, and nicht nocht concealed.

You can see to what and whom that goes back. Is it or is it not to William Dunbar? And there is what is perhaps the most famous of MacDiarmid's short poems—"The Watergaw":

> Ae weet forenicht i' the yow-trummle
> I saw yon antrin thing,

A watergaw wi' its chitterin' licht
Ayont the on-ding;
An' I thocht o' the last wild look ye gied
Afore ye dee'd.

There was nae reek i' the laverock's hoose
That nicht—an' nane abune;
But I ha'e thocht of that foolish licht
Ever sin' syne;
An' I think that mebbe at last I ken
What your look meant then.

If you are going to understand the bulk of Scottish poetry, now and to come for some time, you must understand such poems as these. There is no space or place here to deal with the great body of work—much of it unequal and esoteric—that belongs to MacDiarmid's name. It can just be stated that, in fundamentals, Mac-Diarmid is the most important man in Scottish poetic literature of the last quarter of a century, and is likely to be for more years yet.

In contrast let me give you one verse of one of Edwin Muir's poems that does deal with Scotland. It is called "Scotland 1941".

We were a family, a tribe, a people,
Wallace and Bruce guard now a painted field
And all may read the folio of our fable,
Peruse the sword, the sceptre and the shield.
A simple sky roofed in the rustic day,
The busy cornfields and the haunted holms,
The green path winding up the ferny brae.
But Knox and Melville clapped their preaching palms.

And huddled all the harvest gold away,
Hoodicrow Peden in the blighted corn
Hacked with his rusty beak the starving haulms.
Out of that desolation we were born.

No, Mr. Muir and his colleagues of the renaissance are not fond of Knox and others like him. They think Scotland's cultural development was delayed centuries by their work and theology, and the effects of them.

Many of the disciples of MacDiarmid, Gibbon and Muir are coming to their maturity. They are a potent force among the intelligentsia. They mean little or nothing to the great body of reading Scots. These are still thirled to the past and to what they can understand. Who shall blame them? Yet, we know, art must advance, if advancement this is.

Scottish literature, as I have pointed out, is at its best and to a great extent poetic.

Our best prose writers and our second best are too well known to the world to need more than reference here. Scott and Stevenson, and such as Neil Munro and John Buchan—the two latter most Scottish when they were most young.

There were writers such as Ian Maclaren and Crockett, who had their day and vogue, but along with that household name in Scotland, Annie S. Swan, they wrote tales for auld wives, and the auld wives still read them. George Douglas Brown, in a single novel, *The House With the Green Shutters*, shattered the Scottish world built up by Maclaren, Crockett and Barrie, and died. Grassic Gibbon took up Brown's work in the newer way, and he, too, died. The superstitious may see something in their deaths. The young men of Scotland see life and the future in the work of Brown and Gibbon, and are following hard after. Scotland, literarily, is today one of the most interesting countries in the world, one of the most alive. This is not a dawn in which it is good to be alive; it is getting fairly far into the morning, and with the advancing day, work progresses.

In work that belongs both to Scotland and a wider world we have Eric Linklater, whom I have mentioned more than once, and there is Neil Gunn, more Scottish, in general, than Linklater, and yet with a wide general public. Neil Gunn has the north highland temperament, which is something different from the Celt of the western mainland and the islands. You find this northern temperament in his work. It is clear cut, and yet behind the clarity is something of the twilight of the mind and spirit; again he seems to unite two aspects of his country.

With the great upcome of Scottish writers has come an outbreak of periodicals and publishers. The work they give to the world is more essentially Scottish, in every way, than has been known since the eighteenth century. This outbreak was necessary; economically and otherwise it was impossible that such work could emanate from London. Barrie, for instance, did not need a Scots publisher—nor did Fiona MacLeod—such as Fionn MacColla does. It is good, also, to find authors who are Scots in actuality or by descent coming home. Such are Compton MacKenzie and Moray McLaren.

Yes, Scotland, strange as it may seem, is becoming a magnet to keep those we have and to bring home such as have strayed.

2

ART

IN the Scottish Arts Club in Edinburgh one afternoon a noted Scottish painter, who had lunched rather well, suddenly entered the lounge and crossed to the group among which I sat listening to good conversation.

Suddenly this visitant pointed a skinny finger at another noted Scottish painter and said, "What is art?" The second painter looked up lazily, and said, just as lazily and in his west-country accent, "That's a hellofa big question."

So it is, but it's also a complicated question when nationality is mixed up with the basic matter, and this matter of nationality, especially in the British Isles, tends to include the snobbery of centralisation. Or perhaps, I should say, tended to include, for, because it has been found out, centralisation is going to take some very bad knocks, and that right soon. And Scotland is going to administer some of them. At any rate, I think and hope so.

In this matter of art, Scotland, over and over again, has been rather shabbily treated, and mostly by the art critics and writers on art. I have myself been enrolled among the art critics for over a quarter of a century, but, because I am Scots, I have, of course, not been among the art critics who were foolish about Scottish art. That cuts both ways: I have not been foolish about Scottish art just because it is Scottish. In that quarter of a century I have watched art and Scottish art change, and, in the latter case, grow in stature and strength. I have battled with metropolitan snobs, a pitiable rather than despicable band, but one so easy to defeat, because, while I have known both London and Scottish art, they have known only one end of the critical mahl-stick.

In my time I have watched so many movements come to a kind of fruition, in art, in literature and music. The only thing to say about them is that, where they have had some basis, however fanatic, they have added something to the fabric of their art, and faded out or merged again into the general pattern. I wonder what happens to all those zealots and their hangers-on when their little day is gone. The hangers-on, I suppose, move on to the next movement.

It is all this sort of metropolitan nonsense and its earlier equivalent that has prevented Scottish art from getting its due. That is not a matter of years, but of centuries.

The matter is gradually being redressed. That, of course, is also due to what is happening in Scottish art today—another facet of the renaissance. For a time Scottish art, during the last twenty-five years, was part of Scotland's division. There was established what was Scotland's Salon des Indépendents—the Society of Scottish Artists. These were our "fauves", and the S.S.A. was, in its early days, in rather piquant contrast to the Royal Scottish Academy. That was still something of a watershed, but twenty-five years ago most of the water ran towards the past. Year by year I have watched the Academy and the S.S.A. get nearer and nearer. The "wild men" have won their A.R.S.A.'s and R.S.A.'s, until today there is little, hardly a paper wall between them. That is one of the differences between art in Scotland and art in London. The Royal Academy's exhibition at Burlington House would be laughed off the walls in Edinburgh, if only for its dull monotony. I'm not so sure about Glasgow; there the Fine Art Institute has tended to be a Scottish Burlington House. Some years ago it suddenly dawned upon Scottish art connoisseurs that there had been a reorientation of art in Scotland. All that was implicit once upon a day in the world-famous Glasgow School had gone from Glasgow. The Edinburgh School had taken its place. But that is in tradition.

Art in Scotland, modern and known, as I have told you, began in the east, but the north-east, in Aberdeen. The pioneer was the George Jamesone, of whom I have spoken. He was born on February 8, 1587, the day, as has been pointed out, on which Mary Queen of Scots was executed. His father was an architect, and young Jamesone was a student at Marischal College before he took to painting. That he went to Antwerp and studied there is pretty certain, but that he was a pupil of Peter Paul Rubens and a fellow-student of Van Dyck has yet to be proved. That, besides being a painter, he was a man of independent mind and something of a character—as Raeburn in his time also was—is pretty certain. He painted Royalist and Covenanter alike, but his sympathies were with the first, and he was in trouble for his allegiance.

There remain quite a fair number of his works—in Aberdeen, in Edinburgh and elsewhere. The chief complaint against them is that they tend to be stiff in pose, but when we come to tone and sympathy with the people he is painting, the critics adopt a rather different tone. He did, as far as his experience and ability could go, get his people on to canvas, and his painting of dress has its detail and delicacy. Among the best of his works are the unflattering but natural "Lady Mary Erskine"; a portrait of the Young Montrose; and, again a young person, the portrait of Thomas, Lord Binning. But he was a pioneer, and began his work in a place that was cut off largely from any centre of art in Scotland or England, though it must be remembered that Belgium, where he received his training, was in many ways as near to Aberdeen as London was. Scotland's trade with the Lowlands lasted for a long, long period and had its effects on art in Scotland as much as upon anything else. Jamesone died in Edinburgh, in 1644, and lies in an unknown grave in Greyfriars Churchyard—the place of the Covenanters. He who did not care for them.

It is interesting, in relation to Jamesone, that one of the next names of note in Scottish painting was a Fleming, Sir John Medina. He was popular, but not a really good artist. A pupil of Jamesone, it is said, John Michael Wright, found the noblest prospect inviting, and in London he had some success. From the north again came the next in succession, William Aikman, a Forfarshire laird who sold his estate for art's sake. He, too, went to London, but there they were all outshone by such as Lely.

With the eighteenth century we come towards the first realisation of something notable in Scottish painting, something that even today is known to people beyond the Scottish Border. First we have Allan Ramsay, son of the author of *The Gentle Shepherd*. Both in his art and his life Ramsay had "that damned charm" which, when a Scot has it, seems to be there in abundance. Ramsay was the prototype of the fashionable painter, whose day and vogue seems to be passing. He knew all the best people, though some, like Voltaire, were among the best because of their brains. Among others who may be mentioned before we pass to the high art light of this century, are David Allan and John Runciman. Portraiture was not their claim to fame. They were men who, to a certain extent, were breaking new ground. I like Runciman's "The Road to Emmaus" and I like Allan's spirit in following his flair in spite of its lack of popularity—he was the forerunner of our pastoralists. But the time was not ripe, and Allan had not the strength either of art or character to bend things to his will.

And then came one who was everything that Allan was not, one who corresponded in his way to Robert Burns in poetry, who set the name of Scotland—in his time, since and today—high enough in the annals of art for us to admire him even for that alone. But if we find that others will not set him where we do, there are his portraits for us as consolation, and none can admire and appraise the portraits of Henry Raeburn like a Scotsman. Where the Scots lover of art is concerned the work of Raeburn is in his brain and bone.

What a galaxy of Scottish character! There has never been anything quite like it since, and I should not like to say that that is because there has not been the same galaxy of character; but there is something in that. There are few things in connection with Scotland that I could love more than to have the Raeburns collected in one great exhibition and to spend days and days going from one to the other, in studying the contrasts, in puzzling out what was behind each face, each pose and look. And, besides all that, there would be the enjoyment of Raeburn's colour,—this may seem heresy to some—his treatment of this or that feature, his use of light. Something of this enjoyment can be found even in the comparatively small but varied collection in the National Gallery of Scotland.

Raeburn was first and last a portrait-painter, and, whether he knew it or not—and I rather think he did—that is what he was ordained to be. Happy the man who follows out his proper destiny. There was that in him which enabled him, apart from his gifts as pure artist, to get out of those of his sitters who had them the essences and subtleties of character. As Sir James Caw has said, so fine was the impact of character on the painter and so well could he pass that impact on, that "to recall the Raeburns you have seen is to recall not so much a gallery of pictures as a number of people you have met personally".

And yet there is always the art aspect of Raeburn's work, but it is so blended with this matter of psychological delineation that it is often difficult to separate the two. You can in such a painting as that of the Macdonell of Glengarry—in which the tartan and the Scottish garb received its first and still, perhaps, its greatest treatment. You may, perhaps, because of the subject in such as Mrs. James Campbell. But when you come to such a work as Lord Newton—and, in his painting of women he was superb in his own way—to Mrs. George Kinnear, your thoughts are a mixture. You are enjoying the painting as painting, but you are also trying to fathom things that lie far beyond mere pigment. Raeburn was not by any means the last great Scottish portrait painter, but he was and is certainly the greatest.

Two names can be mentioned soon after that of Raeburn. One is Sir John Watson Gordon, the other Andrew Geddes. Neither was a Raeburn, nor a copyist of the master. Both had something individual. Gordon, in some of his portraits, seems to delve even a little deeper into certain aspects of Scottish character, but his surface work was not quite so brilliant. Geddes had that in some of his work—"Summer", for instance—that seems to make him the Renoir of his day.

Then came something that took on a shape equally as Scottish in its style as Raeburn's portraits did—Wilkie's *genre* paintings. There is no denying that he had predecessors—the Dutch and Flemish painters—but in time Wilkie worked out his Scottish salvation. To any country dweller Wilkie's "Penny Wedding" and "Blind Man's Buff" are the true counterpart of jollity today in any of the remoter and simpler districts of Scotland. Wilkie was a forerunner, and immediately and for years afterwards, the subject picture, the picture that told a story became one of the great stand-bys of any and every exhibition. That, of course, was only what was happening in every country that had any art. But Scotland came later to this type, in any great proportion, and, of course, the majority of the subjects were Scottish. This was a great thing for Scottish history, not only of the past but what was then contemporary. We have now a pictorial record of Scottish life in the nineteenth century. Because of a change in the attitude towards subject and treatment in art, this record is something of which we shall have little or nothing for our day, so far as art is concerned. But then we have the camera and the cinema, and that, in part, is the reason why story and subject pictures have become things of the past so far as art is concerned. As the art of colour photography develops we shall miss them less and less, and, indeed, the story picture had outlived its day except among the very unsophisticated. The historical picture in Scotland particularly attracted both painter and public, because—as you may have noticed—in Scotland we cannot get away from our history. If not entirely an obsession, it is something of a passion with us, even now. A historical book attracts a Scottish public. We are intensely atavistic, and I should not be surprised if, where an Englishman revels in Bradshaw, a Scotsman would rather climb up and down a genealogical tree.

The next figure in Scottish art who might be mentioned after Wilkie is George Harvey. One would not put him, in his Scots pictures, quite so high as Wilkie; that is, perhaps, more a matter of technique than anything else; but, in spirit and truth to type and atmosphere, Harvey did work that makes him a live figure in art today, when his type of art is so far behind us. Harvey was not a great artist, sometimes merely competent, but what sets him up and apart often is the sincerity of his work. His whole heart was in what he was painting, whether it was a Covenanting scene, a picture of sheep-shearing or of children skailin' from school. Heart, with all that he could muster of head, are the chief features of an artist who has lasted when others have been forgotten. He has his decriers and he has his admirers, and both have a certain amount of right on their side.

Mention of Harvey reminds us that, in 1837, the Royal Scottish Academy came to its official and Royal status. It came out of clashes and rivalries in the quest for a society that would unite artists in a body and do the best for art and artists; and it was the end of many attempts that had been made to establish such an academy. Even in those far-off days, London, by withholding a charter, could rule and interfere with Scottish affairs, even of those of art. Harvey was the Academy's fourth president. Today, in spite of all changes and chances, the Academy still flourishes, and, as I have said, is alive compared with the art museum which is assembled annually at Burlington House.

Sir George Harvey was, in a way, the institutor of what many would call the kailyard school in painting, but that can be so only in retrospect. There was nothing else with which to compare it in the days in which Harvey and his successors were painting. That is the trouble with the bright young things when they deal with art. They will not look at it in historical perspective. In time their own works will have to face the same attitude in bright young things of tomorrow.

There are in this school many pictures that have the same fine feeling that Harvey could impart—such as Faed, or more incisive in character drawing, such as Erskine

13

Nicol. When the flood-tide came of story and historical picture, it brought on its wave such men as Orchardson, the delicate and atmospheric, and Pettie, more robust. One or two men stood out and apart in the general procession. Earlier than those I have just mentioned were two, and they were both Aberdonians, William Dyce and John Phillip. Both began in a way they did not continue, and both stand apart, in their work or their attitude or their subjects, from the native stream of Scottish art. They did not stay at home.

Dyce, academic and correct, is known in a big way by his frescoes executed for the Houses of Parliament at Westminster; in a smaller but, perhaps, more permanent way, by certain portraits and by such exquisite gems of Pre-Raphaelitism—he became strongly attached to that movement—as "Titian Preparing for his First Essay in Colour" (now, appropriately, in Aberdeen Art Gallery). This has a *primavera* atmosphere in every way. Phillip began as a second-rate Wilkie, but he found himself in Spain. His paintings of Spanish life and colour have something of the Old Masters whom he studied so assiduously, but he gave to his work a broader and more lively reflection of life. There was a time when Phillip was regarded with great reverence. That has passed, but among painters, and even critics, his work is still treated with respect. Phillip, incidentally, reminds us how many Scottish artists who have achieved fame came from the humblest domestic circumstances. It is the story that you will find in all the arts and professions in Scotland, the lad o' pairts who finds his way to the top.

Concurrent with such work as I have mentioned, there was going on in Scotland the development of the art of landscape. This began, in the eighteenth century, with Nasmyth and the Rev. Mr. Thomson of Duddingston, the latter a name still much respected in the history of art. This parish minister with a gift for painting enjoyed a great vogue. He was a romantic and the source of his romanticism was the Scottish scene, especially where there was grandeur and history allied to it. For instance, Fast Castle, of which you have heard. But, for all his vogue, and for all the spirit of his work, he remained essentially an amateur, though a highly gifted one.

For myself, in earlier Scottish landscape, I prefer the livelier work of such as Sam Bough—who came from just over the Border, but became essentially Scots. I think the spirit of his work is the spirit of what the man was—lively and Bohemian, kindly and scathing; in short, a worthy. From Thomson I leap to Horatio McCulloch, the man who settled the Scottish landscape for many generations to come. Those of an older generation will remember those eternal hills wropt in mist, the valleys, the lochs, the waterfalls—eternally repeated, well or ill—that adorned parlour walls, in reproduction, of course. They alternated with the lesser Millet pictures, such as "The Gleaners" and "The Angelus", or with Landseer's dogs or deer. Well, Horatio McCulloch began it all in Scots. Again, we cannot entirely blame him for the beginning; it was something new in its day. But even McCulloch seemed to realise in part what he was doing. It has been alleged that he practically made the turning-out of such works into a factory, and was not averse from signing works of the kind turned out by pupils. In that he had precedents in older and old masters. The work of McCulloch and the long, wearisome procession which came after him did, however, bring Scottish art into a certain kind of disrepute, and "McCullochism" took a great deal of dislodging. In fact, even today you will see on exhibition walls the last gasp of it by men who ought to know better now.

But, over against what McCulloch was doing, we had what is now recognised as one of the glories of nineteenth-century Scottish art—the work of William McTaggart. The glory of McTaggart has been most reasonably and finely set out in splendid volume by Sir James Caw, his son-in-law, a fine and knowledgeable man who has, in his day, done perhaps the greatest service that any Scot has done for Scottish art, both as Director of the National Gallery and as writer and critic.

Whether he knew it or not, McTaggart was a pioneer. He anticipated the impressionists, or, at any rate, he was an impressionist before their influence ever penetrated the art of Britain.

At his best McTaggart was a painter of seascapes and of fisher-folk at work and at play. He was, also, an exquisite delineator of childhood. There are works of his which deal with the countryside, and there he does, I think, in his delicate way what Van Gogh did more heavily, more sensationally, with more eccentricity. But it is in his seascapes that he reaches his best, that he is most himself. After all, why not? He was born and reared in Machrihanish, on the west coast, fit training-ground in impression for the artist he came to be. By the way, when he did come to training, McTaggart was a pupil of one of the greatest teachers Scotland has ever known, Scott Lauder. What Scottish art of the nineteenth century owes to Lauder has, in part, been recognised.

McTaggart was not the perfect artist, and, considering what he did achieve in certain aspects of his art, we cannot be regretful. In drawing and composition there are some defects. But, when we come to the effects of light and the lightness of atmosphere, we have a genius here, a poet and an observer who cast aside the academic trammels that he might have freedom. And the result today? His name and fame and work stand higher than, probably, they ever did. In his day, like so many pioneers and forerunners he puzzled where he did not antagonize. But, before he passed on, he had seen and known his recognition.

In the eighties of last century in Scotland, in Glasgow, something was happening, almost accidentally, almost unknown to the artists themselves, something that was going—as we say now—to put Scotland and Scottish art on the map of the world.

Up to this time art had been associated mostly with Edinburgh, which was the official home. The men who formed this loosely attached group—and who might have been most surprised to hear themselves described as the "Glasgow School"— included John Lavery, George Henry, E. A. Hornel, E. A. Walton, Alexander Roche, James Paterson, W. Y. MacGregor, Joseph Crawhall, Arthur Melville and James Guthrie—later a president of the Roya Scottish Academy.

They were influenced by the French Impressionists, and, of course, rather revolted by the stereotyped in contemporary Scottish art—"McCullochism" and the story picture. And, of course, they were given the usual treatment meted out to innovators and rebels. The conventional, in and out of art circles and the academy, would have none of their work. That did not worry the new men, who had their ideas and ideals; they despised the academy even more than the academy did them.

Bit by bit they began to work as a group—and besides Glasgow, Cockburnspath and Kirkcudbright were their rallying places, two places still the haunts of art groups. They were joined by other adherents and became quite a considerable school. They went their way, having basic affinities, but variety marked their work, and also their later careers. Hornel, of them all, rejected academic honour, Lavery became famous and fashionable. But Guthrie led the way to the academy in 1888, and most of the rest followed.

If they were unpopular in Scotland, they were not so among the more advanced painters and connoisseurs in London, and, even more so, on the Continent, where admiration and honours were their portion. Their works are to be found in galleries far furth of Scotland. In time, as always happens, they were merged in the art of Scotland, generally, because they had so influenced that art that they were no longer ootlins.

Besides Lavery, Sir James Guthrie became one of the most generally famous of the men of the school. He has left us, besides some very fine early work, later portraits which rank among the best of his generation and more.

On the fringe of the school, but not quite in it, was the painter and limner who was to become one who would put on paper and canvas the very essence of Scottish landscape. This is an artist whom I have mentioned much before—Sir D. Y. Cameron. There are those who set his etchings unduly high, I think, above his work in colour. Granted the magic of his line and depth of bulk in etchings—some of which are ranked among the greatest in this branch of art—I still think that his paintings have the same qualities, with the added joy of pure, lovely colour. He was poet-painter and a man in whom the spirit mattered much. Certain of these things have made him an artist apart in Scottish art. In etching he combined the architecture of great fanes with the grandeur of mountains, such as Suilven, but in his painting I prefer him best among loch and hill, though he could give us noble impressions of buildings such as Stirling Castle. He was an asset to Scotland and Scottish art.

Besides Cameron, Scotland has produced one or two other etchers of international fame. William Strang belongs more to London than to his native land, but there is something Scots in his portraiture. Muirhead Bone is a man of the world in etching and roves from country to country in search of subjects, but he also has his roots in Scotland. More Scots than any in subject and in personality is James McBey, an artist who has carried on the tradition of Rembrandt, extending both the range of subject and technique. McBey began as a bank clerk in Aberdeen, and for his earliest work used an amusingly but ingeniously contrived home-made etching apparatus, part of which consisted of a common clothes mangle. His 1914–18 etchings, done with the minimum of line and maximum of suggestion, got part of their technique from that which the artist learned when catching the magic glimpses he has given us of the Moray Firth. Bone piles line upon line to entrance and fascinate us, McBey takes line upon line away to set our imaginations working, and into space we put what is not there in actuality but in reality. It is something comparative to the drama of silence which certain of the French dramatists have made their own.

Among the artists of the last forty years or so in Scotland another stood out for all Scots who love art, and Scotland. He was S. J. Peploe. To see a chronological exhibition of Peploe's work is to watch the evolution of the art of one man and also to watch the evolution of art and, especially, the art of Scotland in the twentieth century. From the rich texture and colour quality of the early work, bit by bit we pass to the drier, thinner but much more fascinating later periods. We also pass from the objective to the subjective, for that was part of the progress of Peploe, and let it be said that he took with him in his train some of the best of the younger artists of the generation before the present. Peploe found his native soul in places such as Iona, he gave us revelations of subject and treatment in the way in which he could give curious intensity to the painting of a boiled lobster. There was anything but still life behind and beyond Peploe's *nature morte*.

In Scottish art of the last quarter of a century and more, Scotland reverted to the Auld Alliance with France, and particularly with the work of one French artist, Cézanne. Cézanne-ism was for a time almost an obsession and a hindrance in certain Scottish art circles, but bit by bit we are working out our own salvation. There have been other influences, even to that of the French extremists, but we are, I think, evolving a really native school.

In this, one name already famous in Scottish art might be mentioned, William McTaggart, grandson of the pioneer of that name with whose work I have already dealt.

The sculptor of Scotland gets little credit in any book or article that deals with Scottish art, but, if less in bulk than painting, it is none the less fine and enterprising

13A

in quality. In other days we had Pittendrigh MacGillivray, whose work again and
again managed to convey in portrait and imaginative busts the two sides of the
Scottish character, the Celtic and the Sassenach, because he combined the two in
himself. Today we have men, and women, who are reaching out to the new and
the subtly imaginative, and if I mention Whalen and Sturrock, they are merely
token names. There are many others.

One of the most important things in Scottish art today is that it is not confined
to one centre, one school. Up and down and across the length and breadth of the
land we have artists, working in isolation and in groups. There are schools, and in
them there are men who are not only fine artists in themselves but admirable teachers.
Gillies and Bliss, Sutherland and Sivell, Cowie—all are names that will have their life
as artists, but just as great will be their work for Scottish art in the pupils they send
out. The tradition of Lauder is very much alive in that way today. Here again in the
graphic arts Scotland was never more alive, and few countries are as much alive.

3

MUSIC

MUSIC and drama—and especially music—seem, on the surface, to have been for long the Cinderellas of the arts in Scotland. It is not that Scotland has ever, I expect, been without its music—it is the land of the lilt, of the stroud, of the melody for fiddle and bagpipes, but, compared with Italy in earlier days, Germany and Austria and France in later ones, Scotland was for long primitive and elemental in its music. As for drama, heaven knows we have always had that in plenty in the raw, but, except for what we get in the ballads, we had too long nothing to show the world.

How far can we blame the Reformers for this state of affairs in both these arts? Or were we too long, in the arts as in life, cut off from the contacts that would have helped us by learning and emulation to build up schools of both music and drama? Yet there was a time when we were nearer the Continent than we have been since, and certainly nearer than we are in these days of national imprisonment. I cannot but believe that in the days before Knox we—with our Lowlands and French and Italian connections, and with the Old Religion in full bloom—did not import as well as the adornments of our churches and cathedrals the music that was to be found in churches and cathedrals abroad. There can be little doubt that, when the gold and silver vessels, the vestments and adornments were destroyed or melted, that the music books were burned and the singing canons and choristers were scattered and silenced. With the coming of the Reformers the austere beauty of plainsong would gradually give place to a wail-and-bawl of metrical psalms and paraphrases. Even the music that grew up in the Anglican places of worship in the days of Elizabeth and James could not be imported, except in secret. In any case, in the Scottish kirks there were no kists of whistles, no little bands of instrumentalists such as even village churches had in England; just that which was heard in Scots kirks into the nineteenth century and is still heard in remoter Highland churches today. At its worst this church music, if so it can be called, is a pitiful, drawling caterwaul, and with its grace (save the mark!) notes is equalled only—as I have said —by the singing I have heard by Chinese coolies.

Whatever may have been in the churches, in the homes and in the inns, there must have been playing and singing of some primitive kind. Our heritage of song shows that. But, meantime, we were missing the greater music. We hear little of that until about the mid or later eighteenth century when, in such towns as Edinburgh, Glasgow and Aberdeen, we have record and trace of concerts and musical societies. These societies, however, performed what all the other societies up and down Britain were performing—Handel, then as now—especially, eternally "Messiah"—seems to have been the great stand-by. They had their touring celebrities as we have today, and the cities seem to have interchanged their artists, as we are beginning to do again, but now not with any great success. That idiotic shibboleth of the nineteenth, and to some extent, the eighteenth, century still exists—that no artist can be of any good unless he or she is not British, or, in our case, not London. That was a form of snobbery that came to both England and Scotland with the rise of the *nouveaux riches* of the industrial revolution. They took art under their golden wings, but, unlike Midas, almost everything they touched turned to dross. In Scotland, as elsewhere, they were a vulgar, pretentious, half-baked lot. Their descendants still remain and we have a new lot as aftermath of the profiteering of two great wars. I should hate to batten on blood and sweat and toil.

Well, music, to a great extent, was a lost art in Scotland, as well as Britain, for the greater part of that, aesthetically, dreadful century, the nineteenth. That was the fault of the upper and upper middle classes. They encouraged the wrong things wrongly. Where the stream ran more freely and purely was among the lower middle classes and the working-folk. In most things of any spiritual value these classes were the saviours of Scotland—and England—but especially of Scotland, where the lower middle classes and the working-classes have been the salt of the Scottish earth for nearly a century now. The others were too much occupied imitating and toadying to London and English ways, and mostly making a poor hash of it. All they earned were the pitying smiles of their models.

Where there was music that mattered in Scotland during this period was in the choirs and orchestras which sprang up in every city and town. They were not afraid of Scots music, and the peak night of many of these organisations, everywhere, was the annual Grand Burns Concert. Not only this annual event, but concerts everywhere and at any time of the year, brought out a race of singers and players of Scots song and instrumental music the best of whom were through and through the genuine article. They did not sing braid Scots with an Englishy pronunciation, clipping their vowels and doing away with the apostrophes. If these had only known, the best of the English aristocrats, like some of the Labour Party statesmen today, had no final "g" in their possession—huntin', shootin', fishin', is an grained reality, not a skit.

The music, judging from old programmes, that these choirs performed was not always of any great merit, because, if they were going to keep abreast of the times and sing and play works other than Handel, Haydn, Mozart and Mendelssohn, they had to sing and play the second-rate because only the second-rate was being written.

Had Scotland no composers, then or before? It is a curious fact that music of any value in the north in the eighteenth century seems to stop short at Newcastle with Charles Avison, who is having a little vogue at the present time. Of course, there were the melodists such as Niel Gow and his son and others like them, the writers of pibroch, of marches, but, though these had their own value and, I think, could have greater building value now, they were not in the great stream of world or even European music, and, actually, of course, there was only European music, if one includes Russia in that.

If one takes Scottish music and includes it in the British category there were only two names which remain—A. C. Mackenzie and Hamish MacCunn. Certain works of both are still played, Mackenzie's as a kind of tribute to his place in musical history, MacCunn's because they have a definite Scottish tang. Of the two I think MacCunn was the greater, and might have been even greater still if he had not had to fight against all sorts of antagonistic circumstances. His chief claim to a hearing is his ubiquitous "Land of the Mountain and Flood" overture. I do not know, but is it not possible to find in his work something other that might represent him? His songs are neglected, unduly, and his cantata, "Bonny Kilmeny", might be oftener performed by Scottish choral societies, even if only as a diversion from the rather stereotyped programmes of so many of them.

Modern Scottish music—and it does exist—began, I think, with J. B. MacEwen, and he, again, does not get his full due in Scotland. That nineteenth century dies hard.

What is coming to flower in music in Scotland today began somewhere between 1900 and 1914, and nearer the latter date. It is an interesting and curious fact that two of the men who have made music what it is in Scotland today were not Scotsmen—Sir Donald Tovey and Dr. C. Sanford Terry—the one attached to the University of Edinburgh, as musician, the other to the University of Aberdeen, as historian. And both are world-famous. What Tovey did for music in Edinburgh and among the serious students of Scotland is almost impossible to estimate, but you are for ever coming across the results of his work and his personality, and it is something that will last, because the Tovey tradition will be handed down. Like all musicians, Tovey, I suppose, longed to be a composer. He was, of course, but his *magnum opus*, the opera, *The Bride of Dionysus*, which I heard on its first performance in Edinburgh, was, if I may say so, characteristic of such as Tovey. Everything was there in the music, except what makes for permanency. It would not have mattered, even if we did hear echoes of other composers, and not always operatic ones, the something that was needed was wanting. I should not have mentioned this opera, except to show that Scotland had come alive, musically, and Tovey had done a great deal of the spade-work.

As for Sanford Terry, whose friendship and encouragement I was honoured to have, what he did for the north-east of Scotland in music has never been acknowledged, no more than his great and tremendous work for Johann Sebastian Bach. Wherever you go in the civilised world of music today, the name and music of Bach cannot come up but Sanford Terry is mentioned. And yet, since his death, not a pamphlet, not a brochure, not a monograph has been written about him. That, of course, is not Scotland's fault alone. Sanford Terry made music in north-east Scotland what it is today. There was—in the years before 1914—the great performance of Bach's "Passion According to St. Matthew", with the famous interpreter of the Evangel, Gervase Elwes, in the part. That was in Aberdeen! That performance began something that still bears fruit. I have been laughed at for saying that Aberdeen is a Bach, Brahms and Beethoven town, but it is. These especial composers of world music do, in some way, accord with the characters of the Aberdonians. And to performances of their works, Aberdonians do flock. Today the universities of Aberdeen and Edinburgh are, I make bold to say, the pre-eminently musical of the four; Aberdeen's upcome being due to the hard work of a Yorkshire-man, Willan Swainson. In Aberdeen you will hear season after season a fine body of university singers perform the B minor Mass, the "Missa Solemnis", Verdi's Requiem, Vaughan William's "Sea Symphony" and other works of this great British composer, and we can judge the quality of the performances of these works from what we hear broadcast and what we hear on visits to other musical centres. Aberdonians, also, are devotees of chamber music. The club there has not only a full membership of hundreds, but a yearly waiting list. It was one of the few clubs in Britain that carried on its activities during the war of 1939-45, through constant sirens and blackout; few provincial towns had more alerts.

Apart from the B.B.C., Scotland has only one large orchestra, the Scottish Orchestra. This is a body with a fine history, of work and of conductors. Its qualities have grown in recent years, and today it is an orchestra that—in spite of the futilities which certain London and Edinburgh critics (remember it is an orchestra with Glasgow headquarters) utter—cannot be dismissed easily from British orchestral history. There is a type of musical criticism that is founded not on music but on personal fads and prejudices, and some matters even less admirable than these.

And Scotland is a land of choirs. The Glasgow Orpheus Choir, and its conductor, Sir Hugh Roberton, are world-famous. Roberton, of course, has been the great spirit of this vigorous and exquisite body of singers, most of whom are working-folk, and by certain people—who put other things before music, will tell you behind their hand, "They're Reds, you know"—are suspected as having hidden propaganda in their accidentals. This choir has not only brought secular Scottish folk-music to a fine art, but have done the greatest amount of good in teaching the religious body how the Scottish psalm tunes should be sung.

Next to folk-song these Scottish psalm tunes, rightly done, are an integral part of the musical folk-life of Scotland. They appeal to all, of almost any denomination of religion; you cannot escape them; they will sing them at a football match as the Welsh sing "Land of my Fathers"; they will sing them at any sort of meeting; you hear the bells peal them on a Sunday; and they have recitals of them Sunday after Sunday in the churches in town and county. The psalm tunes have come to their full fruition as folk-music.

With all this laid aside, has Scotland any composers today? Is any headway being made in the creative aspect? The answer is—Yes. We have not a horde, but a selective few, as yet. One or two names are known to every cultured Scotsman, and of these one beyond the bounds of Scotland.

There is Ian Whyte, still in his forties, and coming to maturity. He is conductor of the B.B.C. Scottish Orchestra. He is essentially Scottish in every way, a product of the Dunfermline school of music, with London training on top of that. Mention of Whyte and Dunfermline suggests that here tribute should be paid to the late David Stephen, a man and a musician, who was Whyte's mentor at Dunfermline, and himself an essentially Scottish composer. He has left a fine legacy.

Whyte is pianist, conductor and composer—and a personality—and will one day have to choose which of all of them he wants to be pre-eminently. At present his life is mainly divided between conducting and composing. His works of importance are increasing in number and bulk, and include a symphony, a pianoforte, concerto, tone poems and a host of smaller works and arrangements. He is heart and soul— and mind and brain—in Scottish music of tradition. He has ideas as to what should be done with that music nowadays, and if its modernistic transmogrifications seem to the conventional and the ordinary body like adding wrong notes—which has been said—Whyte knows what he is doing. For myself, I think his best work is yet to come, and I think it will come. His "fauve" days are over, and, in a medium that still inclines to the left in music, he will do something for Scotland that is worth waiting for.

Along with Whyte must be set a slightly younger man, Cedric Thorpe Davie, in charge of music at the University of St. Andrews, and bringing up the standard of music there. Like Whyte, he has composed his symphony, and he has much else to his credit in arrangement and original composition.

There remain three other names which I would mention—W. B. Moonie, Francis George Scott and Erik Chisholm. Mr. Moonie, like Tovey, has an opera to his name, but native Scottish opera will never mean a great deal until we get a new

Beggar's Opera to Scots words and lyrics. That, too, I think, is going to come, and the sooner librettist and composer get down to it, the better. The way has been shown in the United States, in *The Brigadoon*; but we must go better than that in both words and music and in authenticity.

Erik Chisholm inclines to the Celtic side of Scotland, and he has written pianoforte works and ballets on Celtic themes. He is a strong modernist, and that prevents wide fame. Talking of ballet, Scotland has its balletomanes. That is not strange; remember that, if ever there was a dancing country, it is Scotland. Go to our Highland games, of which I have told you, go to our concerts, go to any town or country ballroom and watch the dancing of Scottish dances. There is the ready-made stuff of a native ballet. When are we to realise this in Scotland? There are plenty of composers, plenty of dancing teachers and dancers. What is wanted? The dynamic and co-ordinating impulse.

And Francis George Scott? A puzzling figure in our art. A Scot to the backbone, one who appreciates Scottish poetic literature like a littérateur, and so, when he sets it to music—and he is essentially a composer of Scottish *Lieder*—we get double value, the value of the literature and the music with which he interprets it. But, alas, only a minority appreciate. Is he too early, must he have gone from us before we realise his stature in Scottish music? It is not the fault of such men as Whyte and the art of singers such as John Tainsh if Scott has not had his due. But a new generation is coming up: they may be Scott's men and women.

Much of what I have written of music in Scotland applies to Scottish music in general, to—that word again—Sassenach music. There still remains that great body of melody, the Gaelic airs, from Highlands and Islands. I should like everyone who loves music and, especially, folk-music to see and hear the annual Gaelic Mod, which is a movable feast, so far as venue, as they say, is concerned. It takes place in a different Scottish centre each year, and, I am happy to relate, nowhere has it been more successful than in the granite city of Aberdeen, where Celtic art and Celtic feeling are supposed to be at the bottom of the financial list. If you wish to experience community feeling and art at their best, then visit a Mod—or, failing that a *ceilidh*—and you will understand why the Gael, even today, when many say that especial community is breaking up, will last in community for a gey while yet.

People who do not know, think of the Gael as a sorrowful and sad person and that all the works that come out of his life are of that nature. A Mod will teach you different. Of course, you will find sorrow, sadness, mysticism and whimsy, but some of the loveliest as well as the happiest moments of a Mod are when the songs that are being sung are of work or humour. Among the Gaelic singers are humorists—not comedians, that gives a wrong impression—who can keep an audience of a thousand

in a constant ripple of merriment, and, perhaps, half of that thousand do not understand a word of what is being sung.

I am sorry to end on a note of controversy, but, at the same time, I could not
close a chapter on Scottish music without a further tribute to a great native genius,
who excelled as collector, arranger and interpreter. I allude—let me say at once—to
the late Margaret Kennedy-Fraser. It is the fashion in certain circles in Scotland to
decry and attack Mrs. Kennedy-Fraser's work. Again, I say, right away, that those
people are traitors to Scotland and Scottish good. Many of them have never lifted
a little finger or gone a foot's length to do anything for the songs which, they
pretend, are their dearest treasure. Only their silly tongues wag. You can never get
from these detractors exactly what it was that Mrs. Kennedy-Fraser did that rouses
their woolly ire. They belong to the same school who insist upon writing of the
Cuillin while their happiest hunting-grounds are the streets of Glasgow and their
climbing the heights of Mount Florida.

Margaret Kennedy-Fraser has done more for Hebridean and Highland folk-song
than anyone else in Scotland or the world. If she turned them into an art-form, then
they were capable and worthy of that transformation. The credit goes to the songs
themselves as well as to their transmogrifier. And who has ever interpreted these
songs on the level of art as she did? There is no reason why they should remain sea-
tangle and heather, or should not be admired in another setting than their original.
That is to deprive the world of the Gael's own pleasure, a very selfish attitude. There
is in this attitude to Mrs. Kennedy-Fraser something of that attribute of a certain
type of Gael which in the past and, if persisted in in the future, has held and will hold
Gaeldom from keeping the place it wants to keep in the world. It is an attitude that
will destroy Gaeldom, and God forbid that that should take place, for the sake of
something in Scotland's soul.

Of the art of Mrs. Kennedy-Fraser as singer and interpreter let me say that I
consider her as having been Scotland's Elena Gerhardt. An evening for me at one
of her concerts was an evening of varied pleasure and enchantment. I can see that
fine figure, that face, with something of the eternal faery changeling in it, poised on
the platform and held ready for what was to come, and according to what was to
come was the type of poise and the expression on the face. Always she prepared
herself for the feeling and the atmosphere of the song she was about to sing—so
does Elena Gerhardt. If it was a song of mysticism or sorrow, the eye looked into
infinity or upon death or disaster. If it was a song of battle or defiance, the eye lit
up with that expression, and if it was of tender playfulness or humour, then the
body unbent and the eyes were those of the elfin creature her face suggested.

A great artist in every way went from us when Margaret Kennedy-Fraser's body
took its way to Iona and her spirit to Tir-nan-Og.

4

DRAMA

WE have no records of the drama in Scotland in the sixteenth and seventeenth centuries because we had no Shakespeare, no Ben Jonson—although, as I have told you, Jonson was in Edinburgh and visited Drummond the poet at Hawthornden. It is a curious fact that, although Scotland always seemed to the people of the south, for long, as a place devoid of anything except savages and mountains, the artists always found their way to the country. I think there is a lot in that. It is the opinion of far-south England. The people of Northumberland, Cumberland, Yorkshire and Lancashire are our "buddies", and, whatever they think, know us for kin. I should like to see the Scottish Border extended to include those counties. We are kin in language and character. We are not like the people below that line, nor are they. God made the Cheviots, and the people of Scotland and northern England accepted them as a dividing line. It was wrong, and still is.

We are dealing with drama, and let me take a very little matter to back up my theory of the link between us and northern England. Harold Brighouse wrote a play—one of the best one-acters—called *The Price of Coal*. It was written in the broadest Lancashire dialect. A Scot saw the possibilities and translated it—not a difficult job—into Scots. That play was more often, professionally and by amateurs, played in Scots than it was in Lancashire dialect. Look at the work of the present-day Lancastrian who has ever done real justice to his native county—Thompson—and you will find that he has as many Scots readers, almost, as Lancastrian. We are at home with Mr. Thompson's people, their words are ours as much as they are those of the Lancastrians. No, the dividing line is wrong. It was not the line once upon a day. But dividing lines are fading out in certain ways, although I cannot forget that there are other important matters that still divide us.

But—drama. There must have been a feeling for drama in Scotland, even after Mr. Knox and his horde tried to squeeze everything artistic out of our Scottish lives. When Master Fletcher, of London, and his players went on a tour of Scotland, in King James the VI's day—with a company that, as you have read, may have included one Will Shakespeare—he was fêted by the magistrates of Aberdeen and made a burgess of the town. That is an honour that has always been reserved for the most notable.

It is not until near the end of the eighteenth century that we hear much of drama in Scottish cities. In the country—as compared with the present day—it did not exist. But, in the country then, nothing existed except the dour fight for life. Today is rather different, as you shall hear.

Bit by bit the cities of Scotland came nearer London in matters theatrical. And London was not unaware, as it is today, of the money-making possibilities of tours in Scotland. London "stars" came to Scotland with Shakespeare and those dreadful plays which, today, no one except the most academic researcher can read. It is amusing to think that the day after tomorrow only the academic researcher will be reading much of what is produced in the theatres today, and, I should think, he will put most of the plays of today even lower than those unreadables of the eighteenth century, in a certain large way. He will think what trivial people we were. There is triviality and triviality—but look at our triviality and consider the Restoration drama. There you had triviality brought to classic heights. We can't do it. And the reason—money, in short; a matter which does not affect us here.

Out of the Scottish-written drama of the time comes one phrase which has rung down the years to the detriment of drama in Scotland. It is the cry of the gallery boy when Home's play of *Douglas* was produced in London—"Whaur's yer Wullie Shakespeare noo?" Well, where is he and where is Home? Try reading the play and you will know.

It is a curious fact, but the man who helped to establish something like a Scottish theatre was not a playwright, but a novelist—Walter Scott. For years and years, for generations, there circled the Scottish cities a dramatic version of *Rob Roy*. As I have told you, that freebooter was more in Scottish minds than many a better man, until at last he and the play were ousted by modernity. Even the outlying places began to see the unconsciously funny side of *Rob Roy's* fustian. Yet, today you will still meet aged people who say: "Ah, there's naething noo in the drama like *Rob Roy*." Quite right.

Other long-stayers on the Scottish stage were *Jeanie Deans*—taken out of *The Heart of Midlothian, Cramond Brig* and *Mill o' Tifty's Annie*, a play founded on the old legend of Fyvie Castle and its trumpeter, Andrew Lammie. This last is the ballad made dramatic. I should not be surprised, however, if one of these days these old plays might be given a new short life—as period pieces and curiosities.

The Scottish theatre, so far as original work was concerned, was dormant for nearly a century. There was no lack of theatres—every city had, at least, one—but they were inhabited by that bane of the provincial drama—the "London company". Of course, they were no more London than my foot, which is very much always on Scottish ground. They were just fifth-rate tourers. We had the occasional tour of the London "stars" such as Henry Irving and Ellen Terry, and the annual visits of such as Barry Sullivan, Osmond Tearle and—two Scotsmen—Edward Compton (Mackenzie) and William Mollison. But of Scots theatre there was nothing, using theatre in the sense of dramatic body as a whole.

Then came the kailyarders and J. M. Barrie, and I should not like to say which was worse—no theatre or these, except for the theatre genius of Barrie. If only our dramatists would learn from him in that way.

The dramatisation of MacLaren's *The Bonnie Brier Bush* was another *Rob Roy* and, as a matter of fact shared the week's bill in the Scottishly famous touring company of John Clyde, a name which still holds in the annals of Scottish drama.

Barrie's first contribution to Scottish drama was a "kailyarder", *The Professor's Love Story*, of which so little is thought that it is not included in his collected works. But it is still being played by amateurs. I, myself, was taken to see it in 1916 by Edward Compton, whose daughter, Fay, and H. B. Irving were playing it then. Even then I thought it rather wish-wash. Barrie's best Scottish play (*Mary Rose* is just whimsy-whamsy that might belong anywhere) is *What Every Woman Knows*. That may not be the best play for Scotland, but it was a contribution to the Scottish theatre, and, having thick skins, we can put up with it. Its technique, especially that of the first act, is great—I know only one first act like it, and that, too, is a dialect play, Stanley Houghton's *Hindle Wakes*. Once again, in *Shall We Join the Ladies* Barrie did a first act of such technical cleverness that he could not go on with it. But Barrie was an *émigré* playwright: Scotland and the Scots were of use to him only as a plaything, as a sentimental hold, and as a place and people he could return to when we wanted to be nicely idolised. Bernard Shaw—who is partly a Scot—is somewhat alike in this way, except that Shaw never used Ireland as Barrie did Scotland; Shaw was too big for that. Barrie, intellectually, was a little man, exquisite, but a gnat, complete with sting.

What have we had then, in Scotland, dramatically, apart from Barrie? We have had the Graham Moffat comedies—*Bunty Pulls the Strings*, *A Scrape o' the Pen* and others, all in the kailyard tradition. And Moffat wrote one one-act comedy, *The Concealed Bed*, which for fun and actuality has never been outdone. They are all half-forgotten now. It is a curious thing that, every so many years, a Scots play catches London, but only every few years. You can put any dialect from Lancashire and Yorkshire to Devon steadily on the London stage, and London will lap it up, but you must be careful of Scots; every theatre manager fights shy of it. Why? Ask those curious pieces of humanity, the theatre managers. They take plenty of money out of Scotland, but they are very, very shy of putting any into it. The cinema is going to teach them a lesson which they may—but, probably—will not learn, until it is too late.

Between 1919 and 1939, however, a revolution took place in Scotland in the matter of the drama. There had been an attempt before 1914, in Glasgow, to establish, not exactly a Scottish national theatre, but something rather like it—the Glasgow Repertory Theatre. That was a time when, founding on that glorious piece of British theatrical history, Miss Horniman's Manchester Repertory Theatre and the Dublin Abbey Theatre, some part of the theatre tried to put its house in some sort of intelligent order. Only now is that planting coming to partial fruition. In another few years London will not be the centre of the theatre world. The regions, the counties will have knocked London's silly drama on the head. One of the reasons will be that London is no longer the place of the leisurely, pleasure-loving patrician. In fact, there will be few patricians left. London may even learn from the provinces and adjust its theatre accordingly.

The Glasgow "Rep" did do something for Scotland theatrically, though the few Scots plays it did attempt were beneath contempt, dramatically. They were again kailyarders—why do southerners think that that is the only attitude people in Scotland have to literary and dramatic life? It is the blight of the "quaint", something that intelligent Scotsmen have to fight tooth and nail. It is allied to the wrong attitude to Mary Queen of Scots and Prince Charlie.

The people who kept Scottish drama going until the professionals were ready to give us something of our due were the amateurs. You would be surprised to know what the amateur drama has been in Scotland in the last twenty or more years. Of course, there was amateur drama in Scotland before that, but it was, somehow, different. It was slap and stick, it was very bad technically. The plays they played were professional rubbish—from *Black-Eyed Susan* to *East Lynne* and *The Octoroon*, all the tushery of the professional stage. And how badly they played them I can remember from my boyhood days. Even then I was a critic.

I have found that really good professional actors and playwrights—many of them have graduated from the amateur rank; no sneer in the word rank—do not despise the amateur actor or playwright. Emlyn Williams, for instance, has expressed himself to me very finely on the matter, and he is both actor and playwright.

Well, the amateurs in Scotland, aided by one of the finest pieces of good work ever sent out from London—the Arts League of Service—and headed by a great Scotswoman, Eleanor Elder, have done something for Scottish drama that will, in time, become something of the greatest importance in the British theatre. There is Lowland Scots solidity and there is Highland fantasy, and between the two we shall, I think, produce a theatre that will be as famous in the world as was the Glasgow School of Painting. I can see that we are heading that way, and I am in touch with this movement, practically and aesthetically, right down to rock bottom.

There arose in Scotland in the 'twenties a body called the Scottish Community Drama Association—you see, democratic Scotland was there in the word "Community"; that is Scotland essentially—and that association has made Scotland drama-conscious from the Mull of Galloway to Cape Wrath. If only you were present, as I have been, both in an official capacity and as a spectator, at the S.C.D.A. festivals, and I have officiated as adjudicator in almost every area of Scotland, you would know that drama has become part of the Scottish consciousness as nothing else has. Unfortunately, it has driven music somewhat out of the picture. But that will right itself in time.

The best amateurs of Scotland submit themselves, every year, to public criticism at S.C.D.A. festivals. That and competition make for a really good standard of amateur drama. I should say, apart from association football, there is nothing in Scotland so hotly debated as the points of drama technique. Isn't it curious, and somewhat amazing? This Scotland that so long avoided drama like the devil. It is a poor district that has not its dramatic society, and the various societies tour like repertory theatres. Yes, the drama is part of the life-stream of Scotland today. London, already, has actors and actresses whose names appear in bright lights, and they have come out of this great amateur movement in Scotland. I can name half a dozen right off the reel. And there are others whom the cinema has claimed.

In the professional theatre there has been in Scotland that God-sent man, James Bridie. I am quite serious in my description of him. James Bridie has meant and means to Scotland something that Scotland will only realise in time. He did not begin as a Scottish dramatist. He has never had a struggle for recognition—his first play was accepted right away—but, for all that, he is a bonnie fechter, and he has had to fight for his Scottish drama. Heaven help his opponents!

It's a curious thing—Barrie, I have said, was half fey. Bridie is pixie or leprechaun. —unfortunately we have not got a word in Scotland to describe him, kelpie is no use. But if ever there was a dramatist who was essentially Scottish, it is James Bridie. He has a great intellectual foundation and wide knowledge—his plays, incidentally, show that—but, he has got, also, thank heaven, a Scots sense of humour, and that is something which is like nothing else in the world. It is not like English or American humour—remember that great genius of the music-hall stage, Harry Lauder; his humour they say is now out of date; it was not "wise-cracking", it was something much more slow yet subtle—Scottish humour has a tang that is like our caller air and the line of the hills. Well, Bridie puts that into character and plot, into dialogue and situation. But he is the leprechaun in this way—see his eyes sparkle behind his glasses, and you will know what I mean—that he will not keep the conventional dramatist's straight line. He hops and leaps; he kills good characters early in a play because he thinks they have served his purpose and are gone; he will not toe the line.

Early in his career as a dramatist certain very professional creatures in London tried to kill him—that was when London mattered dramatically, as it does not now, so far as Scots are concerned. Today he is going strong while certain of those creatures are going down. No; James Bridie is the crown and top of drama in Scotland, and I could swear every young dramatist in Scotland from now on will want to be a Bridie. But, alas, they must have his foundation and his genius.

That is the one serious trouble with Scottish drama, where this great amateur movement is concerned, so much of it lacks the top-storey. It never gets beyond the kitchen, and in that kitchen they do not even read the important news about Scotland. There is, led by leftish political folk, a new drama arising in Scotland, which is going to triumph over the kitchen "comics". Already the districts, as we say, are kicking against kitchen comedies; they want something that means something to the folk for whom they are acting. If the demand is there the supply, will, in time be forthcoming. But, in Scotland, drama today—what a curious overturn! —is definitely part of the national life.

There are in Aberdeen three fine granite edifices which stand side by side—the public library, a church and His Majesty's Theatre. They are known jocularly in the city as—Education, Salvation and Damnation, the last sobriquet a tilt at what used to be the attitude of the unco guid in Scotland towards the drama. There are still in Scotland not a few people who would as soon enter a house of ill-fame as enter a theatre. They regard the two as adjuncts. Actors and actresses are even worse than their official status in Britain—rogues and vagabonds.

Devotees of the drama in Aberdeen, however, point to the huge statue of Sir William Wallace, the great apostle of Scottish freedom, which stands on its plinth before the theatre. His outstretched hand and arm point towards the theatre doors!

Yet, as I have told you, Aberdeen is one of the few places in Scotland in which we have any trace of the medieval drama. That, as I say, came out of the church, and it is a curious repetition of history that, today, the Church of Scotland has gone back to the drama. In Edinburgh it has now its own little theatre, its own directors of drama and its own dramatic company. The plan is to send the company and the kirk's plays throughout the length and breadth of the land.

EPILOGUE

NOW the task I have loved, and hated, is almost done. Like everyone who writes —no matter how much loved the subject may be—I wish there were some instrument that could record, without my having to write them, all the thoughts that arise in the mind. If that could be so, again, as every writer knows, there would be more masterpieces, and there would be in existence masterpieces such as the world has not yet seen.

Henry Harland, on the title of his book of stories, *Grey Roses*, has this sentence: "The conception was a rose, but the achievement was a rose turned grey".

In the still hours of the night, just before sleep comes over you, the most wonderful sentences, it may be whole paragraphs, form themselves in your mind—you seldom get as far as a whole chapter, for by then you are asleep. In the morning they have, very often, gone altogether, or, if recovered in part, they are never quite the same or quite as good as the originals. They are like a translation. Well, that is what happened to what I hoped might be some of the best of this book. Some were not suitable for the kind of book I was supposed to be writing, but embroideries on the theme of a certain chapter.

While I was at the chapter on Edinburgh, for instance, I, naturally, thought much of Mary Queen of Scots and John Knox, and there came to me sentences about the relationship of the twain. They ran something like this:

"I can imagine Knox as, down the corridors of Eternity he pursues Mary of Scots, as he wished he could have done along the dim passages of Holyrood, crying, 'Mary, Mary, I really loved ye. What I did and said was only another aspect of my love. I kent then and I ken now the solution to all our quarrels and divisions, but it wasna possible, nor possible to utter it then. Now it is too late.' But he will never, in all Eternity, find Mary, because, clear of the nets of wrong and right, no longer a queen or even a woman, she is happier than ever she was, even at the best moments of all her troubled life. Now she is, as she was in those happiest moments of mortality, busy at her prayers and praises, not to and of men, but of God, a very different God from that of John Knox. And I wonder which has found that God in His reality is nearer their differing conceptions."

On paper they may seem foolish sentences, but the originals to me seemed right and good. Yet, even in that translation there is something of one of the great problems that, even today, occupy Scots and, in some ways, divide them in their allegiances. Scotland, as I have elsewhere indicated, is in some ways a divided country. That can be seen as the plays and books on Mary and Knox mount up year by year, and are treated as if they were matters of the moment, just as in the affair and *affaires* of Prince Charles Edward Stuart. Scotland is still like that, to too great an extent.

But Scotland is also united, and I hope always will be, on one matter—Scotland. It is towards that unity, and out of the hope that temporal things will come to matter less and less, will achieve a synthesis, that certain parts of this book have been written. The book is for Scotsmen as well as men of other countries, who love their own countries as much as I and other Scots love ours. If I have been able, in the smallest part, to bring the look and the tang of Scotland, past and present, into the pages of a book, my labours have not been lost.

As I write and look up from my writing, I see the autumn sun dropping behind a range of low hills. The day has been crystal clear, with a caller Scots wind blowing —and, incidentally, causing a considerable series of showers of gold from the trees. The bow window of the room in which I write is an enclave of light in this dimming inn parlour. The bull's eyes in the panes are like whorls of water with the stone set at the centre. At the top of the fields, across the road, are the silhouettes of three hay-ricks; round the corner, I know, is the stackyard, filled, and at morning a symphony in gold *à la* Whistler or George Clausen. Robin is twittering, the rowans are swinging red from the deep green boughs of the trees that stand on either side of the house. Beyond the southern fields are the Mearns hills, row upon row of them, every shape of every one of which I have come to know and love.

It is an unmistakably Scottish landscape—with long vistas through a long howe; new vistas because of the cutting of the trees in war-time; and, where there still are trees, they march up the heights and into the hollows, a dark green army; the corner of a loch gleams in the setting sun. To work I have to turn my back, else I should stand looking at the landscape till dark, and even after.

Yes, this is essentially Scotland, though not of the remoter highlands and the high mountains. It is very dear to me, because of its beauty and because that beauty is part of Scotland. Were I given my choice I should live nowhere else—despite the rigours of winter soon to come. This is Scotland, my ain land, my ain folk. I am Scots. Where else? Nowhere. What else? Scotland yet, always and only.

INDEX